THE
BECKET CONFLICT
AND
THE SCHOOLS

THE
BECKET CONFLICT
AND
THE SCHOOLS

A Study of
Intellectuals in Politics

BERYL SMALLEY

ROWMAN AND LITTLEFIELD
Totowa, New Jersey

First published in the United States 1973
by Rowman and Littlefield, Totowa, New Jersey

LIBRARY OF CONGRESS CATALOGING IN PUBLICATION DATA

Smalley, Beryl.
The Becket conflict and the schools.

Includes bibliographical references.
1. Thomas à Becket, Saint, Abp. of Canterbury,
1118?–1170. 2. Scholasticism. 3. England—
Intellectual life. I. Title.
DA209.T4S6 1973   942.03′1′0924 [B]   72-14254
ISBN 0-87471-172-X

Printed in Great Britain

IN MEMORIAM
MATRIS NOSTRAE SUIS OMNIBUS AMABILEM

7/30/74 E.B.B.

Contents

Abbreviations

A.H.D.L.M.A.: Archives d'histoire doctrinale et littéraire du moyen âge

Ancient Libraries: M. R. James, *The Ancient Libraries of Canterbury and Dover* (Cambridge, 1903)

Baldwin, *Masters*: J. W. Baldwin, *Masters, Princes and Merchants. The Social Views of Peter the Chanter and his Circle* (Princeton, New Jersey, 1970)

B.G.P.T.M.: Beiträge zur Geschichte der Philosophie und Theologie des Mittelalters

Brady, 'Peter Lombard': I. Brady, 'Peter Lombard: Canon of Notre-Dame', R.T.A.M. xxxii (1965) 277–95

B.R.U.O.: A. B. Emden, *A Biographical Register of the University of Oxford to* A.D. *1500* (Oxford, 1957–9)

D.N.B.: Dictionary of National Biography

Draco: *Draco Normannicus*, ed. R. Howlett, *Chronicles of the Reigns of Stephen, Henry I and Richard I* ii (Rolls Series, 1885)

E.H.R.: English Historical Review

Ep. Cant.: *Epistolae Cantuarienses*, ed. W. Stubbs, *Chronicles and Memorials of the Reign of Richard I* ii (Rolls Series, 1865)

Eyton: R. W. Eyton, *Court, Household, and Itinerary of King Henry II* (London, 1878)

Foreville: R. Foreville, *L'Eglise et la Royauté en Angleterre sous Henri II Plantagenet (1154–1189)* (Paris, 1942)

G.F.L.C.: A. Morey and C. L. N. Brooke, *The Letters and Charters of Gilbert Foliot, Abbot of Gloucester (1139–48), Bishop of Hereford (1148–63), and London (1163–87)* (Cambridge, 1967)

Gilbert Foliot: A. Morey and C. N. L. Brooke, *Gilbert Foliot and his Letters* (Cambridge, 1965)

Gloss: *Biblia Sacra cum Glossa Ordinaria et Nicolai Lyrani, Additionibus Pauli Burgensis ac Matthaiae Thoryngi* (Lyons, 1598)

Glunz: H. H. Glunz, *The Vulgate in England from Alcuin to Roger Bacon* (Cambridge, 1933)

J.W.C.I.: Journal of the Warburg and Courtauld Institutes

Knowles: D. Knowles, *The Episcopal Colleagues of Archbishop Thomas Becket* (Cambridge, 1951)

Knowles, *Becket:* D. Knowles, *Thomas Becket* (London, 1970)

Letters of Arnulf of Lisieux: ed. F. Barlow (Camden Society, 3rd series, lxi, London, 1939)

Lottin: O. Lottin, *Psychologie et Morale aux XIIe et XIIIe siècles* v (Gembloux, 1959)

Maccarrone, 'I Papi': M. Maccarrone, 'I Papi del secolo XII e la vita commune e regolare', *Pubblicazioni dell' Università del S. Cuore,* scienze storiche 2, serie terza, Miscellanea del Centro di studi medioevali III, i (1962) La vita commune del clero nei secoli XI e XII, 349–99

M.A.R.S.: Mediaeval and Renaissance Studies

Mat.: *Materials for the History of Archbishop Thomas Becket*, ed. J. C. Robertson and J. B. Sheppard (Rolls Series, 1875–83)

Medieval Libraries: N. R. Ker, *Medieval Libraries of Great Britain* 2nd ed. (London, 1964)

M.G.H.: Monumenta Germaniae Historica

Pacaut: M. Pacaut, *Alexandre III. Etude sur la conception du pouvoir pontifical dans sa pensée et dans son œuvre* (Paris, 1956)

P. L.: Patrologia Latina, ed. J. Migne

Poole, A. L. Poole, *From Domesday Book to Magna Carta 1087–1216* (Oxford, 1951)

Rep. Bibl.: F. Stegmüller, *Repertorium Biblicum Medii Aevi* (Madrid, 1940–61)

R.H.E.: Revue d'histoire ecclésiastique

R. W. Hunt, 'English Learning': R. W. Hunt, 'English Learning in the Late Twelfth Century', T.R.H.S., 4th series, xix (1936) 19–42

Saltman: A. Saltman, *Theobald Archbishop of Canterbury* (London, 1956)

Schneyer: J. B. Schneyer, *Wegweiser zu lateinischen Predigtreihen des Mittelalters* (Munich, 1965)

S.G.: *Studi Gregoriani*, ed. G. B. Borino (Rome, 1947–60)

Southern: R. W. Southern, *Medieval Humanism and other Studies* (Oxford, 1970)

Spic. sac. Lov.: Spicilegium sacrum Lovaniense

Study of the Bible: B. Smalley, *The Study of the Bible in the Middle Ages*, 2nd ed. (Oxford, 1952)

Thaner: *Die Summa Magistri Rolandi nachmals Papstes Alexander III.*, ed. F. Thaner (Innsbrück, 1874)

T.R.H.S.: Transactions of the Royal Historical Society

Webb: C. C. J. Webb, *John of Salisbury* (London, 1932)

Works of John of Salisbury

Letters, i: *The Letters of John of Salisbury. The Early Letters (1153–1161)*, ed. and transl. W. J. Millor and H. E. Butler, revised by C. N. L. Brooke (London, 1955)

E. D. P.: *Entheticus de dogmate philosophorum*, ed. C. Peterson (Hamburg, 1843)

Hist. pontif.: *Historia pontificalis*, ed. and transl. M. Chibnall (London, 1956)

Metal.: *Metalogicon*, ed. C. C. J. Webb (Oxford, 1929)

Policr.: *Policraticus*, ed. C. C. J. Webb (Oxford, 1909)

Foreword

An invitation to give the Ford Lectures at Oxford in 1967 was an honour and a challenge. The Ford Lecturer by statute must choose a subject within the field of English history. The lectures must embody original research. The audience consists of undergraduates, graduate students and colleagues. My research on medieval thought and learning had not focussed on English history previously and the results were too specialized to appeal to a large audience. *The Becket Conflict and the Schools* struck me as the only possible solution to my problem. The role of medieval scholars in politics had interested me ever since Sir Maurice Powicke gave his Ford Lectures on Stephen Langton in 1927. Here was a chance to make late and partial repayment of what I owed to him and to his friend and collaborator in Langton studies, Mgr. George Lacombe. The subject had a further advantage: so many books, both learned and popular, had appeared on Archbishop Thomas and his conflict with Henry II that I could take a general knowledge of the historical background for granted. The number of studies has multiplied since 1967. My debt to Professor Raymond Foreville, Dom David Knowles and others will emerge on almost every page. These scholars gave me a starting point and their achievements dispensed me from repeating an often told story. I have merely alluded to the narrative, which can be found elsewhere.

Fortune favoured me in that Dom Adrian Morey and Professor C. N. L. Brooke were already working on the career, character and writings of Gilbert Foliot, bishop of London and Becket's chief opponent in his lifetime. I have drawn upon their massive learning. They have helped me personally by answering my enquiries too. Dr Henry Mayr-Harting told me of the Gervase of Chichester transcripts at Westminster Abbey and generously lent me his photographs and his notes on Gervase. Mlle M. T. d'Alverny sent me data from unpublished French archives. I have tapped the brains of many colleagues, too numerous to mention here. Dr J. I. Catto and Mr T. A. Reuter in particular supplied useful information. Dr R. W. Hunt put his inexhaustible store of patience, acumen and scholarship at my command, as he always has. The Bodleian Library staff has propped up a demanding reader with kind efficiency over many years.

The Governing Body of St Hilda's College granted me a term of sabbatical leave to prepare the lectures. The Principal and Fellows, Mrs Menna Prestwich in particular, did everything in their power to ease the strain of lecturing. I am very grateful to them all.

The lectures enlarged themselves when I turned them into a book. At least one important paper appeared too late for me to use: 'Henry II's Supplement to the Constitutions of Clarendon' by M. D. Knowles, Anne J. Duggan and C. N. L. Brooke, *English Historical Review* lxxxvii, 1972, 757–71. Professor Braxton Ross has a note in press in the same review on a contemporary French scholar's criticism of Becket's behaviour as chancellor; his discovery fits nicely into my chapter on Becket. Dr Ignatius Brady kindly kept me informed on the progress of his studies on the writings of Peter Lombard, which have now appeared in the Prolegomena to *Magistri Petri Lombardi Parisiensis Episcopi Sententiae in IV Libris Distinctae* (Spicilegium Bonaventurianum iv, 1971). I had not time to knit his re-dating into the gist of my argument; but he has saved me from repeating the old errors. A new edition of the Becket dossier is promised and is in competent hands. Meanwhile I have had to rely on the *Materials* in the Rolls Series *faute de mieux*. For the sake of economy I have not given the Latin of texts translated or paraphrased where it is easily available to readers. Bibliography has been cut to the bare minimum needed as evidence for my statements. A comprehensive list of studies on all the subjects and persons mentioned would have swollen my book to double its size. Modern authors have been indexed except for works which come into the table of abbreviations and are quoted *passim*. My spelling of biblical names and translation of quotations normally follow the medieval Latin Vulgate and the Douai version. The latter comes closest of the English translations to what a medieval writer had on his desk or in his memory.

December, 1972   *Beryl Smalley*

Introduction:
Intellectuals and Politics:
Detachment or Commitment?

Loysir et liberté
C'est bien son seul désir:
Ce seroit un plaisir
Pour traicter verité.

L'esprit inquieté
Ne se fait que moysir.

Liberté et loysir.

Leisure and liberty for the pleasure of treating of truth: disturbance
makes one moulder. Des Periers expressed one extreme of the intellectual's ideal. It is seldom attainable. The scholar poet hoped to
realize it by having a clever, emancipated queen as his patron; but
even Margaret of Navarre did not save him from the consequences
of his unorthodox pursuit of truth.[1] At the opposite pole we find
study conceived as an instrument of action. Skipping over countries
and centuries, I quote John Stuart Mill on the role of intellectuals in
the House of Commons: 'To put ideas into their heads and purpose
into their hearts'.[2] Jowett's Balliol, with its ideal of public service,
represents a wider application of the same theme. Learning must be
'useful' and lead to the betterment of all. T. H. Green would serve
as the apostle of this theory, to the joy of undergraduates, who
wanted 'earnest effort to bring speculation into relationship with
modern life, instead of making it an end in itself', and 'fearlessness
in the expression of opinion, ... instead of the present deadly
reserve'. Green scouted the notion that a man's philosophy has
nothing to do with his politics.[3] The objective may be reform,

[1] *Oeuvres françoises de Bonaventure Des Periers*, ed. L. Lacour i (Paris,
1856) 169; see L. Febvre, *Origène et Des Periers ou l'énigme du "Cymbalum
Mundi"* (Paris, 1942) 16.

[2] *Autobiography*, ed. H. J. Laski (London, 1924) 166; see J. Hamburger,
Intellectuals in Politics. John Stuart Mill and the Philosophic Radicals (New
Haven/London, 1965).

[3] M. Richter, *The Politics of Conscience. T. H. Green and his Age* (London, 1964) 159. For various views on the question whether political ideas
have a philosophical basis see A. Gewirth, 'Philosophy and Political Thought
in the Fourteenth Century', *The Forward Movement of the Fourteenth
Century*, ed. F. L. Utley (Ohio, 1961) 125-7.

revolution or conservatism; but on this view of his function the intellectual commits himself to political action or at least propaganda. Yet
here too his role presupposes that the Establishment will be indifferent, tolerant or friendly; otherwise the teacher may lose his post.

Many intermediate attitudes are possible between the two extremes
of detachment for the pursuit of truth and commitment to action.
Public service and a role in politics will expose the intellectual to
compromise and careerism. He may be tempted to sell himself to
his employer. The deeper his plunge into politics the more he must
waive his principles. He will sometimes choose or have thrust upon
him the part of adviser, prophet or critic as the only alternative. Such
a limitation may be self-imposed in the name of purity: office con-
taminates. 'Even as a government supporter, the intellectual should
keep to his role of critic, in other words, *penser et non effectuer.*'
The task of criticizing does not admit of perfect detachment, since
it entails publicizing one's ideas and perhaps open protest.[4] At some
times and places the intellectual may have isolation forced upon
him willy nilly, since his comments go unheeded; he may be dismissed as an 'egghead' by public opinion outside his own circle. In
that case he will have to break through the barrier, if necessary by
violence, or resign himself to passivity. There may be no third
course.

The dilemmas of modern intellectuals and their various responses
have become a favourite subject for study. They emerge without
credit; indeed their historians generally put them in the wrong. If
detached, they are blamed for living in ivory towers or for being
'alienated'. If committed to action, they make a mess of it, exposing themselves as dogmatic, unpractical and gullible. 'An intellectual in politics is not necessarily a figure of fun', is all that a recent
apologist can say for them. They supply models for the anti-hero in
fiction. Writers can manhandle the intellectual at pleasure because
he falls into a recognizable category. The question whether non-
intellectuals have made a better showing in public or private life can
never be answered. It does not lend itself to a book or a thesis. The
intellectual, on the other hand, offers a sitting target.

The attack on modern intellectuals adds interest to the record of
their prototypes in the middle ages. These form an even more
clearly definable group, since learning centred on schools and universities from the late eleventh century onward. When few men

[4] S. de Beauvoir, *La force des choses* (Paris, 1963) 427, 650.

were literate and Latin, the language of book lore, belonged to the clergy, pursuit of higher studies in institutions created a conscious élite. The graduate, whether clerk, monk or friar, wore his Master's title as a badge, just as knighthood marked a social distinction among laymen. Hence an 'intellectual' was an academic by profession, a scholar or 'schoolman' as historians call it. Naturally, therefore, the schoolmen have been treated as a closely knit group, which could be either committed or detached *en bloc*. Opinions as to which it was have differed according to the viewer and are contradictory. The conflict has turned mainly on the question whether the schoolmen were committed agents of the Church and the papacy or whether they remained detached and independent. My survey of historical judgements on their role in politics is not meant to be comprehensive, but I hope that my illustrations are typical.

At first the schoolmen were accused of being committed, not for ideological reasons, but for self-interest. The offensive began with Marsilio of Padua; it was launched in his *Defensor pacis*, 1324. Marsilio traces the papal 'usurpation' of civil power in the West, which included control of education and learning. The popes realized that the schools would serve them as a means, and a very powerful one, to strengthen their hold on the bodies and the minds of Christians. They appropriated as their right what Christian emperors had granted to the Church for motives of piety and respect. So it came about that universities under papal control formed centres of subversion against the civil power. Marsilio saw the schoolmen as mercenaries engaged to fight for the popes. They sold themselves in order to safeguard their degrees, wrongly supposing that their titles derived from papal rather than from civil authority:

> Bishops today . . . subject colleges of learned men to themselves, withdrawing them from their allegiance to secular rulers, and use them as no slight, but very powerful means to defend and perpetuate their usurpations against secular rulers. Learned men do not want to lose their professional titles, since they desire the ease and the glory which possession of such titles brings. They believe that they owe their titles solely to the authority of the Roman and other bishops; so they obey the latters' directives and oppose any persons, whether rulers or subjects, who go against what they consider to be the authority of the bishops.[5]

[5] *The Defensor Pacis of Marsilius of Padua*, ed. C. W. Previté-Orton (Cam-

B

The pope, therefore, had 'sophists and false teachers and preachers of Holy Scripture' at his bidding to stir up subjects against secular princes. Force of habit played into his hands. Inveterate misinterpretation of Scripture had conditioned men to accept all those papal claims which Marsilio would expose as baseless. His remedy for the evil was not academic freedom, but civil control. Education ought to be a function of lay society, subject to the secular government just as much as any other matter touching the public welfare. Willing commitment to the State should replace corrupt subservience to the Church. Marsilio called for a new type of professor, who would fight the enemy and draw better lessons from Scripture.[6] His friend and collaborator, Master John of Jandun, agreed with him that the intellectual ought to commit himself: armchair philosophers should be expelled from the commonwealth or merely tolerated as parasites.[7]

This is trenchant enough, but the tone grows sharper. Protestant polemic revived Marsilio's attack on the schoolmen, independently, yet not accidentally. There is one difference, in that Marsilio's subtle analysis of motives was beyond the reformers' grasp. They saw the schoolmen as volunteers, not mercenaries, in the devil's army, foundation members of the Great Conspiracy to pervert true religion to superstition. Again they were blamed for distorting Scripture to suit their purpose. Worse, they added to Scripture the teaching of other writers, which was more easily manipulated. As Peucher, Melanchthon's son-in-law, put it, they wove 'a doctrine opposed to the Gospels out of Plato's opinions and Aristotle's arguments' so as to keep men in subjection to Rome. Scripture proved insufficient to authorize new abuses; then they turned to the *Sentences* of Peter Lombard, whose name sounded in the pulpits more often than Christ's. Not only theologians, but canon lawyers also supported Roman tyranny and the Roman hierarchy. As for the friars, they were sired by Roman tyranny out of superstition.[8]

bridge, 1928) 340; I quote with a few changes from the translation by A. Gewirth, *Marsilius of Padua. The Defender of the Peace* ii (New York, 1956) 298.

[6] ed. cit. 109, 111, 308, 334–42, 412.

[7] L. Schmugge, *Johannes von Jandun (1285/9–1328)* (Pariser historische Studien v, Stuttgart, 1966) 71–3.

[8] *Chronicon Carionis expositus et auctus a Casparo Peucero* (Wittenburg, 1580) 493, 502–3, 436–9, 440, 482–4; G. Falco, *La polemica sul Medio Evo* (Biblioteca della Società Storica Subalpina cxliii, Turin, 1933) 52, 66, 78.

The Erastian element in Protestantism led to the revival of Mar-silio's charge that the schoolmen subverted civil government as well as teaching false doctrine. The friars in particular, as university men, looked like sedition-mongers and trouble-makers. Paradoxically enough, John Selden compared them to Puritan extremists. He knew enough of medieval history to note a curious parallel. Puritans were endowing lectureships in English parishes to correct the short-comings of ignorant or backward parish clergy in preaching to the people. The lecturers were graduates for the most part and strove to reform the Church of England on Protestant lines. Selden disliked their zeal, which reminded him of the old quarrel between regular and secular clergy: 'Lecturers doe in a parish what the ffryers did heretofore; gett away not only the affections, but the bounty that should be bestowed on the Minister.'[9] The friars had been papal agents; the lecturers cried 'No popery!' louder than moderate men could approve. Universities bred both types of enthusiast.

Thomas Hobbes underlined and expanded the thesis that uni-versities endangered the peace of the commonwealth. He followed Marsilio in tracing it back to their origins in the middle ages. In *Behemoth* Hobbes gives a short history of the medieval schools as instruments of papal politics:

> The profit the Church of Rome expected from them, and in effect received, was the maintenance of the Pope's doctrine, and of his authority over kings and their subjects, by school divines. . . . It was an evident argument of that design, that they fell in hand with the work so quickly. . . . From the universities it was, that all preachers proceeded, and were poured into city and coun-try, to terrify the people into an absolute obedience to the Pope's canons and commands . . .[10]

Leviathan tells us how the 'school divines' propagated 'the King-dom of Darkness' by expounding Scripture according to the papal sense: 'The power of the pope was always upheld against the power of the Commonwealth principally by the Universities.' The effects had lasted: 'It is no wonder that they yet retain a relish of that subtle

[9] *Table Talk of John Selden*, ed. F. Pollock (London, 1927) 49, 71, quoted with other examples by Christopher Hill, *Society and Puritanism in Pre-Revolutionary England* (London, 1964) 80.
[10] *The English Works of Thomas Hobbes*, ed. W. Molesworth vi (London, 1840) 184–5, 213–15.

liquor, wherein they were first seasoned.'[11] Hobbes saw the schoolmen as both bribed and willing agents of Rome. Again like Marsilio,
he prescribed not freedom but service to the sovereign as his remedy.
'The right teaching of youth in the universities' would forestall subversion. He offered a doctrine compounded of his new mixture of
authority and reason.

The revival of biblical scholarship in the nineteenth century
brought the schoolmen's politics under fire again. The school divines
had expounded Scripture according to the four senses. The method
had long been discredited; it embarrassed even Catholic apologists
for the schoolmen.[12] New ideas and techniques in exegesis made the
four senses look even more absurd than formerly; they were seen to
have political implications as well. Dean Farrar, whose views were a
mixture of broad church and evangelical, considered medieval
exegesis in his comprehensive survey. He blamed the four senses as
'advantageous to hierarchical usurpations'. The schoolmen 'made a
standing dogma of "the obscurity of Scripture", which was thus kept
safely out of the hands of the multitude'. But this Victorian clergy-
man was a widely read scholar; he knew his sources. While deploring
their aims and methods, he admired medieval teachers as men.
They impressed him as dedicated and unselfish, however misguided.
The 'deceived or deceiving schoolmen', as Hobbes called them, get
the benefit of the doubt in Farrar's *History of Interpretation*.[13]

The Romantic reappraisal of the middle ages brought up the
opposite view: the schoolmen were free from political pressures and
detached in their attitude. Liberal Catholics in France held them up
as an example to prove that one could be both a Catholic and 'a
friend of liberty and learning', in Ozanam's words. If the Church
could be shown to have fostered learning and liberty in the middle
ages, she might do so again.[14] Montalembert, historian of the monks
in the West, found time to praise the freedom enjoyed by medieval
scholars. Their universities, he noted, were 'lively, free, sometimes
even rebellious':

[11] ed. Blackwell's Political Texts (Oxford, 1949) 454, 225, 408.

[12] See for instance A. Duquesnel, *Histoire des letters au Moyen Age* (Paris,
1842) 165.

[13] F. W. Farrar, *History of Interpretation* (London, 1886) 246, 296–7, 302.
On Farrar see D.N.B. supplement ii, 9–12: on his scholarship see Owen
Chadwick, *The Victorian Church* ii (London, 1970) 67, 108.

[14] F. A. Ozanam, *Oeuvres complètes* (Paris, 1855) ii, 394–6; vi, 67–70, 88.

... the masters' independence was equalled only by that of the ardent, rowdy young; they tackled daily a thousand questions which would frighten the straitlaced orthodoxy of today.[15]

The schoolmen received freedom of thought as a posthumous gift from their Catholic historians. Others contributed. An allied trend in nineteenth-century thought exalted 'groups within the State' as a bulwark against tyranny. Distribution of power among corporate bodies would protect the individual citizen both from the central government above and from Jacobinism below. Hence a revival of corporations on medieval lines was desired.[16] Medieval *studia* suggested a shining example. Their constitutions had an attractive element of democracy, but not too much of it. Milman described Paris university as 'a state within a state, a city within a city, a church within a church'. Here humble friars would 'teach the teachers of the world'.[17] Hastings Rashdall built a lasting monument to this view in his *Medieval Universities*. He had no sympathy for scholasticism, which he regarded as obscurantist, but much for the schoolmen's capacity to organize themselves. They did so efficiently enough to raise *studium* to a level with *sacerdotium* and *imperium*:

> The university, no less than the Roman Church and the feudal hierarchy headed by the Roman Emperor, represents an attempt to realise in concrete form an ideal of life in one of its aspects. Ideals pass into great historical forces by embodying themselves in institutions. The power of embodying its ideals in institutions was the peculiar genius of the medieval mind...[18]

Rashdall's picture has kept all its freshness. *Studium* is still presented as 'a third force' in medieval politics, confronting *sacerdotium* and *imperium* on equal terms, and able to ally now with one, now with the other.[19]

The detachment ascribed to medieval scholars could serve in

[15] *Les moines d'Occident* i (Paris, 1860) ccxlii, ccxlix, cclvii.

[16] See G. Martini, *Cattolicesimo e storicismo* (Naples, 1951) 10.

[17] *History of Latin Christianity* (London, 1854) i, 18; iii, 346–7; v, 42; see Duncan Forbes, *The Liberal Anglican Idea of History* (Cambridge, 1952).

[18] *The Universities of Europe in the Middle Ages* (Oxford, 1895), new edn by F. M. Powicke and A. B. Emden (Oxford, 1936) i, 3.

[19] See for instance S. Stelling Michaud, *L'université de Bologne et la pénétration des droits romain et canon en Suisse aux XIIIe et XIVe siècles* (Geneva, 1955) 13.

polemic of a new kind. It found classic expression in Julien Benda's
La trahison des clercs (1927). Benda used it as a stick to beat his contemporaries, especially the fascists. Intellectuals of the twentieth century were prostituting themselves to the demands of governments
and parties. They descended into the political arena and distorted
the truth, instead of seeking and presenting it objectively: 'The clerk
hired by seculars is a traitor to his calling.' Benda saw their treason
as a modern phenomenon. The clerks of the middle ages never justified hatred and slaughter, however powerless they were to stop them.
Humanity, thanks to the teaching of the clerks, honoured the good,
even when doing ill. Benda thought that circumstances permitted
freedom in the interval between the fall of the Roman empire and
the rise of nation states; there were fewer temptations to treachery:
the universalism of medieval culture made it easier to embrace the
things of the spirit. His personal tastes and upbringing led him to
sympathize with the abstract, supernatural quality of medieval culture, as he imagined it at least.[20]

It seems hard to reconcile these two opposing views, but Professor
Jacques Le Goff has tried to do so in his stimulating little book *Les
Intellectuels au moyen âge* (1957). His method is to distinguish two
phases in the academic history of the middle ages. First came the
pre-university phase, when teaching was still uncentralized. The
master would move from one place to another, taking his pupils
with him. The student for his part circulated freely and sampled the
teaching of masters as he chose. This lack of organization or co-
hesion favoured a comparative freedom of thought. But the scholars'
need to protect themselves led to the second phase, formation of
privileged bodies of masters and students. The members of these
new institutions submitted to the papacy in return for the granting
of privileges and for defence against local hostility. Submission
bought security at a price. The popes, while showing some broad-
mindedness, fostered universities in order to tame them. Intellectuals
became 'to a certain extent, but certainly, papal agents'. The alternative to papal supervision would have been 'la laïcité', an untrans-
latable term. Here it means independence of the ecclesiastical hierarchy, rather than dependence on the lay power. Le Goff implies that
medieval scholars might have snapped their fingers at the papacy.
The freedom of the pre-university phase might have continued. Alas,

[20] *La trahison des clercs* (Paris, 1927) 198–9; *La jeunesse d'un clerc* (Paris,
1936).

it was a 'might have been'. We return to the view of Marsilio and Hobbes that the schoolmen sold themselves to guarantee their comforts and status. Far from liberating them, as some historians have supposed, organization put fetters on intellectuals. Le Goff's is an anticlerical view, though he presents it gently and reasonably.

A different approach is possible: the schoolmen have been fitted into world histories, where they figure as unconscious or only partly conscious manifestations of forces shaping society at a certain stage in its development. Again judgements have varied. Now they are blamed for being detached, instead of praised. To Hegel their tournaments of thought and mental gymnastics typified the long night of the middle ages.[21] Karl Mannheim characterized scholasticism as 'remote from the concrete problems of life', the inward-looking mode of thought peculiar to a caste which had acquired monopolistic control of moulding the world outlook.[22] The sheer exuberance of medieval universities impressed Gibbon; he saw the schoolmen as caretakers for the humanists: 'their misguided ardour might be directed to more manly studies.'[23] Comte charged them with a more dynamic role. They were committed to the task of creating a better society within the limits imposed on them by their time. The apostle of positivism felt an odd kinship with the schoolmen. *His* new philosophy should lead to action and so to the creation of a more orderly social system. *Their* speculations, a function of medieval Catholicism, marked a rung in the ladder leading up to positivism. Anticlericals and Catholics alike had missed the schoolmen's significance; only the positivist could judge them calmly and equitably. Comte admired the medieval Church for her separation of spiritual things from temporal. By this means, he thought, she had brought morals into politics and had set a standard. He approved of her conquest of authority and of the right to judge in spiritual matters: he even sympathized with Thomas Becket. The building up of 'special institutions' for the 'speculative class' raised the schoolmen to new dignity and power, a dress-rehearsal for the modern philosopher's guidance of society. The speculative class 'set itself up in the midst of society

[21] 'Vorlesungen über die Philosophie der Geschichte', *Sämtliche Werke*, ed. H. Glockner xi (Stuttgart, 1961) 503, 518.

[22] *Ideology and Utopia. An Introduction to the Sociology of Knowledge* 3rd edn London, 1966) 9–10.

[23] *The History of the Decline and Fall of the Roman Empire* cap. lxvi (Everyman's Library, London, 1954) vi, 379.

in a permanent state of calm, enlightened observation, yet in no wise indifferent, of practical daily life.' It worked indirectly, by moral influence alone. He realized that his 'speculative class' had close links with the papacy, but that did not shock him. The popes were drawn to support the new intellectual movement and wisely accepted whatever in it was not directly hostile to themselves.[24]

The marxist view of medieval intellectuals is that they helped to build up the superstructure of feudal society. They supplied the justifications for the dominance of landlords, great or small, weaving the veil of 'feudal, patriarchal, idyllic' relations between exploiters and exploiters, which the bourgeoisie would tear down. 'We are all marxists nowadays': all would agree that the social teaching of the medieval Church was hierarchical and that criticism of the lords stopped short of advising their victims to rise in self-defence. But social teaching accounted for a small part only of the schoolmen's activities. Their particular role within the framework of the Church still remains to be determined.

Certain errors can be cleaned off at the outset. Many of the generalizations that I have reported rested on scanty knowledge of what the schoolmen wrote and did. It could not be helped. Much of what they wrote has been made available only within the last fifty years. The task of sorting, identifying, dating and editing scholastic writings is still far from complete. But we know enough to dispel the idea that the schoolmen were 'remote from the concrete facts of life'. They engaged in the abstract speculation which has given them a bad name in some quarters, true enough; but they also discussed 'concrete' problems such as taxation in its various forms. They observed and considered the import of facts in the life around them. Novelties interested them. *Primum vivere, deinde philosophari* is a modern scholar's judgement on their attitude to the corporations and guilds which sprang up in the social life of the twelfth and thirteenth centuries; the schoolmen contributed to their development, 'en lui fournissant une première élaboration intellectuelle'.[25]

The real breakthrough in modern studies of the schoolmen has

[24] *Cours de philosophie positive*, 2nd edn v (Paris, 1864) 232–4, 238, 246, 390. See D. G. Charlton, *Positivist Thought in France during the Empire 1852–1870* (Oxford, 1959) 24–50; H. Gouhier, 'La pensée médiévale dans la philosophie d'Auguste Comte', *Mélanges offerts à Etienne Gilson* (Etudes de philosophie médiévale, hors série, Toronto, 1959) 299–313.

[25] P. Michaud-Quantin, *Universitas, expressions du mouvement communautaire dans le moyen âge latin* (Paris, 1970) 341.

been to reveal what they did outside the schools and who paid them. We no longer see them in an exclusively academic setting. Knowledge of their sources of income and of their careers has enlarged and complicated the problem of their detachment or commitment in politics. Most students would follow up their degrees by teaching, perhaps for a lifetime. A piece in a thirteenth-century letter book calls upon colleagues to attend the funeral of 'that admirable doctor, who cried like a young swallow from morning unto night and meditated like a dove; devoting himself to his pupils, he died teaching and he taught dying'.[26] Even when he remained in the schools, as in this case, the master had to supplement his income from fees if he was to live comfortably. An unbeneficed teacher would suffer the humiliation of eating at another's table as a poor dependant.[27] The solution, north of the Alps at least, was to get a benefice, generally in a cathedral or collegiate church. For that one needed influence, exerted by one's family or by a patron. But few masters grew old in the schools; most of them resigned their chairs sooner or later to seek a career in ecclesiastical or secular government. The growth of bureaucracy in the twelfth century offered dazzling prospects to the graduate. Popes and prelates, abbots, princes, kings and queens employed masters as secretaries, advisers and diplomats. The wave flowing into government from the schools began about the third decade of the century and spread unevenly, according to the means and needs of employers, but inexorably. Masters educated abroad crossed both the English and the Irish Channel; the king of Connaught had a Master Laurence as his chancellor by 1175.[28] Historians of government and of *studia* join hands to uncover the masters' influx into the civil service. The richest reward was a bishopric. Kings used the Church to finance their servants, though chapters would sometimes elect a professor. Subsisting on inadequate fees and scrounging for external support did not appeal to the majority of

[26] A. Huillard-Bréholles, *Vie et correspondance de Pierre de la Vigne* (Paris, 1865) 301–2; see Isa. xxxviii, 14.

[27] See the letter to Alexander III written by Master Odo, 1166–7, begging the pope to provide for his successor in his Paris chair, printed by J. B. Pitra, *Aanalecta novissima* ii (Frascati, 1888) xxxix–xl; on the date see Brady, 'Peter Lombard', 289. Master Odo himself had been well off as chancellor of Notre-Dame.

[28] *Irish Historical Documents 1172–1922*, ed. E. Curtis and R. B. McDowell (London, 1943) 23. Master Laurence's origins and the places where he studied are unknown.

masters. There were no research institutes in the middle ages; endowment of colleges in the universities began only in the thirteenth century. The rise of the Mendicant Orders, vowed to poverty and study, opened up new perspectives; but an uninterrupted career of writing and teaching was reserved for the most gifted friars. St Thomas Aquinas owed his privilege to the fact that his superiors perceived his genius. Most friar graduates had to take their share of pastoral work, administration and business, as their Order needed them.

Scholars, therefore, were neither self-sufficient nor self-supporting. Many were unashamed careerists; all wanted their bread and butter; they had opportunities. The wheel had turned full circle. Their prototypes in the ancient world, Greek philosophers and rhetors, had served their cities or the imperial government as ambassadors, mentors and magistrates, as well as lecturing to pupils. The familiar and lucrative 'fusion of erudition and politics' reappeared just as soon as the medieval *studia* began to train men for the business of government.[29] This is not to deny that intellectual curiosity and pursuit of learning as a good in itself inspired the rise of the schools.[30] Most people have mixed motives. The schools would have been smaller and poorer had they recruited none but utterly dedicated scholars.

Our new evidence on the masters' careers makes it impossible to generalize on the question whether 'they' were detached or committed in politics. Did teaching in the schools have a political slant? If so, did the teacher put it into practice subsequently? Did he, after indoctrinating his pupils, do what he had recommended when he went off to serve a ruler or become one himself, as bishop or perhaps as pope? To collect evidence for the answer involves the study of individual masters. What did a master teach and what happened to him after he left his chair? Such evidence is hard to come by; but some gallant efforts have been made to collect and interpret what we have. Sir Maurice Powicke, that leaper over academic walls, connected Stephen Langton, the Paris theologian, with the English arch-

[29] G. W. Bowersock, *Augustus and the Greek World* (Oxford, 1965) 30–31 and passim.

[30] H. Grundmann, 'Vom Ursprung der Universität im Mittelalter', *Berichte über die Verhandlungen der sächsischen Akademie der Wissenschaften zu Leipzig, philol. hist. Klasse* ciii (1957) 37–65, defends *amor sciendi* as the primary motive in the rise of the schools.

bishop who had a hand in *Magna Carta*. Previously, Langton had been cut into two: continental scholars had studied him as a theologian and biblicist; writers on English history noticed him only from the date of his nomination to the see of Canterbury by Innocent III. Powicke believed that the evidence for both parts of Langton's career sufficed for a synthesis: the archbishop consistently applied his teaching on the rights and duties of kings and subjects and on the limits to obedience when he tackled the problems which faced him in England. The Powicke view of Langton both as a thinker and as a statesman has laid itself open to criticism;[31] but *Stephen Langton* was a pioneering book; it broke down specialisms, in order to connect what the experts had separated. It encouraged others to collect evidence for the role of scholar bishops in English politics. The *magistri* tended to be reformers. Robert Grosseteste in particular stood firm on his principles as bishop of Lincoln, though he was untypical in his refusal to compromise.[32] The inquiry continues.

It reaches full momentum in Professor J. W. Baldwin's *Masters, Princes and Merchants. The Social Views of Peter the Chanter and his Circle*.[33] The study begins in Paris, where the author examines the teaching of Peter the Chanter of Notre-Dame and his pupils and associates on moral problems of current concern to clerks and laymen, subjects and rulers. Baldwin gives us a comprehensive survey of the opinions held by a group of masters, which included Stephen Langton, for the period *c*. 1170–1215 on the norms of Christian conduct both inside and outside the schools. We follow them when they serve on commissions or go on preaching tours and when they take office as prelates. To measure their actions against their teaching is to find a high degree of consistency. But could they exert enough pressure to get their standards accepted either in canon law, as applied in the Church courts, or in secular law and practice? Some of their recommendations, but not all, passed into the decrees of the Lateran Council of 1215. Lay society, on the other hand, proved

---

[31] F. M. Powicke, *Stephen Langton* (Oxford, 1928); *The Christian Life in the Middle Ages and Other Essays* (Oxford, 1935) 130–46. For criticism see J. C. Holt, *Magna Carta* (Cambridge, 1965) 188–9; R. W. Southern, 'Sir Maurice Powicke 1879–1963', *Proceedings of the British Academy* l (1965) 285.

[32] M. Gibbs and J. Lang, *Bishops and Reform 1215–1272* (Oxford, 1934); W. A. Pantin, 'Grosseteste's Relations with the Papacy and the Crown', *Robert Grossesteste, Scholar and Bishop*, ed. D. A. Callus (Oxford, 1955) 178–215.

[33] Princeton, New Jersey, 1970.

stubborn. Neither princes nor merchants would behave as the masters thought that Christians should. The ecclesiastical authorities did not try hard enough to make them, as the Chanter and his circle saw it. The detailed rules which they proposed to prevent oppression and cheating in all walks of life were honoured in the breach. These masters set their sights too high; but that is not the point of Professor Baldwin's study. He shows that their casuistry was intended to guide contemporaries through the moral choices which beset them in marriage, business, government and litigation. As theologians they dealt with social facts and had a sense of mission. Their role was to lead the clergy in reforming the Church and the laity. Hence the privilege as well as the duty of clergy loomed large on their horizon. They were high churchmen. The reader will finish *Masters, Princes and Merchants* with a picture before him of deeply committed, disillusioned men, who acted upon their principles to the limit of the possible.

This is the fullest study of elusive data which has appeared so far. The mist has lifted patchily from later periods in the history of the scholars' role in politics. Historians have responded to the challenge of the controversies between Boniface VIII and Philip IV and to the polemics of fourteenth-century quarrels by proposing theses on academic reactions to them. What goes for one period need not apply to others. My subject in this book is just the Becket conflict. Chronologically it falls into a crucial period in the history of the schools. I have had to push back into the 1120s in order to investigate the early education of those who joined in the quarrel between Becket and Henry II. I shall touch on the Chanter and his circle near the end, so as to gauge the effect of 'murder in the cathedral' on academic opinion. Universities did not exist in name and barely in fact before about 1200. Intellectuals in the pre-university phase should have been free agents, according to Le Goff; they had not yet submitted to the papacy. It should be feasible to test his thesis, at least in so far as it concerns Becket and his friends and antagonists as former students or masters. The evidence for their doctrine and their careers is overwhelmingly rich, in spite of some nasty gaps here and there. Records survive in sufficient quantity to enable us to reconstruct the outlines of their careers both in the schools and afterwards. Thanks to modern scholarship we know what Robert Pullen and Robert of Melun taught in the schools and we can get some idea of what John of Salisbury and Herbert of Bosham learnt from their masters. Above all we have literary evidence in the form of letters, polemical pieces, and *Lives* and *Miracles* of St Thomas. Robertson assembled most of it in his *Materials*. A critical study of the dossiers put together to make up these accounts of the conflict is still to come; but we now have excellent editions of the letters of Arnulf of Lisieux, of the early correspondence of John of Salisbury and of Gilbert Foliot's letters and charters. The letters written during the dispute give us a rare opportunity to compare the official propaganda put out by Becket and his secretaries with what some of the persons involved confided to one another in private. The letters and the *Lives* between them bring the characters in the story to life; we get to know them as people. The role of individual scholars in politics could hardly be better documented than it is here. The conflict put careers and lives at stake. Scholars who took part in it had to decide first of all which opinions they held to be right; in this they would be influenced by the teaching of the schools; then they had to choose whether to sacrifice themselves for the cause or whether to compromise. In either case, they had to justify their decision on grounds of principle or expediency.

Faced by *embarras de richesses*, I decided to concentrate on the theologians or 'masters of the sacred page'. It is not a watertight division: Becket was an amateur, not a professional; John of Salisbury is better known as a classicist or 'Greats' man; many of the participants had studied canon law as well as theology; but I have neither the competence nor the courage to study the lawyers as a separate group. My inquiry begins with a short account of the relations between the papacy and the schools from the late eleventh to about the mid twelfth century. In the same chapter I shall outline the teaching of the schools on the relations between *regnum* and *sacerdotium* and on 'the liberties of the Church', since the Becket conflict raised these issues in an acute form. It is better to avoid the terms 'Church and State': secular and ecclesiastical government overlapped; Catholic rulers belonged to the polity of Latin Christendom and fought out their quarrels in that framework; the secular State was unheard of. I shall touch on the teaching of the *Artes* (trivium and quadrivium) in so far as it affected the theologians' presentation of their arguments. Rhetoric as studied in the Arts course governed the technique of drafting letters and propaganda. Masters Robert Pullen, who became papal chancellor, and Robert of Melun, who died as bishop of Hereford, will then make a bridge

between the teaching of the schools and politics in England on the
eve of and during the conflict. Next I shall examine the careers
and ideas of Herbert of Bosham and John of Salisbury. Both stand
out among the *eruditi sancti Thomae*, the learned men whom Becket
assembled in his household; both served Becket as advisers and
secretaries; Herbert was his master of the sacred page. The *eruditi*
deserve to be studied as individuals and as members of a group,[34]
but here I shall limit myself to three of them: the third is Master
Gervase of Chichester, who comes into the last chapter of the book.
In the chapter on Becket himself I have tried to describe the theologians' influence on him and how he reacted to it. I go on to Pope
Alexander III. He was another intellectual in politics; he had to
adjust the theories of the schools to the double crisis of his relations
with the emperor Frederick Barbarossa and Henry II. 'The Case
against Becket' will outline the arguments put forward by Henry
and his counsellors and defenders. My last two chapters deal with
the aftermath of the murder, the first with the effect of the martyrdom and the Becket cult on scholars in England and abroad, the
second with changing attitudes in England. We end with Master
Ralph of Diss, the dean of St Paul's.

Thus summarized my journey suggests a package tour. It is less
strenuous than it sounds. I have had to turn aside to dig into the
evidence in tiresome detail. Some tourists will prefer to rest in the
coach rather than follow their guide into nettles and thickets. In
'Conclusions' I look back at the road we have covered to find an
answer to the question whether my theologians were detached or
committed. The personnel includes a wide variety of characters in a
wide variety of situations; so there may be more than one answer.

The Becket conflict still sparks off passions and provokes value
judgements among its historians. I admit, though it makes for
dullness, that I cannot take sides in the triangular confrontation
between Henry, Becket and Alexander III. It centred on privilege
of clergy and broadened out into the wider issues of papal and
clerical rights in general. Modern arguments on either side strike me
as anachronistic. Privilege was built into the structure of medieval
society. A person who benefits from privilege will naturally want to
defend and enlarge his particular kind. Why should ability to fight
on horseback as a knight have carried more privilege than ability

---

[34] Dr Mayr-Harting tells me that he hopes to undertake such a study of
Becket's *eruditi*.

to read Latin as a clerk? Those historians who have blamed Becket as a trouble-maker because he defended clerical immunities have not shown themselves conspicuously anxious to renounce their own privileges in their own times. On the other hand, his apologists would hardly wish his claims for the Church to be revived today. History decided against ecclesiastical liberties and theocracy in the long run; but it decided against Angevin despotism too. Another admission: again at the price of dullness I cannot judge my characters as good or bad, saintly or selfish or even as big or little men. I shall not treat them *de haut en bas*, but simply ask of a scholar what opinions he professed and whether he acted on them when the crunch came. His difficulties call for sympathy, which I offer gladly. Moral judgements lie outside my scope.

I
The Teaching of the Schools

Innocent III expressed the relationship between the papacy and theologians concisely as he saw it in a formula which seems designed to prove the view of Marsilio and his successors. The pope was writing to Master Prepositinus in 1203. Prepositinus had taught theology at Paris and was now *scholasticus* at the cathedral school of Mainz; here he had sided with the anti-papal schismatics. Innocent admonished him:

> Have you forgotten what you have not only learnt but also taught, that the servant stands or falls with his master, that God is our judge and that it is sacrilegious to dispute the judgement of the prince [i.e. the pope]? . . . The Holy See expected better things of you.[1]

Prepositinus gave in. The pope was master and the masters were his servants, according to Innocent. No earlier pope would have put it so confidently; but it represents a hardening of the relationship between patron and protégés which goes back to Gregorian reform.

A synod held by Gregory VII in 1078 renewed a decree which dated from 626 after a lapse of over two and a half centuries: all bishops should have *artes litterarum* taught in their churches.[2] The popes went on to protect the bishops' employees by insisting that they should charge no fee when they granted licence to teach to a

---

[1] G. Lacombe, *La vie et les oeuvres de Prévostin* (Le Saulchoir, 1927) 33–4. I have slightly abridged in translation: ... An oblitus fortasse es, illius quod sepe non solum legisti, sed etiam docuisti, quod servus suo domino stat seu cadit, et qui nos iudicat Dominus est et instar est sacrilegii de iudicio principis iudicare? ... Ideo autem graviter te corripimus et utinam efficaciter corrigamus, quia dolemus te conversum esse in arcum perversum, de quo apostolica sedes aliud cogitavit.

[2] V. Ussani, 'Gregorio VII scrittore nella sua corrispondenza e nei suoi dettati', S.G. ii (1947) 341–2.

qualified master.[3] As the number of scholars attending schools in places far from their homes increased, the problem of their status arose: they were 'stateless' and 'lawless' and had no appeal against local attempts to exploit them. The popes came to their rescue. Scholars sheltered under privilege of clergy, as it came to be defined at canon law. The umbrella of papal patronage was by no means stormproof. Its very frailty led the popes to intervene in special cases and on special occasions. A key issue in the Gregorian reform movement was that the Church should offer a career open to talent, as we should put it. Wealth, birth and service to a prince should no longer be the sole criteria for promotion. They continued to carry weight, but less than formerly. The programme appealed to scholars who depended on their brains to rise in the world. It followed logically that masters and students sought papal recognition and privileges when they began to unite in guilds and corporate bodies.[4] Popes and scholars formed a mutual help, if not always a mutual admiration society. They relied on one another because they had no alternative.

Theologians looked to papal favour more than any other group of scholars. It was costly to proceed from the Arts to one of the higher branches of study, theology, medicine or law. Desire for support during the course and reward for capital outlay afterwards was common to all. Law and medicine offered better prospects than theology, which was a gamble from a career point of view:

Galen gives you wealth and so does Justinian's law;
From these you gather grain, from the others only straw.

The latest research on this famous quip has traced it back to an unknown English writer of the late twelfth century.[5] The sentiment he expressed was by no means new. It dated from the specialization in disciplines of the early twelfth century. Theology or *sacra pagina* hived off from canon law studies. Demand for legal experts exceeded that for theologians. The acknowledged 'queen of the sciences' had less obvious usefulness than law in the eyes of employers, electors

[3] P. Delhaye, 'L'organisation scolaire au XIIe siècle', *Traditio* v (1947) 211–268.

[4] P. Kibre, *Scholarly Privileges in the Middle Ages* (Publications of the Medieval Academy of America lxxii, 1961) 7–9, 85–8.

[5] S. Kuttner, 'Dat Galienus opes et sanctio Justiniana', *Linguistic and Literary Studies in honour of Helmut A. Hatzfeld*, ed. A. B. Crisafulli (Washington, 1964) 238–46.

C

and patrons. No papal pronouncement could alter the law of supply and demand; the Curia itself needed lawyers. But Christian doctrine obliged the popes to pay lip-service to the claims of theology as the best training for cure of souls, and hence of high office in the hierarchy. St Gregory's *Rule of Pastoral Care* put the claim too forcibly to be ignored. The popes offered praise always and promotion sometimes, as when Robert Pullen was raised to be cardinal and then papal chancellor.

The schools of theology performed two functions, both of which concerned the pope as head of the Church. The masters were slowly building up a body of doctrine on subjects hitherto undefined, and establishing a sacramental system by a process of discussion and synthesis. This part of their work is the better known. Modern scholars have discovered, classified, identified and edited many *quaestiones*, sentences and early attempts at systematic treatises. We have studies on the schools of Laon and of St Victor, of Peter Abelard, of his disciples and critics and of the *Porretani*. They are not a happy hunting ground for the student of political thought. Relations between *regnum* and *sacerdotium* seldom figure among the subjects discussed in the schools. Hugh of St Victor makes an exception; he had an unusually wide range of interests. The conspiracy of silence suggests a reaction against the polemics of the 'Investiture Contest'. The questions at issue between empire and papacy had been settled or shelved before it ground to a halt in 1122. The period between about 1100, when the school of Laon was flourishing, to the schism of 1159 marked a pause. The schism of 1130 hardly disturbed it, since the emperor took St Bernard's side; St Bernard spoke for the majority of northern princes and bishops. Not that the popes abated their claims, but masters had no reason to defend what was not openly denied. They put their energy into clarifying doctrine by means of speculation and worked for the moral reform of the Church: a reformed clergy would teach and discipline the laity. The time had come to carry out this part of the Gregorian programme. Responsibility fell upon the willing shoulders of masters of the holy page.

Master Anselm of Laon, a shrewd and serene character, did his best to forward reform. He objected to the rigged election of Waldric, Henry I's chancellor, to the bishopric of Laon on grounds of irregularities and of unsuitability in 1107. Anselm brought the case to the Curia, but Paschal II decided in favour of Waldric and his money, according to Guibert of Nogent. Anselm accepted the pope's decision. His suspicions of Waldric were confirmed when he accompanied Waldric on a journey to England and perceived that his wealth was dishonestly come by; but the master of Laon must have been on good terms with Henry I or he could hardly have made the journey. As dean of Laon he tried to keep peace in the rebellious town and fulfilled his duties so conscientiously that they interfered with his work of glossing the Bible.[6] His real contribution to reform was to hold a school to train future priests and prelates in preaching and pastoral care. This represents the second function of the early schools.

The Gregorian reformers laid stress on preaching, which inhered in their concept of *sacerdotium*. A bishop had *ministerium praedicationis;* it was his duty to teach and preach and to supervise teaching and preaching in his diocese. The duty went right down the scale to the humblest priest. Ordination conferred power to preach the word as well as to administer the sacraments, although its exercise was subject to the permission of superiors. A more legalistic view of preaching, which dwelt upon the jurisdictional element in its exercise, became current only in the thirteenth century.[7] Masters of the holy page would preach themselves and they would train cadres. The condition for training was to set an example: practise what you preach. The masters of Laon held a school of piety. Their teaching pointed the way to conversion to a religious Order or to the mission field. Robert of Bethune had this experience. Doubting his own competence to understand the Scriptures,

> He betook himself to the famous Catholic masters William of Champeaux and Anselm of Laon. The writings of the holy fathers had taught them truly what to think of the divine Scriptures and what to preach and to venerate.

His studies led Robert to join the Order of Canons Regular. Later, as bishop of Hereford, 1131–48, he befriended poor scholars and he obeyed the pope, attending the council of Rheims in spite of illness.[8]

---

[6] Guibert of Nogent, *De vita sua*, ed. G. Bourgin (Paris, 1907) 139–44; *Study of the Bible*, 50. On Waldric, see D.N.B. vii, 812–13.

[7] M. Peuchmaurd, 'Le prêtre ministre de la parole dans la théologie du XIIe siècle', R.T.A.M. xxix (1962) 52–76.

[8] ed. H. Wharton, *Anglia sacra* ii (London, 1891) 300–1, 308, 314. The *Life* is contemporary, written by a chaplain of Robert's.

St Gilbert of Sempringham studied the liberal arts and theology
and qualified as a master somewhere in France. The date of his
birth, 1089, makes it likely that he went to Laon, though the canon
of Sempringham who wrote his *Life* does not specify. Gilbert turned
to religion upon leaving the schools and founded the Order called
after him.[9] It is remembered for the help it gave to Becket when
he was hiding after the council of Northampton. He also received
money from the Order sent to him in exile, at some risk to Gilbert
and his canons.[10] A conversion to the mission field is recorded by
Helmold in his *Chronicle of the Slavs*. The clerk Vicelin travelled
to Laon after teaching Arts at Bremen, because Anselm and Ralph
were so eminent as teachers of the holy page. Vicelin avoided superfluous questions in order to concentrate on what would suffice him
for sober understanding and character formation. He began to lead
a more ascetic life after thus receiving God's word. Three years later
he returned home. St Norbert ordained him priest and he served
Duke Henry of Saxony as missionary to the pagan Slavs.[11]

It appears from these three examples that conversion happened
as a result of study; it was not a reaction against scholasticism. Note
the contrast between Robert, Gilbert and Vicelin on the one hand
and Richard Rolle of Hampole on the other: Rolle gave up his
studies at Oxford in disgust about 1315 and became a solitary.[12]
The schools had ceased to be a path to virtue. Yet the masters of
Laon had immense success in the more worldly task of equipping
their pupils for prelacy. When some canons of Laon visited England
on a tour to collect money for building, they met alumni all along

[9] *Vita*, ed. W. Dugdale, *Monasticon Anglicanum* vi, 1 (London, 1830)
v... patriam suam deserens, in Galliarum se transposuit regiones... Ado-
lescans... in scola virtutum didicit maturius morum disciplinam, et cuius
postea erat magister, coepit mox totius honestatis fieri discipulus. Institutus
est itaque tamdiu liberalibus et spiritualibus studiis, donec magistri nomen
mereretur et gradum...
See R. Graham, *S. Gilbert of Sempringham and the Gilbertines* (London,
1901) 1-4.

[10] ibid. 17-19: Knowles, *Becket*, 100.

[11] ed. B. Schmeidler, M.G.H. *in us.schol.* (1937) 87-92. Vicelin probably
attended the school of Laon after Anselm's death, when his brother Ralph
was still teaching, 1123-6. Vicelin studied only 'quae sobrio intellectui et
moribus instruendis sufficerent'.

[12] *Richard Rolle Le Chant d'Amour (Melos Amoris)* i, ed. F. Vanden-
broucke, with a translation by the nuns of Wisque (Sources Chrétiennes 168,
Série des Textes Monastiques d'Occident xxxii, 1971) 19-20.

their route, beginning with the archbishop of Canterbury, William of Corbeil (1123–36).[13]

The trials of Abelard and of Gilbert of la Porrée sent up a smoke-screen of polemic on the role of the schools. It should not blind us to the dull, workaday services which masters rendered to the Church. In fact they spoke up for themselves and climbed out of the fog. Master Alan of Lille (d. 1203) gave them a high place in the ecclesiastical hierarchy when he compared it to the divine. Masters of the holy page corresponded to cherubim, having 'fullness of knowledge'; they stood only one step lower than contemplatives, corresponding to seraphim. The masters' part in the divine plan was to guide men to knowledge of God. Each rank in the hierarchy had its opposing group of demons. Those opposed to the masters tried to pervert good government to tyranny.[14] Alan's juxtaposition of ideas brings out the responsibility for teaching and training prelates which he allotted to theologians. *They that are learned shall shine as the brightness of the firmament* (Dan. xii, 3), the pope wrote to doctors of theology in 1219.[15] The Laon tradition had established itself.

An account of teaching techniques will be in order here. Our proliferation of courses, such as pastoral theology and social psychology, was quite foreign to the medieval schools. It never occurred to the masters to devise a syllabus to train their pupils in 'decision making'. Yet they had the equivalents. It was all lumped together into lectures on Scripture. *Lectio* itself served as an omnibus term: to 'read a book' meant both to read it to oneself or to others, and to hear it lectured on by one's master.[16] The lectures on *sacra pagina* given in the schools combined exegesis in the strict sense of biblical study, reinforced by textual criticism in varying degrees, with homiletics, based on the text and its earlier commentators. Homiletics offered character formation, *instructio morum*. When Vicelin chose

---

[13] *De miraculis S. Mariae Laudunensis*, P.L. clvi, 974–88.

[14] M.-T. d'Alverny, *Alain de Lille* (Paris, 1965) 231–3.

[15] G. Le Bras, '*Velut splendor firmamenti*: le docteur dans le droit de l'Eglise médiévale', *Mélanges offerts à Etienne Gilson* (Toronto, 1959) 372–388.

[16] Guy II of Chartreux, *Epistola de vita contemplativa* (d. 1188) ed. E. Colledge and J. Walsh (Sources Chrétiennes no. 163, Paris, 1970) 110: Auditus enim quodammodo pertinet ad lectionem: unde et solemus dicere non solum libros illos nos legisse quos nobis ipsis vel aliis legimus, sed et illos quos a magistris audivimus.

it as his special subject at Laon, we must suppose that he attended lectures on the holy page. Students of *Artes* could pick up some notions on ethics from the teaching on ancient philosophers before they went on to learn about the Christian dispensation.[17] The activities of early-twelfth-century masters in this field are less well documented than their production of sentences and *quaestiones*. Fewer commentaries on Scripture have survived and they have been less carefully studied. Master Anselm of Laon and his pupils and colleagues compiled a *Gloss* on the whole Bible, which became an indispensable *instrument de travail* in medieval classrooms. But they did not mean it to be an original contribution. Otherwise their record as commentators is meagre from the point of view of survival.[18] The same thing applies to masters in other schools. Master Alberic, a pupil of Anselm, taught the holy page at Rheims for eighteen years, 1118-36; nothing of his work remains.[19] Simon of Poissy, who taught John of Salisbury at Paris, left nothing either. However, we can use bits and pieces of evidence and read between the lines.

Two masters, Robert Pullen and Geoffrey Babion, used their lecture courses as material for sermons; so we can reconstruct their teaching, although we cannot read it in the original form.[20] One of our earliest specimens of the homiletic type of commentary derives from the lectures of Master Ivo of Chartres, called 'the younger' to distinguish him from the canonist bishop of Chartres. Ivo on the Psalter did become popular enough to survive in many copies.[21] He was a pupil of Gilbert of la Porrée and the link is suggestive. The future bishop of Poitiers made his mark as a philosopher and

---

[17] Ph. Delhaye, '*Grammatica* et *Ethica* au XIIe siècle', R.T.A.M. xxv (1958) 59-110; R. Bultot, 'La *Chartula* et l'enseignement du mépris du monde dans les écoles et les universités médiévales', *Studi medievali*, series 3, viii (1967) 787-834.

[18] B. Smalley, 'Les commentaires bibliques de l'époque romane: glose ordinaire et gloses périmées', *Cahiers de civilisation médiévale* iv (1961) 15-22; R. Wasselynck, 'L'influence de l'exégèse de S. Grégoire le Grand sur les commentaires bibliques médiévaux', R.T.A.M. xxxii (1965) 186-91; Lottin, 153-74.

[19] J. R. Williams, 'The Cathedral School of Reims in the time of Master Alberic, 1118-1136', *Traditio* xx (1964) 93-114.

[20] See below, pp. 117, 242.

[21] *Rep. Bibl*, no. 5337; B. Smalley, 'Master Ivo of Chartres', E.H.R. l (1935) 680-6: R. B. C. Huygens, 'Guillaume de Tyr étudiant', *Latomus* xxi (1962) 822-7.

theologian, but he also won fame as a commentator on the Bible. His obituary notices dwell on his commentaries on the Psalter and the Pauline Epistles, which expanded the Laon *Gloss* on these books and were called the *media glosatura*.[22] John of Salisbury praised him as 'the most excellent preacher of grace among the school doctors of our time'. *Gratiae praedicator* implies a likeness to St Paul. John describes Gilbert's method as a lecturer: wherever his text gave an opening, he would attack heretics, explaining what passages of Scripture the heresiarchs used to defend themselves, how their heresies arose and for what reason.[23] Ivo of Chartres supplemented his master's teaching on Scripture by producing a fuller, more homiletic type of commentary on the Psalter; Gilbert had warned against heresies; Ivo saw to the more practical business of *instructio morum*. We need not see him as an innovator. He would have used earlier school books among his sources. His homiletic lecture course just happens to be one of the first we have.

The marriage between exegesis and homiletics was of long standing. But the masters had a new purpose. What abbots had done for their monks in *collationes*, that masters would do for their pupils in lectures. They brought St Gregory's *Rule of Pastoral Care* up to date and reorganized the gist of his teaching around their text. They differed from monastic homilists in looking outwards rather than inwards. Certainly they spoke of conflicts between virtues and vices in the soul; but they preferred to focus on society. They harped on the theme of the duties and corresponding failings of each rank of the social hierarchy. Priests and prelates got the full treatment: masters exalted their duties and status and scolded them for falling short of the high standard required of them. Here we impinge on

[22] N. M. Haring, 'Epitaphs and Necrologies on Bishop Gilbert II of Poitiers', A.H.D.L.M.A. xxxvi (1970) 59, 69–70, 79. A Christmas sermon preached by Gilbert, probably between 1140 and 1153, consists for about two-thirds of quotations from his commentary on Boethius, oddly framed in the liturgy; it points to his particular interests, which ran to philosophy and theology; see N. M. Haring, 'A Christmas Sermon by Gilbert of Poitiers', *Mediaeval Studies* xxiii (1961) 126–35.

[23] *Hist. pontif.* c.xiii, p. 28: Fuit autem inter scolasticos etatis nostre doctores excellentissimus gratie predicator, et qui ceteris subtilius et fortius, quotiens inter legendum se locus ingerebat, impugnans hereses edocebat a quibus articulis scripturarum eas eruere et tueri conati sint heresarchie, et que quibus originem dederint, et a quibus et qua ratione et quibus auctoritatibus fuerint condempnate.

It is natural to take *inter legendum* as referring to lectures on Scripture.

political theory at last. The good bishop must defend his church and his people against lay tyrants. His subject led the master to make statements on the relations between *regnum* and *sacerdotium*. Such comments appear more often in lectures on Scripture than they do in *quaestiones* because the genre demanded that they should. I wrote 'statements': allusions would be a better word. The masters generally touch on opinions which had been current since Gregorian reform or earlier. They take for granted points of view which they regard as familiar. We have to put their teaching into its background.

Their tendency was to uphold the superiority of the spiritual over the temporal power and papal supremacy over the Church. There were shades of opinion; but I shall not go into the niceties of discussions on 'the two swords'. The disciples showed two swords to Christ according to the Gospel; he said *it is enough* and he commanded St Peter to sheathe his sword. It was generally agreed by the mid twelfth century that the two swords signified respectively the spiritual and temporal power. Peter received the sword of spiritual power directly from Christ in virtue of his office as head of the Church and passed it on to his successors in his chair. When Christ commanded him to sheathe his sword, he referred to the sword of temporal power. It was not permitted to the pope and clergy to wield the sword of temporal power themselves: as churchmen they might not be party to the shedding of blood. Physical coercion belonged to the secular ruler, who must exercise it on the Church's behalf. Argument turned on the degree of independence which the secular prince might have in ruling over his subjects. Did he receive his sword directly from God or as a delegation of power from the pope as representative of St Peter? Should he be resisted if he ruled tyrannically and oppressed the Church? Should the clergy respect the temporal power as ordained by God in all cases? Should they rely on spiritual weapons only, arming themselves with prayer or perhaps excommunication? Gregory VII had mobilized lay subjects to fight against the Henricians: should his precedent be followed if a lay ruler tyrannized? These were thorny questions. It was better to let sleeping dogs lie. Theologians did not concern themselves with the consequences to be drawn from the 'two swords' theory until they ceased to be matter for academic speculation and became actual, with rare exceptions, as we shall see.

What part, if any, did masters of the holy page play in formulating the theory of the two swords? St Bernard was the first to express it precisely in a letter to Pope Eugenius III, written towards 1149:[24] St Peter and his successors held both swords, one of which was delegated to the lay power. Intensive research on the history of the idea has shown that the underlying concept and even the metaphor were not new. St Peter Damian (d. 1072) is said to have been the first to compare the two swords of the gospel to *regnum* and *sacerdotium*.[25] A closer parallel to St Bernard's formula occurs in a commentary on the Canticle by John of Mantua, a secular priest or clerk in the household of Countess Matilda of Tuscany; he wrote it between spring 1081 and autumn 1083. Professor Bischoff discovered the commentary and edited passages from it as long ago as 1948; seekers of precedents for Bernard's formula have tended to overlook it, because the article is shrouded in an unlikely title and buried in a *Festschrift*. John of Mantua used his commentary as a setting for polemic in favour of the Gregorian cause, as supported by his patroness, the friend and most faithful ally of Gregory VII. The pope, in John's view, wields the 'sword of heaven', that is of spiritual censure. Christ commanded St Peter to sheathe his sword, that is the 'sword of the world', but not to throw it away. The sword of the world signifies power exercised righteously under papal authority. St Peter sheathes his sword at the divine command when he authorizes the secular powers. So John calls upon Matilda to fight for St Peter with the sword of the world.[26] The whole argument supposes that the pope as vicar of St Peter has two swords; he ratifies the use of the temporal sword by secular rulers, provided, John

---

[24] P.L. clxxxii, 463–4; and *De consideratione* iv, 3 (*Opera*, ed. J. Leclercq and H. M. Rochais, iii, Rome, 1963) 454; see H.-X Arquillière, 'Origines de la théorie des deux glaives', S.G. i (1947) 501–21.

[25] H. Hoffman, 'Die beiden Schwerter im hohen Mittelalter', *Deutsches Archiv für Erforschung des Mittelalters* xx (1964) 79.

[26] B. Bischoff, 'Der Canticumkommentar des Johannes von Mantua für die Markgräfin Mathilde', *Lebenskräfte in der abendländischen Geistesgeschichte. Dank-und Erinnerungsgabe an Walter Goetz*, ed. W. Stammler (Marburg, 1948) 41: Animadverte quod Dominus Petro in gladium ruenti dixit 'repone gladium in vaginam'. Qui enim precepit gladium in vaginam custodiri, non precepit omnino debere abici. Non enim proici, sed repone et loco suo redde. Locus gladii iusta est potestas ab auctoritate Petri non divisa. Huic dimittit Petrus gladium divino imperio, quando eius vicarius laudat et firmat potestates in seculo. Ad hanc vaginam iussit Magister suus imponere, ne, qui sacerdos erat, sua propria manu militiam gereret. Sed ipse cohercendo gladio celi, tu autem gladio mundi, contra heresim pululantem et maiorem partem mundi subvertentem vindictam exercete.

implies, that they wield it righteously, that is, in St Peter's cause. Henry IV and his allies, who fought against St Peter, get some hard knocks in the commentary.

It is impossible to believe that John of Mantua invented the application of the biblical text to his polemic. He refers to the two swords obliquely, expecting his readers to know what he means. His aim is less to theorize than to encourage Matilda and to justify her for making war on the Henricians. The formula must have been current in Gregorian circles before the 1080s. Nor could St Bernard have copied it from a book written over sixty years earlier, and soon forgotten. The fact that it became commonplace from the mid twelfth century onwards suggests that he did not put it into circulation either. The two swords of St Peter, one of them delegated to the lay power, led an underground existence from the Gregorian reform until St Bernard referred to them, in the sense that we find no mention of them in any known writings. They must have had currency in speech in the schools; they may even have appeared in writings such as biblical commentaries which are now lost.

Master Hugh of St Victor described the relationship between the two powers in his *De sacramentis* (*c.* 1131-7),[27] without quoting the texts on the two swords: he argued for the superiority of the spiritual power on the traditional ground that the higher rules the lower. *De sacramentis* spread so fast and was so much read that it is worth resuming a well-known passage. The primacy of *sacerdotium* belonged to the very fabric of Hugh's account of the history of salvation, which he focused on the Church. He defined the Church as 'the multitude of the faithful, the aggregate of Christians'. The aggregate embraced two orders: the laity stood on the left and the clergy on the right. Faithful Christian laymen were allowed to possess earthly things, but to the clergy only spiritual things were committed. Hugh included sources of revenue among 'spiritual things'; he went on to find prototypes in the Old Testament. The tribe of Levi, which represented the clergy, was supported by tithes and oblations and victims of sacrifice, whereas all the other tribes of

---

[27] D. Van den Eynde, *Essai sur la succession et la date des écrits de Hugues de Saint-Victor* (Spicilegium Pontificii Athenaei Antoniani, Rome, 1960) 100–3, 207. Book II of *De sacramentis* was written after the summer of 1134. See II, ii, 2–8, P.L. clxxvi, 417–22. I have partly followed the translation by R. J. Deferrari, *Hugh of Saint Victor on the Sacraments of the Christian Faith* (Cambridge, Mass., 1951) 254–9.

Israel received their portions in heredity. Hence there were two lives, two peoples and two powers, the earthly and the heavenly, each having grades within itself:

> The earthly power has the king as its head. The spiritual has the pope. To the powers of the king pertain all things that are earthly and made for the earthly life. To the power of the pope pertain all things that are spiritual and attributed to the spiritual life. Now the more worthy the spiritual life is than the earthly and the spirit than the body, so much does the spiritual power precede the earthly or secular in honour and in dignity.

Hugh drew the consequence that the spiritual power had to 'establish the earthly, that it might exist', and had to judge it if it were not good; but the spiritual power could be judged by God alone. Royal or imperial power was consecrated, blessed and formed by the priesthood. He allowed some discretion to the earthly power in making just distribution of lands and revenues and in granting rights to clerical overlords. A secular ruler might grant them jurisdiction. They could not exercise such rights in person, if they involved shedding of blood, but might delegate secular officials to do so according to secular law. Hugh safeguarded the rights of the secular ruler: churchmen owed him obedience in administering the lands he had granted them; but his rights stopped short in spiritual matters. A secular judge might lay hands upon a layman if he sinned, but not upon a clerk. Spiritual causes belonged to the Church. Secular justice must respect holy places, holy days and the right of sanctuary.[28]

De sacramentis made a strong claim for *sacerdotium*, in spite of the author's desire to be fair to *regnum*. The Church establishes, judges, blesses and 'forms' or instructs the temporal power. Hugh defended clerical immunities as a corollary. His teaching lived on at St Victor and was put into practice. The Chronicle of Wigmore

[28] P.L. clxxvi, 420–22: Secundum personam aliquid licet; et aliquid non licet, quemadmodum saeculari iudici in personam laicam, si peccaverit, manum mittere licet, in clericum non licet. . . . Secundum personam ergo iustitia violaretur, si iudex saecularis in ecclesiasticam personam manum mitteret. Secundum causam, si ecclesiastica negotia examinanda susciperet. . . . Secundum locum, si loca sacra violare praesumeret; et confugientibus ad illa etiam reis et pro suis sceleribus condemnandis inordinate violentiam inferre tentaret. Secundum tempus, si sacris et solemnibus diebus reverentiam non exhiberet. . .

Abbey illustrates it. Wigmore was a daughter house of St Victor on the Welsh border. The canons kept in close touch with the Paris abbey in the early years; there was exchange of personnel and journeying to and fro. The canons of Wigmore refused to pay taxes to their secular patron on grounds of principle and would defend their property rights by appeal to the Roman Curia.[29] The Paris Victorines supported Becket warmly.[30] Their position as endowed religious *vis-à-vis* the papacy differed from that of secular masters in that they did not depend on papal favour for their careers. But they had reason to be grateful to the popes for sponsoring their Order. St Victor and her daughter houses belonged to the Canons Regular or Canons of St Augustine. This Order had grown up under the wing of the reformed papacy. Popes Honorius II, Innocent II and Adrian IV were all three Canons Regular themselves.[31] The 'Rule of St Augustine' attracted intellectuals because it encouraged study and teaching as part of the religious life. The Victorines kept open school at Paris. The experiment of reviving up-to-date and original teaching in the cloister was a brilliant success in the lifetime of Hugh and his pupils. By favouring the Order, the popes promoted learning and religion simultaneously.

Interest fused with conviction to persuade masters of the holy page that they ought to defend the papacy and *sacerdotium*. The defence only smouldered in the calm of the early and mid twelfth century. We see the odd flicker, but nothing spectacular. The schism of 1159 and the Becket conflict made it burst into flame.

The two swords of the Gospel and the Old Testament levites bring me to the darkest and most controversial part of my subject, political allegory. It was a form of Bible punching, a way of explaining Scripture used in lectures and other writings, when texts were quoted for a political purpose. It always happens, whenever texts are regarded as having authority, that the exegete finds a way to make them agree with the ideas of his time. He will explain that the literal sense signifies something more relevant or edifying; it has a deeper meaning. The spiritual interpretation of sacred literature went back to antiquity. Cynic and Stoic philosophers explained

---

[29] J. C. Dickinson and P. T. Ricketts, 'The Anglo-Norman Chronicle of Wigmore Abbey', *Translations of the Woolhope Naturalists' Field Club* xxxix (1969) 428–33. These disputes can be dated roughly 1148–61.

[30] See below, p. 55.

[31] Maccarrone, 'I papi', 349–98.

the fables of the gods as signifying natural truths or moral lessons. Medea's vengeance on Pelias teaches us to avoid relaxing pleasures and to live hygienically. This ancient witch undertook to restore flabby old men to health by means of hot baths (her cauldron) and exercises (disjointing limbs). She rejuvenated an old ram by cutting him up and boiling him, but the treatment killed Pelias. The latter signified a person who had gone too far in self-indulgence for her cure to work. Medieval exegetes, to do them justice, never thought up anything more fanciful than the philosophers' picture of Medea as a physiotherapist (she invented hair-tinting according to another version).[32] Greek, Jewish and early Christian traditions all contributed to the medieval interpretation of Scripture by means of allegories and moralities. It was part of a wider outlook. Not only Scripture, but the whole of creation had a hidden significance:

> It is a good thing to seek the flowers of a mystic meaning among the thorns and thistles of this world.

I quote from the *Dialogue of the Exchequer!*[33]

The spiritual interpretation of Scripture, allegorical, moral or anagogical, had to be based on 'the literal foundation'. The literal or historical sense was attracting scholarly attention in the early twelfth century in various centres, notably at St Victor.[34] According to the allegorical sense the Old Testament foreshadowed the New Testament and the Old was fulfilled in the New. The moral (also called 'tropological') interpretation revealed Christian moral teaching anywhere on the sacred page. The anagogical looked forward to the 'Last Things' and the end of time. Complicated rules governed the deduction of the spiritual senses from the literal and their content had to agree with Catholic doctrine. Both were elastic: the rules allowed plenty of freedom and Catholic doctrine was developing. The Church needed new arguments to support new claims; political allegory supplied them. It grew up quite naturally in the framework of the traditional allegorical and moral interpretation. The levites of the Old Testament with their special place and privileges

---

[32] J. Pépin, *Mythe et allégorie. Les origines grecques et les contestations Judéo-Chrétiennes* (Paris, 1958) 109-10, 149.

[33] *Dialogus de scaccario* ed. and transl. by Charles Johnson (London, 1950) 26. See below, p. 229.

[34] For recent evidence see B. Smalley, 'An Early Twelfth-Century Commentator on the Literal Sense of Leviticus', R.T.A.M. xxxvi (1969) 78-99.

foreshadowed Christian priesthood; it followed that the clergy should have an equal or better place and as many or more privileges. The two swords of the Gospel could signify relations between *regnum* and *sacerdotium* because the word *sword* traditionally stood for 'the sword of the word', that is preaching, rebuke or censure; as there are two swords, the other must signify physical enforcement of what was ordered by the first.

It seems that political allegory originated in the polemics of Gregorian reform.[35] Gregory VII did not use it; his understanding of Scripture was too direct and simple. But reformers used it before and after his pontificate. Both Old and New Testaments contain more precepts and examples recommending obedience and respect to the powers that be than justification for rebellion against a bad ruler. Biblical prophets were generally unarmed. So exegetes forged them armour. *Engagés* themselves, they engaged their authors. Reform stimulated 'novelties', as its opponents complained. New ideas came up in political theory, in canon law, in the writing of hymns,[36] and nowhere more markedly than in the teaching of Scripture. John of Mantua's commentary on the Canticle, already mentioned, will show how a mere twist in the traditional interpretation could adapt it to his polemic. John set his account of the relationship between the two swords into his explanation of the text: *The beams of our houses are of cedar, our rafters of cypress trees* (Cant. i, 16). A house or building in Scripture normally signified the Church and its parts the members of the Church: pillars signified the apostles or doctors and so on.[37] John followed convention when he made *the beams of our houses* mean spiritual powers or prelates of the house of the Church. He went a little further when he made *our rafters* mean earthly powers or secular rulers. Then he drew the consequence: earthly powers are set under spiritual, as rafters are set under beams; as rafters are there to support the beams, so the function of secular princes is to enforce the prelates' teaching, 'that the knight may make good by his sword what is lacking in the word of the priest'.[38] The text of the Canticle, on John's interpreta-

[35] My pupil Mr I. S. Robinson is studying this subject.

[36] See J. Szövérffy, *A Mirror of Mediaeval Culture. St Peter Hymns of the Middle Ages* (Transactions of the Connecticut Academy of Arts and Sciences xlii, 1965).

[37] J. Sauer, *Symbolik des Kirchengebäuden und seiner Ausstatung in der Auffassung des Mittelalters* (Freiburg-im-Breisgau, 1902).

[38] Bischoff, op. cit. 41.

tion, gave added authority to his argument from the two swords of the Gospel; it strengthened his defence of *sacerdotium*.

It is surprising that the Gregorians got away with it. The imperialists made much of texts enjoining obedience to secular rulers in the literal sense. They could have countered political allegory either by exposing it as partisan and subjective or else by using it themselves and turning it against the papalists. Their attempts to expose it as a method were half-hearted and ineffective and they did not try to snatch it from their opponents' hands. The reformers were too clever for them. Political allegory was too much embedded in tradition to be picked out for attack; the Gregorians' use of it soon became traditional in its turn. The notion of expounding Scripture by means of allegories and moralities had to wait for the rationalist climate of thirteenth-century Paris before it was seriously questioned; even then the attack on it failed.[39] For the moment the Gregorian view of sacred history won through. *Sacerdotium* was foreshadowed by Melchisedech, who typified Christ as king and priest, and by the levites; it was realized in the Christian priesthood under St Peter. Ernst Kantorowicz described political allegory as 'monopoly by exclusion'.[40] It is a happy phrase for the way in which masters of the holy page put priesthood at the centre of their teaching. I shall choose three examples to illustrate the use of political allegory in the schools, and in polemic arising from the schism of 1159 and the Becket conflict.

My first example has the merit of being gross and clear. The poet Walter of Châtillon studied and taught in a number of schools; he counts as a scholar, though he had varied experience as a courtier. Walter composed verses in favour of Alexander III's case against the imperialist anti-popes, probably soon after 1168. He says in his prose introduction that he will attack the anti-popes with theological arguments and will draw his authorities from both the Old Law and the Gospels. To summarize the poem: we begin with the flood; Noah's ark prefigures the Church amid the waters of the world. Noah signifies the pope, who steers us in the ark of the Church over the deep waters of the world, and who has no peer upon

[39] See my forthcoming paper 'St Thomas and the Old Law', *Mediaeval Studies*.

[40] 'Deus per naturam, Deus per gratiam' reprinted from *Harvard Theological Review* xlv (1952) in *Selected Studies by Ernst H. Kantorowicz* (New York, 1965), 133.

earth. Therefore it follows (we should note the *ergo*) that 'Caesar' (Frederick I) is no member of the Church unless he submits to the pope. Mother Church must be free; Caesar dishonours her by making her his bondwoman. He has divided the seamless robe of Christ, which signifies unity in the faith, by creating schism. The Law commanded: *Thou shalt not wear a garment which is woven of two sorts* (Lev. xix, 19). That the emperor has done by meddling in ecclesiastical business (the papal elections), although a layman. If Caesar had power in papal elections, then the mixture of clerical and lay would mean a schism indeed, and clerks would lose their sway:

> privarentur clerici sua dicione.

Walter's last line hits the nail on the head. His verses include a statement on the two swords: Caesar receives the use of the temporal sword from the pope, who holds the spiritual sword and who has pastoral care.[41] The poem interests us because Walter versified the stock arguments of the schools, which he had heard at Paris and perhaps elsewhere. He takes both the doctrine of papal superiority and privilege of clergy and the technique of political allegory for granted. It is true that Walter satirized the vices of the clergy in other poems. He drew on school clichés there too. Masters of the holy page would denounce clerks for being unworthy of 'their sway'. The most loyal churchmen were the sharpest satirists, as Walter would have learnt. He attacked Henry II as a tyrant after Becket's murder.

My next example comes from a letter of John of Salisbury. He wrote it during the Becket conflict in defence of Becket's stand for the liberties of the Church. The recipient was Gilbert Foliot, bishop of London, who had taught as a master of the holy page and would be sure to recognize, if not accept, the allusions to Scripture in John's pamphlet. He puts forward the freeing of the children of Israel from bondage, the resistance of the Maccabees, and David's victory over Goliath; David took a stone from his shepherd's bag (for *shepherd* always understand pastor or prelate) and killed Goliath; so a bishop must defeat the evil intent of wicked rulers. All these examples teach

[41] F. J. E. Raby, *A History of Secular Latin Poetry in the Middle Ages* (2nd edn, Oxford, 1957) ii, 190–204; K. Strecker, *Moralische-satirische Gedichte Walters von Chatillon* (Heidelberg, 1929) 134–6.

us to uphold the liberties of the Church. John clinches his argument
with a final appeal to the levites:

> God commanded that the Levites, figuring priesthood, should
> be immune from public burdens, as we read in Numbers, and
> subject only to the orders of the high priest.... If the clergy has
> not succeeded to the privileges of the tribe of Levi, then the
> Apostle's words are vain and all the interpreters of the Scriptures
> mislead us. Whence it should be clear to all that those who fight
> for the Church's liberty have a most righteous cause.[42]

Political allegory in John's eyes has established itself as the standard
orthodoxy. To doubt his examples would be to doubt both St Paul
and the Fathers.

My third illustration is Master Herbert's account of how he taught
the holy page to his archbishop; Becket had appointed Herbert to
be his master in divinity:

> ...he embraced the holy image-bearing Scriptures with deep
> attention and devotion, in order that by his new learning he should
> shake off the old ignorance, which long commerce with the world
> had brought, so that he, a new bishop, should be reformed to the
> new image of a bishop.[43]

Herbert calls the Scriptures *imaginariae* because they teach by means
of images or allegories. Fallen man is reformed by grace to *the image
and likeness* of God, in which he was first created.[44] On this analogy
Becket learns to understand scriptural imagery under Herbert's tui-
tion, as worldly ignorance has prevented him from doing before. He
reforms himself in the light of his new knowledge to the image of
the good bishop, as he found it in Scripture or as Herbert found it

---

[42] *Mat.* vi, 94–6: Sed profecto in figuris sacerdotii Deus tribum Leviticam a
publicis functionibus, sicut in Numeris legitur, immunem esse decrevit, et
summi tantum pontificis dispositionibus subiacere. . . . Quod si clerus in
privilegiis tribus Leviticae non succedit, et apostolus vanus est, et fallaces
omnes interpretes scripturarum. Ex quo liquidum debet omnibus esse iustissi-
mam esse causam eorum qui pro libertate ecclesiae dimicant.
John is referring in a general way to Heb. vii, 5–12.

[43] Ibid. iii, 204: . . . sacras et imaginarias scripturas summa occupatione et
devotione amplectitur, ut nova eruditione vetus, quam longo iam tempore ex
saeculo contraxerat ruditas propellatur, et nova imago pontificis in novo pontifice reformetur.

[44] Gen. i, 26, II Cor. iii, 18, Colos. iii, 10.

D

for him. We know what that implied for his relations with Henry II.

Père Henri de Lubac has written a learned and sympathetic book in praise of medieval exegesis according to the 'four senses'. Its account of origins and techniques and its wealth of illustration make *Exégèse médiévale* compulsory reading for all students of medieval culture.[45] De Lubac sees the spiritual interpretation as admirably designed to enable the reader or teacher to understand the Bible as a whole; the themes of promise and fulfilment, of foreshadowing and truth and of the final consummation gave unity to a miscellaneous body of writings, which had come to be accepted as canonical. The spiritual interpretation encouraged creative effort within the framework of tradition: the exegete could express his religious feelings and beautiful thoughts. Political allegory distorted a religious and devotional approach to the service of politics. The author leaves it to the end of his book, where he brands it as a mark of scholasticism in decline. He mentions it in connection with the bull *Unam sanctam* of Boniface VIII: here proof texts interpreted in a political sense supported papal claims to possess both spiritual and temporal power. De Lubac admits that the arguments put forward in *Unam sanctam* were of uncertain origin and by no means new.[46] In fact they recall what Walter of Châtillon had learnt in the schools well before 1170: the pope signifies Noah and the ark the Church etc.; *ergo*. . . . If political allegory spells decadence, then decadence had set in during the Gregorian reform. The historian has a right to his personal preferences. He may judge that some of the claims to papal supremacy advanced in the middle ages were unwise and unfounded; he may dislike political allegory for that reason. But it belongs to the story of medieval exegesis from an early stage and cannot just be swept into a corner. Masters of the holy page did not make the modern distinction between religion and politics. They thought that religion called for defence of *sacerdotium*. Political allegory provided the means for them to defend the Church while teaching in the schools and serving her as prelates or secretaries to prelates afterwards. We must learn to live with it if we want to understand their mentality.

[45] There is a shorter book on the same subject, H. de Lubac, *L'Ecriture dans la Tradition* (Paris, 1966); the main one is *Exégèse médiévale: les quatre sens de l'Ecriture* 4 vols. (Paris, 1959–61).
[46] ibid. II, ii, 379–82.

One final hurdle confronts the student of the Becket *Materials*. The theologians in his circle of friends and among his opponents had been through the Arts course and had learnt the rules of rhetoric. Study of this part of the *trivium* began with the reading of ancient texts, but it included training in literary composition. The rules for letter writing as practised in the twelfth and thirteenth centuries have been well charted; we no longer run the risk of taking all statements at their face value. The *captatio benevolentiae* at the beginning of a letter entailed flattery; the writer would then soften up the recipient to grant his petition by exaggeration of need. Edifying sentiments commonly lead up to 'Please do something for my nephews.' The wordiness of twelfth-century writers also puts one off. It was a matter of taste; they preferred fancy to plain. A Paris master even excused himself to a friend who 'blamed him for his style, too simple and straight to the point'; obscurity was 'nobler'.[47]

Rhetoric had another practical purpose. It was taught as an instrument of propaganda, the art of persuasion in writing and speech. Pupils would rehearse their speeches; their practice debates turned on live issues. The English bishops' appeal against Becket was recommended as a theme in the schools, when Quintilian's arguments and allegations were imitated.[48] The clerk trained in rhetoric put his skill at his patron's service to make propaganda for his cause. 'The Arts are swords in the hand of the powerful,' wrote Walter Map.[49] Becket's secretaries knew how to combine propaganda with the art of letter writing. We have a good example in a letter written to Henry II's mother, the Empress Matilda. Becket's friends wanted to persuade her to mediate with her son on behalf of the exiled archbishop. They had little hope of success, seeing that she 'came of tyrant stock'; but it was worth trying.[50] The *captatio benevolentiae* presents her as a kind of St Monica. Complaints against Henry's oppression of the Church follow. But the writer allows for Matilda's maternal bias in favour of her son and suggests excuses. God has granted such wisdom to Henry that it might perhaps be right for the exiles to bear their afflictions as best they can for the time being. Matilda must remember, however, that his successors may be less

---

[47] L. Minio-Paluello, 'The "Ars Disserendi" of Adam of Balsham "Parvipontanus"', M.A.R.S. iii (1954) 118.

[48] *Mat.* iii, 4, vii, 58.

[49] *De nugis curialium*, ed. M. R. James (Oxford, 1914) 7.

[50] *Mat.* v, 149.

wise. Kings may reign after him who will want to devour the Church at a mouthful. Therefore she should urge him not to set a bad precedent. Flattery to both mother and son sweetens the reasons why she is asked to intervene.[51]

A Bolognese rhetor, teaching in the 1230s, hit on a profound truth when he claimed that rhetoric had its origin in the revolt of the angels in heaven. Lucifer had to form a party to rebel against the Almighty. By what other means than rhetoric could he have persuaded nine ranks of angels to join him in so risky an enterprise?[52] Buoncompagno was a wag and he cracked up his subject by stressing its antiquity and its cosmic significance, while showing off his ingenuity. It is true all the same that protestants and resisters need to make better propaganda than conservatives: change is easier to prevent than to force through. It is equally true that a party will depend on the pen in proportion to its lack of swords. We see it in the Becket conflict. Henry had all the swords; the archbishop and his companions in exile relied on propaganda. Urgency drove them to deploy all the arguments that theology and rhetoric had to offer. His murder called for a new effort; his friends propagated the cult of St Thomas. Both before and after they used techniques which they had learnt in their schooldays.

[51] ibid. 142–3.
[52] *Rhetorica novissima*, ed. A. Gaudenzi (Bibliotheca iuridica medii aevi, ii, Bologna, 1892) 255: Prima persuasionis origo fuit in celis, quia probabile sine dubio esse videatur, quod novem angelorum agmina in partem Luciferi sine aliqua persuasione se non traxissent. . .

II

Robert Pullen and
Robert of Melun

These two English masters link up the Becket quarrel to the teaching of the schools. Robert Pullen had both Gilbert Foliot and John
of Salisbury among his pupils. Gilbert remembered his master's
lessons, Becket-hater though he was. John carried them further and
applied them to politics. Robert of Melun, another of John's teachers,
had to reconcile what he had taught in the schools with his policy
as bishop of Hereford at the height of the conflict.

Pullen represented the new evangelical movement among masters
of the holy page.[1] We do not know where he studied or what masters
he had. His teaching career seems to have begun at Exeter, after
which he lectured at Oxford from 1133 for five years. According to
the Oseney annalist, well placed to report on the Oxford schools,
'Master Robert Pullein began to lecture at Oxford on the holy
Scriptures, which had been neglected in England.' The annalist got
it right: the only surviving biblical commentary written in England
in the early twelfth century is monastic, William of Malmesbury on
Lamentations. Pullen's sermons originated in lectures on Scripture.[2]

---

[1] For data and bibliography on Pullen see B.R.U.O. iii, 1525. Fr. F. Courtney
gives a useful account of Pullen's career and teaching, *Cardinal Robert
Pullen. An English Theologian of the Twelfth Century* (Rome, 1954). I cannot agree with him that Pullen was an Austin Canon, probably of Oseney
abbey, Oxford. He argues for this on the grounds that a collection of sermons
in a Paris manuscript, ascribed to 'Magister Robertus Pulo', shows the preacher
speaking 'as a monk to monks' and addresses a monastic audience throughout. But elsewhere Pullen writes as a secular clerk. No source mentions his
being a canon regular; we have no evidence that the canons of Oseney abbey
held a school; it is unlikely that a religious could have held an archdeaconry,
as Pullen did. There has been some doubt as to whether Pullen taught at
Exeter or Oxford or both. The fact that Gilbert Foliot had studied under him
as master at a date before 1133, when Pullen is said to have been teaching
at Oxford, strengthens the case for his having taught at Exeter first and
Oxford afterwards; see below, p. 168.

[2] See below, appendix i, p. 242.

If some of the material goes back to his Oxford teaching, as is likely, he introduced a new genre to England; it was fairly new even in France. A later elaboration on the Oseney annals makes him preach to the people every Sunday. That may be true, but none of his sermons *ad populum* has survived. Then he moved to Paris. John of Salisbury lists him as the second of his masters in theology, coming after Gilbert of la Porrée, who became bishop of Poitiers in 1142, and before Simon of Poissy. John studied theology only, not logic, under these last two masters.[3] Meanwhile Pullen had been appointed to the archdeaconry of Rochester in 1134. There was a story that he refused a bishopric offered to him by Henry I. It would have been an untypical choice on Henry's part. Perhaps Pullen was reported to have said that he 'would have' refused it, to prove the belief in free elections which he expressed in his lectures. He seems to have used the income from his archdeaconry to supplement his fees and tried to hang on to it even when he had a chair. Ascelin, who became bishop of Rochester in 1142, ordered him to return; he accused Pullen of usurping certain episcopal revenues and of disobedience: he trusted to his great learning to get his own way. Ascelin appealed to Rome and confiscated the archdeacon's property. St Bernard intervened on behalf of the absentee. He wrote to Ascelin to renew a plea that Pullen should be allowed to continue his teaching at Paris for a while, with his bishop's consent. The letter carried a threat: Master Robert had many friends at the Curia, who could use their influence on his behalf.[4]

St Bernard wished Pullen to keep his chair because he was needed at Paris as a teacher of sound doctrine. This may seem surprising: Pullen's theology shows the influence of Abelard, although Pullen criticized some of his opinions and held some of the same opinions as Hugh of St Victor.[5] St Bernard probably cared little for the niceties of Pullen's theological doctrine. As a professor he fitted into the Bernardine scheme. Not all men could choose the way of per-

---

[3] *Metalogicon*, 82. It has been deduced from John's statement that Pullen taught both logic and theology. John does not say so, unless it is implied in his remark that Pullen succeeded to the chair of Gilbert of la Porrée, who had taught both. John is categoric that he did not study logic under Pullen: Sed hos duos in solis theologicis habui preceptores.

[4] Ep. ccv, P.L. cxxxlii, 372–3.

[5] Courtney, op. cit. 22–3, 73, 96–100, 278–80; L. Hödl, *Die Geschichte der scholastichen Literatur und der Theologie der Schlüsselgewalt* i (B.G.P.T.M. xxxviii, 4, 1960) 76, 95–8.

fection and enter the 'school of charity' in a Cistercian abbey. Hence Bernard accepted that secular schools were needed to train clergy to teach laymen, making the proviso that the masters in secular schools should limit themselves to subjects 'pertaining to salvation'.[6] Pullen gave the impression of doing so; he knew better than to advertise his debt to Abelard; and he had a name for virtue. John of Salisbury described him as 'praiseworthy for both life and learning'.[7]

It was adventurous on Pullen's part to organize the sum of theological knowledge into *Sentences* (1142–4). He influenced his successors. John wrote that only his later eminence as cardinal and papal chancellor saved him from being called 'a mere hack' by the Cornificians. The latter attacked all the best masters; their scorn guaranteed their victims as sound scholars in John's view.[8] Later writers quoted Pullen's *Sentences* and sometimes ascribed to him opinions not to be found there, which suggests that his oral teaching was remembered. Robert Courson recorded an opinion held by 'Master Robert Pullen and his followers'; it was believed in the late twelfth century that he had a school of pupils, who propagated his teaching.[9]

His lawsuit with the bishop of Rochester may have brought Pullen to the notice of the Curia. Innocent II summoned him to Rome before September 1143; he was created cardinal priest and then papal chancellor about 1144. Pullen must have owed his rise to the highest post in the sacred college mainly to his reputation for learning and his practical ability. The one treatise which he left in literary form shows that he had a clear, elegant style. He lacked noble friends and kinsmen. His powerful backers pushed him forward in recognition of his worth. His spectacular success marked a triumph for the poor master of theology at a time when lawyers were permeating the Curia. St Bernard improved on the occasion by writing to the chancellor to ask him to watch over the new pope, 'our Eugenius', Bernard's former pupil. Pullen has worked loyally and usefully as a teacher. Bernard misses his presence at Paris, but is

[6] J. Châtillon, 'L'influence de S. Bernard sur la pensée scolastique au XIIe et au XIIIe siècle', *Analecta sacri Ordinis Cisterciensis* ix, 3–4 (1953) 269–74.

[7] *Metalogicon*, 82.

[8] ibid, 19–20: Robertus Pullus, cuius memoria bonis omnibus iocunda est, diceretur filius subiugalis, nisi sedi apostolice deferretur, que ipsum de doctore scolastico cancellarium fecit.

[9] Hödl, op. cit. 122, 136–7, 276, 325. For Peter the Chanter's references to Pullen see Baldwin, *Masters* i, 52, 95, ii, 41, 66.

thankful that his friend can now advise the pope and prevent him from making wrong decisions under pressure of business: now is the time for action in God's cause.[10] Pullen either died or lost his health in the autumn of 1146. He befriended the English Church during his few years as chancellor. Perhaps he prepared the way for the promotion of his fellow countryman Nicholas Breakspear, who became a cardinal in 1150 and pope as Adrian IV in 1154. Gilbert Foliot as abbot of Gloucester wrote to congratulate Pullen, addressing him as 'dearest master'. Surprise at the unexpectedness of his rise to power comes out through Gilbert's rhetoric. His rise has caused joy at Canterbury: Pullen has restored the ancient dignity and primacy of the metropolitan see. The abbot of Gloucester cashed in on it. The usual request for help for some of the writer's protégés follows his *captatio benevolentiae*.[11] That the link proved useful appears in a letter written on behalf of Gilbert as bishop of Hereford after Pullen's death. One of Gilbert's clerks had been staying with the chancellor at Rome and was able to deny the claim of a renegade religious to have had papal authority for his reinstatement.[12]

Pullen broached the subject of political theory in his *Sentences*.[13] His discussion is important if only for the reason that he gave it a place in his résumé of theological doctrine. He had a precedent: Hugh of St Victor had discussed the relations between the temporal and spiritual powers in his *De sacramentis*; but the precedent was not followed up in the twelfth century except by Pullen. His theory exalts the Church and the role of prelates within the Church. The second follows logically from the first, since prelates had to enforce discipline and defend ecclesiastical liberties. Pullen writes that the two swords 'are conferred' on the two powers. The Church on earth has need of two swords. Both bear the sign of the cross, which must determine their use. One is deputed to the clergy, the other to the laity. The convenient passive in his verbs dispenses Pullen from stating either that the Church confers the temporal sword on the secular ruler or that the secular ruler receives his sword directly from God. He goes on to explain that the clergy do not wield the temporal sword themselves. He 'proves' the point by means of a political allegory, extending the significance of St Peter's two swords: *Simon Peter, having a sword, drew it and struck*

---

[10] Ep. ccclxii, P.L. clxxxii, 563–4.
[11] G.F.L.C. 84–5, second half of 1145; Saltman, 22.
[12] G.F.L.C. 136–7, 1150–3.   [13] P.L. clxxxvi, 905–6, 919–22.

*the servant of the high priest and cut off his right ear. And the name
of the servant was Malchus* (Jo. xviii, 10). Pullen assumes that his
readers will supply the traditional interpretation of the name
Malchus as meaning 'king'.[14] The two ears signify spiritual and
temporal hearing. St Peter's sword signifies the spiritual penalty of
suspension or anathema, which prevents the king who sins against
Christ or his members (the Church) from hearing God's word. St
Peter contented himself with cutting off Malchus' right ear (that of
spiritual hearing) and thought that the other (the temporal) sword
had nothing to do with him.[15] Two swords, spiritual and temporal,
are needed to bring peace and justice on earth by infliction of
spiritual and temporal punishments: 'these are the two swords
deputed to ecclesiastical discipline'. Pullen does not state that the
secular ruler wields his sword under the Church's direction, but he
implies it. The secular ruler enforces ecclesiastical discipline by
means of temporal punishments. Pullen then draws back and
teaches non-resistance to tyranny: prelates must dissociate themselves from a tyrant's evil deeds, in mind at least. They should not
seek to avenge their wrongs: *Render unto Caesar* etc. The prince
should choose officials who will perform their functions justly.

Readers are left to make out the implications of this teaching as
they will. Pullen is neither conclusive nor original on the subject of
regnum and *sacerdotium*. The important point is that he published
views which could be discussed and interpreted. His mode of argument relied on political allegory; thus he set still another precedent
for its use in the schools and by scholars in their letters, when they
had occasion to argue.

There is more originality and decision in his discussion of the
question: which is the better way of life, the active or the contemplative? A long tradition favoured the contemplative. Rachel
was preferred to Lia in the Old Testament and Mary to Martha in
the New. The question became highly controversial when members
of the Order of Canons Regular claimed that their way of life combined active service with contemplation, and was therefore better
than the way of the secular clergy, on the one hand, and of monks

---

[14] See Raban Maur on Mt. xxvi, 51, P.L. cvii, 1117–18.

[15] The same interpretation of Jo. xviii, 10 appears in Deusdedit's *Libellus
contra invasores et symoniacos, Lib. de lit.*, M.G.H., ii, 346. Pullen refers to it
as though he expected his readers to recognize it without having it fully explained. It must have been current.

on the other: the perfect way of life must include both action and contemplation. Pullen agreed with the thesis, without mentioning the Canons Regular; but he claimed the most perfect way of life for the prelate, not for an Order.[16] Contemplation is better than action in itself, as giving a foretaste of heaven; but the prelate has to care for the souls and bodies of his fellow men. His responsibilities are woven into the very texture of Pullen's *Sentences*; they appear when he goes into detail on the running of the Church.[17] It follows that the good prelate must combine action with contemplation in order to recreate himself sufficiently to bear his burden. If he neglects the inner life, he will start fussing, like Martha. Pullen equates contemplation with *lectio divina*, the study of Scripture. The holy page instructs us on both action and contemplation. Hence it offers the best training for prelacy. St Gregory had taught the same in his *Rule of Pastoral Care*, which Pullen would have had in mind.[18] He sets it into a twelfth-century institutional framework. Preparation for the perfect life, as led by the good bishop, began with the study and teaching of Scripture in the schools. The master of the holy page would then apply it to his conduct as prelate. Pullen presents the bishop as a candidate for the perfect way of life on earth. The bishop has had his training in the secular schools. The cloister is bypassed.

Pullen's own teaching on Scripture, as we have it in his lectures, clarifies that of his *Sentences*. He was addressing clerks, counting himself among them.[19] He supposed that they had some knowledge of the liberal arts; some were already students of the holy page.[20] Most students, he tells them, rely on their masters for an understanding of Scripture. Only a privileged few are taught by God alone; these understand so well that they hear God speaking to them in a

[16] ibid. 933–40.

[17] ibid. 918–19 and *passim*.

[18] II, vii and xi, P.L. lxxvii, 38–42, 48–50. St Bernard gave the same advice to resort to meditation on his soul's health to Pope Eugenius III, in his *De consideratione*, a reworking of *De regula curae pastoralis*; but he wrote it after Pullen's death.

[19] ms Lambeth 458 (see appendix i, p. 242), fol. 147v: . . . reducamus ad memoriam quod clerici sumus, id est a Deo sortiti, preceptores iustitie, promissores castimonie, in numero levitarum assumpti, ut offeramus Deo sacrificia et ponamus super altare vitulos pro populo.

[20] fol. 149v: Hec omnia salva pace vestra diximus, et tamen non omnes qui Liam et Rachel sibi coniungunt salvi erunt, . . . quoniam non ad hoc student in divina pagina ut sint iusti, sed (ut) videantur docti.

familiar way when they consult the Scriptures.[21] It reads like a warning to his pupils: they could not all be St Bernards.

The comparison between action and contemplation comes up twice. Pullen expounds the story of Martha and Mary (Lc. x, 38–42). Here he does mention the monastic life of contemplation, signified by Mary, contrasting it with the active life, involving cure of souls, as signified by Martha. They were loving sisters in the gospel story. They are not so nowadays, which is no laughing matter, but a cause for grief.[22] Pullen is referring to another controversy of the period: whether monks should exercise cure of souls and serve churches; the secular clergy contested this claim and argued that the monk should keep to his cloister to 'pray and mourn' for the sins of the world. Pullen's predecessor at Oxford, Master Theobald of Etampes, had engaged in violent polemic with a monk on the subject towards 1133.[23] If the lectures represent Pullen's teaching at Oxford, we may hear the echo of a local joke about Theobald's quarrel with the monks. Pullen was not attacking monastic claims and he avoided treading on anyone's toes, but the gist of his teaching agreed with Theobald's, none the less. The story of the two sisters leads him to argue again for the superior value of the mixed life. The duties of a good prelate are to help the poor, to give hospitality, to do works of mercy, to preach to the people on suitable occasions and to teach the way of truth. Martha, signifying the prelate, asked Jesus to find her a helpmeet in her work, realizing that she needed assistance. Mary drops out of the picture at this point:

[Martha signifies] bishops who appoint suitable men as arch-

[21] 137v: Audiunt illud quidam ab ipso Domino, quod perpaucorum est, ut eorum qui exercitati sunt sub magnis doctoribus; alii ab aliis audiunt, ut a doctoribus. Hos ab illis secernens, propheta ait: *Celum celi Domino, terram autem dedit filiis hominum* (Ps. cxiii, 16), *celum celi* vocans quos non est necesse erudiri nisi a Domino.... Ad tantam scripture intelligentiam per venerunt ut cum in scripturis consulant eum ibidem loquentem familiariter audiant. *Terram* autem vocat eos qui terrene et adhuc parve intelligentie necesse habent ut a *filiis hominum*, id est a doctoribus erudiantur.

[22] fol. 137: Sunt enim in ecclesia qui propter Deum sanctum amplexantur otium et studium. Sunt alii qui propter Deum proximorum studentes utilitati non solum corporum, verum etiam, quod magis est, excellentius animarum sanctum amplexantur exercitium. Hos per Martham, illos per Mariam significatos habeamus. Ut autem fraterno se invicem diligant amore, Maria non cognata, sed soror dicitur Marthe. Quod quia econtrario fieri videmus, non ridere, ut fieri solet, sed dolere debemus.

[23] B.R.U.O. iii, 1754.

deacons, and set up abbots in monasteries and worthy, discreet priests in their respective churches. Bishops who want to be in sole charge are either lazy and negligent, or they seek their own fame and reward instead of the things of God.[24]

Mary reappears when Pullen reaches the text: *But one thing is necessary. Mary hath chosen the best part.* Here Mary signifies contemplation in general; Pullen makes the same point as he does in his *Sentences.* The prelate has to balance the claims of action and contemplation in his life. One who busies himself wholly with his neighbours' salvation and advantage must be reminded of his own and *vice versa. The best part* is to attend to God, to heed his will and to consider the health of one's soul. The prelate may interrupt his contemplation for a time; *but it shall not be taken away from him.* He must withdraw from business in order to meditate in privacy and quiet. If he considers God's ways and righteousness, he can draw from the spring of life what he will offer to others afterwards.[25] The lesson recurs.[26] Later Pullen gives a tactful reminder

[24] fol. 138: in domo Domini stat qui bonis operibus laborat . . . Sed qui vere est Martha, intelligens se tam frequenti et tam iugi non sufficere ministerio, collegam desiderat, qui partem laboris suscipiat et fructu communicet tam in presenti quam in futura vita. Hii sunt episcopi qui idoneos sibi adsiscant archidiaconos, abbates (bonos?) constituunt in monasteriis (et) presbiteros discretos et dignos in singulis ecclesiis. Qui vero soli pre-esse volunt aut torpent nec labore gravantur aut gloriam sibi et fructum querentes que Dei sunt postponunt.

Some words seem to have been omitted from the text in both MSS. Pullen makes a similar statement fol. 133: Hii vero (episcopi) . . . attendentes se solos non posse sufficere iniuncto officio, sicut ipsi boni sunt, bonos sibi eligunt archidiaconos. Post illos per parrochias constituunt presbiteros eos quos noverunt scientia et virtute preminere inter alios. . . . Sic malus episcopus malos archidiaconos et pessimos presbiteros. . . .

Both MSS have 'archiepiscopos' the first time (Hereford o.2.viii, fol. 83vb) in this passage; the context shows that it is a mistake for 'archidiaconos'.

[25] fol. 139v: *Optimum* est Deo vacare, voluntatem eius attendere, proprie saluti consulere. Quod si intermittatur a prelato, *non tamen aufertur ab eo.* Debet enim prelatus in idipsum redire aliquando ab exterioribus curis, ut receptus in otium et secretum de Deo cogitet. Vias eius et iustitias consideret, et sic a fonte vite hauriat quod aliis propinare valeat.

[26] fol. 140v. Bethel signifies the Church: Que partim activa, partim vita est contemplativa. Activa in temporalium sollicitudine laborat, contemplativa vero, a curis temporalium remota, soli Deo vacat. . . In civitatibus nostris habemus domos et templa, et qui Bethel edificat non solum templa, sed et domos Deo faciat. . . . Per domos subditos, per templa prelatos intelligimus.

that the devil pursues both those who lead the active life and those who dedicate themselves to contemplation.[27] The prelate always dominates the scene. Pullen regards abbots as helpmeets, but the bishop sets them up to act as subordinates.

Mary signifies the study of Scripture as part of the contemplative life. The prelate must hear the Word with Mary before he takes up the duties of Martha.[28] He must know both the Old and the New Testaments.[29] A note of professional pride in his subject sounded in Pullen's *Sentences*; here it rises higher. Proficiency in Scripture and preaching exposes one to the envy of those who, having no good in themselves, try to frustrate it in others, as far as they can. If they cannot dissuade a man from going (to the schools), they put forward false reasons on his return, to show that his precepts are burdensome and impracticable. They promise him better opportunities when he goes; when he comes back, they tell him not to presume to go against custom and the time.[30] Pullen anticipates Stephen Langton's picture of the scholar returning from his studies, eager to preach reform in his native country, only to meet opposition from the bad prelate, who chases him away.[31] We feel the tension already between learning *divina pagina* in the schools, preaching and reform on the one hand, and vested interests on the other. Pullen exalts *divina pagina* over all other sciences. These will find no place in heaven, whereas lectures on the Scriptures will continue and their full meaning will be revealed. He lists a number of texts which the elect in heaven will begin to understand perfectly, instead of dimly as on earth. Medieval monks imagined their chant to be a dress rehearsal for the heavenly choir. Just so, in his different manner, the master of

---

[27] fol. 184: Haud aliter antiquus hostis et eos qui in activa via positi vitia supplantare nituntur . . . et illos qui contemplationi vacant . . . hostiliter insequitur.

[28] fol. 137v.

[29] foll. 152, 153.

[30] foll. 171v–172: Sunt nonnulli . . . qui nec boni in se aliquid habent, et cum in aliis audierint vel viderint non diligunt, sed invident, et eos quos ad divinam lectionem vel predicationem proficisci cognoverint, a bono proposito virulentis dissuasionibus, quantum in ipsis est, revocant. Quod si euntes retrahere nequiunt, redeuntibus obviantes quod dicuntur vel iubentur gravia vel impossibilia falsis, si possint, rationibus comprobant. Euntibus tempus fore promittunt, quo melius et competentius quod proponunt incipiant. Redeuntibus dicunt ne contra consuetudinem suam vel etatem facere presumant. . .

[31] *Study of the Bible*, 251–2.

the holy page was beginning on earth a function which could culmin-
ate in heaven. His lectures transcended their setting in time and
place. They were an academic prelude to the hereafter.[32]
Returning to earth, Pullen deals with the temporal power quite
effectively by ignoring it. He never mentions royal influence when
he lays down rules for electing bishops. The clergy must pray to
God to send a good pastor to a widowed church; otherwise they will
get one who spares his subjects' vices, being carnal himself. The
man of their choice must not agree to his election unless he is 'unwilling and called upon, like Aaron'; that happens when someone is
elected to prelacy 'according to a certain order'. Only a man of virtue, unwilling and called upon by religious men, should accept his
election to a bishopric. He must not presume to hold office, even if
subject to pressure or excommunication, unless he fulfils these con-
ditions.[33] Having taken office, he will have a free hand in his choice
of abbots, priests and archdeacons; so Pullen assumes.

Was he stating the ideal, as he saw it, without any relevance to
practice? Suppose that he was lecturing at Oxford about 1136-8, in
the earliest years of Stephen's reign, then it would have been rea-
listic enough to suppose that 'a certain order' (canon law) would be
observed in ecclesiastical elections and that it was for the clergy to
make a good choice. Stephen's charter of 1136 promised:

> I allow and concede that jurisdiction and authority over eccles-
> iastical persons and over all clerks and their property, together
> with the disposal of ecclesiastical estates, shall lie in the hands

[32] fol. 148v: Dialectica enim sermo duorum est et consistit in solo sermone.
Ibi autem unum labium, unus sermo erit omnium. Ibi legetur scriptura divina,
que non est in verbo et sermone, sed potius in veritate. . . . Ista lectio angelorum erit et ovium electorum. Ista lectio legetur in futuro, scilicet in regno.
Nunc enim obscure et in enigmate percipitur, tunc clare et perfecte intellige-
tur. Tunc primum incipiemus intelligere quomodo *In principio creavit Deus
celum et terram.* . . .

[33] fol. 138-138v: . . . cum prelatis suis viduate fuerint, recurrant ad Dominum; petant et impetrabunt prelatum. Quod quia non faciunt, sepius enim
queritur qui et ipse carnalis vitiis subditorum parcat . . . (potius) quam qui
opus Dei facere velit et sciat. . . . Non ergo nisi invitus et vocatus tamquam
Aaron preficitur. Quod fit quando certo ordine observato aliquis in prelationem eligitur. . . Pollens igitur virtutibus . . . non nisi invitus et vocatus a
religiosis prelationem suscipere debet. Qui vero illis caruerit, nec tractus nec
si excommunicetur accedere presumat.

MS Hereford o.2.viii, fol. 99ra has 'In quo illi qui eligunt maxime notandi
sunt et qui eligitur' after 'in prelationem eligitur. . .'.

of the bishops. . . . . But when sees are vacant and without shepherds, I will commit them and all their possessions into the hand and keeping of the clerks and pious men of the said church, until a new pastor may be canonically appointed.[34]

Stephen had to conciliate both the English Church and the papacy at this stage. He could not follow up Henry I's masterful policy, however much he wanted to. All interested parties understood his dilemma. It would have given Pullen some reason for optimism.

His writings show a serene outlook in any case. Later moralists and satirists gave way to bitterness; not so Pullen. He rebukes the sins of the clergy and calls upon bishops to preach against them and to apply discipline; but he seems to be confident that some bishops will be 'good', and that they will rise to the demands of their calling. The schools will supply men suitably equipped for prelacy.

Pullen's third and last surviving work is an undated treatise, addressed to a friend as 'dear brother', on 'all that is necessary for human life'. Fr. Courtney discovered and edited it. He praises the piece for 'style, rather than for any striking originality of thought'.[35] I think he underrates its originality. Pullen is writing to a secular clerk (real or fictional); he can read his Bible and is highly placed, since he has opportunities to oppress the poor, and is wealthy, although he suffers 'worldly affliction'. Pullen gives him advice on how to save his soul while remaining in the world. The monastic letter, supposed to be written by a religious to a friend, urging him to save his soul by leaving the world and joining an Order, was a favourite twelfth-century genre.[36] Advice on how to gain salvation as a secular was offered more rarely. Pullen makes no suggestion that his friend should flee from the temptations of secular life. He adopts the form of the 'consolatory' type of letter, beginning with comfort and exhortation on bearing one's troubles patiently. Then he proposes rules on all that is necessary for salvation, to be followed by a person living in the world. On the subject of riches, the strictest moralist never denied that a rich man could be saved; that would

[34] *English Historical Documents 1042–1189*, ed. D. G. Douglas and G. W. Greenaway (London, 1953) 403.

[35] 'An Unpublished Treatise of Cardinal Robert Pullen. Sermo de Omnibus humane Uite Necessariis or De Contemptu Mundi' *Gregorianum* xxxi (1950) 192–223.

[36] J. Leclercq, 'Lettres de vocation à la vie monastique', *Studia Anselmiana* xxxvii (1955) 169–97.

have limited God's mercy; but emphasis was generally laid on the dangers of wealth and on the better chances of salvation for one who followed the gospel counsel: *If thou wilt be perfect, go sell what thou hast and give to the poor and thou shalt have treasure in heaven. And come follow me* (Mt. xix, 21). Pullen agrees that the way of perfection is safest; he goes on to explain that not all men can take it. A married man with a family is not permitted to sell all his goods and give to the poor; nor should he seek to dissolve his marriage. Riches do not impede salvation, if rightly used, and if the owner does not love them for their own sake. He must also make restitution for ill-gotten gains. The patriarchs, good kings and some of the holiest men of the Old Testament abounded in wealth.[37] Pullen aims at reassurance throughout his treatise: 'let us do what we can'. He warns against sloth and despair and advises recourse to the sacrament of penance, which was always much in his mind, both as a theologian and as a homilist. Do penance now and beware of a false death-bed repentance. But do not endanger your health by overmuch severity. As the apostle says, *no man ever hated his own flesh, but nourisheth and cherishes it* (Eph. v, 29). He who does not cherish his flesh is not a man.[38] A holy woman who gets raped and enjoys it in spite of herself avoids the taint of whoredom so long as she hates the sin.[39] Further, Pullen touches on a leading idea of John of Salisbury, which John took from Cicero: nature or reason is man's best guide to life. Pullen formulates the principle: 'While reason, the guardian of human nature, functions as watchman, the whole fabric of the human building remains firm.'[40]

John of Salisbury chose his adjectives carefully when he wrote of his master's memory 'bonis omnibus iocunda est'. Pullen set an attractive example to masters of the holy page. He staked out claims for the secular clergy, masters and prelates, without jostling the religious. What was more, his rise in the Church showed that the papacy had taken note of the master's title to preferment. His political theory had something for everyone.

[37] 'An Unpublished Treatise', op. cit. 214–16.
[38] ibid. 216.
[39] ibid. 201–2.
[40] ibid. 201: Uerum dum nature humane custos ratio officio suo inuigilat . . . tota humani edificii fabrica firma consistit.
Fr. Courtney shows that Pullen's main source here was a quotation from St Augustine. The latter uses the word *ratio*, but not the words *nature humane custos*; the emphasis is rather different in Pullen's phrasing.

Robert of Melun was younger than Pullen and he had a more probing mind. His teaching career was longer. Fitzstephen says that he taught dialectic and the holy page at Paris for over forty years.[41] There is no evidence that he studied at Oxford first; more probably he went straight to France.[42] He claimed to have had Hugh of St Victor as his master and he seems to have heard Abelard. John of Salisbury studied dialectic in his school at Paris about 1137. He found Robert a stimulating, sharp-witted teacher, and regretted only that he had neglected to lay a firm foundation of classical learning before he turned to dialectic.[43] Robert has left no work in literary form, not even a letter or a sermon; so we cannot verify John's reproach. As bishop of Hereford he made good his deficiency in rhetoric (if he was deficient) by employing experts: Gilbert Foliot wrote to him (1165-7) about a seisin dispute, thanking him and his notaries sarcastically for their respectful and elegant refusal of his demand.[44] Robert went on to teach theology at Melun, where he had more elbow-room than at Paris. Abelard had held a school there. Fitzstephen must have included the Melun period in his 'forty years' teaching'. Master Robert, now known as 'of Melun', returned to Paris and taught there again. About 1160 Henry II summoned him back to England:

> The king, on the suggestion of Chancellor Thomas, used to recall poor Englishmen of good repute who were living in France, either as monks in religion or as masters in the schools, and set them up in his kingdom. Master Robert of Melun was made bishop of Hereford . . .[45]

John of Salisbury in Archbishop Theobald's household and the king's cousin, Master Roger, who became bishop of Worcester in 1163, were numbered among Robert's former pupils in his home country.[46] Chancellor Thomas Becket could have studied under him, and may may well have met him on a visit to France.[47] We do not know what

---

[41] *Mat.* iii, 60.

[42] B.R.U.O. ii, 1258. An account of Robert's teaching and an up-to-date bibliography will be found in D. E. Luscombe, *The School of Peter Abelard* (Cambridge, 1969) 281-98 and *passim*; I need not repeat references.

[43] *Metalogicon* 78-9, 191.

[44] G.F.L.C. 249.

[45] Fitzstephen, *Mat.* iii, 24.

[46] R. W. Hunt, 'English Learning', 32.

[47] See below, p. 109.

E

Robert did in the few years before his election to Hereford; the statement that he taught at Oxford arose from a muddle; too many Roberts were connected with Oxford and Hereford. Gilbert Foliot was translated to the see of London early in 1163; Robert succeeded to him at Hereford and was consecrated on 22 December.

To return to his academic career: the dates of his movements and of his writings have not been fixed with certainty.[48] He left *Quaestiones de divina pagina, Quaestiones de epistolis Pauli* and unfinished *Sentences*. Recent study of his theology has shown that Robert of Melun resembled Pullen in exploiting the teaching of both Hugh of St Victor and Abelard; but he was more adventurous. Though he criticized Abelard in a constructive way, he attacked St Bernard for having procured the condemnation of Abelard's views as heretical: busybodies meddle in matters outside their competence, he wrote in his *Sentences*. It was the first open defence of Abelard to be launched in the schools. We need not see Robert as a rash enthusiast; he may have been writing after Bernard's death in 1153, and Bernard had failed to maintain his position as undisputed censor of doctrine at the council of Rheims, just as he failed to stem Abelard's influence on theologians. Robert had a good fund of orthodox teaching chalked up to his own account; he had ganged up with the opponents of Gilbert of la Porrée, perhaps through envy at Gilbert's fame.[49]

He discussed political theory in his *Quaestiones* on St Paul. Dr Werner Affeldt has made a thorough study of patristic and medieval commentaries on Rom. xiii, 1–7: *Let every soul be subject to the higher powers. For there is no power but from God: and those that are are ordained of God. Therefore, he that resisteth the power resisteth the ordinance of God. And they that resist purchase to themselves damnation....*[50] It had to be agreed that a Christian must submit to martyrdom rather than obey a command to deny his faith. That was passive resistance. Was it possible to interpret the Pauline text so as to justify active resistance to tyranny? Commentators shied away from the problem with understandable convic-

[48] They depend partly on his relationship to Peter the Lombard; the dates of the Lombard's commentaries on the Psalter and St Paul and his *Sentences* in their various drafts must be established before Robert's can be known.

[49] *Hist. pontif.* 16.

[50] *Die weltliche Gewalt in der Paulus-Exegese. Rom. 13, 1–7 in den Römerbriefkommentaren der lateinischen Kirche bis zum Ende des 13 Jahrhunderts* (Göttingen, 1969).

tion or timidity as the case might be. Robert of Melun was the first
to justify active resistance to a tryant. His originality is all the more
striking in view of his dependence on Abelard on Romans and his
knowledge of Peter the Lombard's teaching; neither would argue
for a right to resist. He argued that the Lombard failed to distinguish between the person and his divine power. A ruler may tyrannize on the pretext that he holds royal office and may oppress his
subjects. The pretext is invalid. Royal power does not excuse tyranny.
A bad ruler's power comes from the devil, not from God, although
a bad ruler may sometimes do God's work by purging the righteous
and punishing the wicked. Lay resistance to tyranny did not concern Robert, who approached his problem as a churchman.[51] He
asks only what part the Church should play in resisting a bad ruler.
Excommunication, if he offends the Church, is Robert's answer.
The sentence should be delayed and due warning given, according
to the offender's rank and to the degree of his guilt. A king should
be allowed a longer delay than others, since his anger might harm the
Church. If he fails to repent in the delay accorded him, then he
should be smitten *pro rigore Ecclesiae*.[52] Excommunication still had a
sharp edge in the twelfth century; Robert does not discuss how it
may affect the ruler's power. Kings are not exempt from discipline;
but if a prelate offends, then his subjects have no remedy.[53] Robert
comments on II Cor. x, 8:

> He usurps power who ascribes to himself what he has not got.
> It pertains to the bishop's power to excommunicate or to loose
> from excommunication, whether he does so rightly or wrongly.[54]

Subjects may warn a prelate not to neglect the health of their souls;
such warning is authorized by Colos. iv, 17: *Take heed to the
ministry which thou has received from the Lord, that thou fulfil*

---

[51] ibid. 161–6; *Oeuvres de Robert de Melun* ii, ed. R. M. Martin (*Spic. sac.
Lov.* xviii, 1938) 152–4.

[52] On I Cor, v, 3–5, ibid. 188: Quidam tamen diutius sunt expectandi et
sepius monendi; quidam minus, secundum ipsarum diversitatem personarum
et peccatorum qualitatem. Ut si rex apud cuius iram strages iacet Ecclesie,
aliquid huiusmodi contra Ecclesiam commiserit, diutius est expectandus quam
alius; tamen si expectatus non resipuerit, feriendus pro rigore Ecclesie.

[53] ibid. 153. Subjects may admonish a prelate and resist him only if they
can do so without scandal, ibid. 189.

[54] ibid. 241: Ad potestatem episcopi enim pertinet aliquem excommunicare,
vel excommunicatum solvere, sive recte faciat sive non.

it. No action is provided for if the prelate refuses to listen.[55] In his *Quaestiones de divina pagina* Robert raises the question whether a judge who gives sentence according to the decrees of the holy Fathers will always judge rightly. He answers that the Church does not err. It should not be said of a judge who keeps to the precepts of the Fathers, which may not be altered, that he has given unjust sentence. The Church's judgements, when made canonically, are always just.[56]

Robert broke with established academic tradition in his exegesis of Romans. The right to resist secular tyranny had been debated during the 'Investiture contest'; but masters had avoided the question when they lectured on St Paul. To raise it was to let the draught of politics blow through the classroom. Robert's high idea of the Church's authority drove him forward.

He wrote nothing else on the subject, as far as we know; but we have evidence on what he taught. It occurs in letters of reproach and persuasion written to him during the Becket conflict. As bishop of Hereford, Robert gave no open support to Becket. Some of the letters urging him to commit himself to the archbishop's cause look back to his professions as a teacher. We may begin with the pope. Alexander ordered the bishops of London and Hereford to admonish Henry on his mistreatment of the Church in June, 1165. They visited the king while he was campaigning on the Welsh border and obeyed their mandate, but without success.[57] It was probably after their failure to mollify Henry that Alexander sent Robert a letter beginning *Miramur plurimum,* the standard opening to a papal reproof.[58] The pope charges him with not having backed his archbishop in defence of ecclesiastical liberties as he should; he has put human fear before fear of the Lord. The letter commands him to show due reverence and obedience and to give manly, unwavering help to Becket in the Church's business in future. The assumption throughout is that Robert was expected and ought to have acted more firmly just because of his record before he became a bishop. Characteristically, however, Alexander ends by ordering him to keep the charge 'altogether secret', until the archbishop and king have

[55] ibid. 267: Ecce auctoritas, ut subditi prelatum moneant ne pigretur in providendis his que ad salutem suam spectant.

[56] *Oeuvres,* op. cit. i (1932) 40–1: Non fallitur Ecclesia, nec sic iudicando debet dici iniuste iudicare a semitis sanctorum patrum non exorbitando, quos non licet immutare. . . . Iudicia Ecclesie canonice facta semper iusta sunt. . .

[57] G.F.L.C. 202–6.

[58] *Mat.* v, 252.

been reconciled, which may God soon bring to pass! This final sentence suggested that the foregoing lecture on his duties was not intended to incite its reader to offend Henry. Robert took the hint. He 'collaborated'. Indeed, he was one of the three bishops who set their seals to the appeal against Becket after the excommunications of Vézelay in June 1166.[59] Alexander still needed to placate Henry at Becket's expense. His dithering gave Robert an alibi in his own eyes, but not in Becket's. Promotion to a see from a chair of theology at Paris carried with it a duty to serve the cause of *sacerdotium* at all costs, as Becket saw it. The exiled archbishop appealed to Robert and his former pupil, Roger of Worcester: their study of sacred letters convinced him that no storm could separate them from faith and obedience to the Holy Roman Church:

> We speak to men who know and who teach the Law. We do not believe that they number among those who hold to the Law, while ignoring the Lord, who wish to seem faithful, while opposing the faith. Such men cheat themselves of their own salvation; they cannot cheat Scripture, which is ever binding.[60]

In other words, Becket called upon Hereford and Worcester to dissociate themselves from Gilbert of London, that plausible cheat, who twisted the Scriptures from their true meaning.

The exiles planned ways and means to make Hereford conform to the type of good bishop as presented in lectures on the sacred page. John of Salisbury had a brilliant idea: he briefed Abbot Ernisius and Prior Richard of St Victor to write to the bishop. Robert had been a pupil and admirer of Hugh of St Victor and had kept in touch with the abbey. The Victorines favoured Becket's cause; they had many ties with England; Prior Richard was the greatest teacher of mystical theology of the day. John suggested to them that Master Robert had been indifferent to money when he was teaching, but had hungered for praise. The judgement has a ring of truth, in that Robert had taught for some forty years without seeking preferment; at least we have no evidence that he did. Therefore, John reasoned, nothing would move him more than exhortation to prove himself to be the type of bishop whom he used to describe in the schools. Thus he would restore his lost repute as one who

[59] Knowles, 97, 105.
[60] *Mat.* v, 344–5; see also ibid. 451, 453.

would *redeem Israel*, that is free the Church from bondage.[61] The abbot and prior saw the point. They sent a letter to the tepid bishop, comparing him to their former colleague, Master Robert. His own pupils and all scholars had expected great things from his promotion to a bishopric; he had inspired them by his example to love learning and virtue. The canons of St Victor in particular had looked forward to the benefits which his preaching and example would bring to the English. They grieved all the more that their hopes remained unfulfilled. Wealth and ambition had corrupted him. His ears would burn if he heard what was said of him now in the schools. The letter reminds him:

> You were wont, people say, in the schools and in talk to com-
> pare such corrupted persons to the breed of dogs. You painted a
> fair picture of the bishop; we wish you would express it now
> in your life and your doctrine.

The writers go on to reproach him for joining in the appeal against Becket. They end by pleading that he may remember his teaching as master, his present office as bishop, their desire and God's judgement, so as to redeem his good name and strive to raise up the Church which is tottering in his care.[62]

The abbot and prior of St Victor suppose that Robert has described the good bishop in his lectures; he has also blamed courtier bishops as belonging to the breed of dogs, fawning upon their masters.[63] It follows that Robert must have given lectures on the Bible of a homiletic kind. It would have been futile to invent such a story: one does not reproach a person for not practising what he has never preached. The text of his lectures has not come down to us;[64] but

---

[61] ibid. vi, 20; see also v, 444-5. John writes to Becket: Si interim Herefordensis episcopus, qui a plerisque videbatur *liberaturus Israel*, in contemptu mundi et peritia litterarum, quarum ab ignaris vel eum ignorantibus creditur habere copiam, vos conturbatores ecclesiae nuncupat. . .

[62] ibid. v, 456-8.

[63] Stephen Langton tells an *exemplum* about 'quidam palatinus canis'; B. Smalley '*Exempla* in the Commentaries of Stephen Langton', *Bulletin of the John Rylands Library* xvii (1933) 128. The point in the Victorine letter is that Robert, now a corrupt bishop, used to attack such persons. As he called them *canigeni* he would have had curial or courtier bishops in mind.

[64] It is possible that Robert's *Quaestiones de divina pagina* represent excerpts from lecture courses which originally contained both literal exposition, including *quaestiones* on theology, and homiletics, which generally went with

they were evidently of the type we have in Robert Pullen's sermons; it is another link between the two English masters.

The bishop of Hereford defended himself against the charge of inconsistency. Fitzstephen tells us that he propounded a tearful question one day in a meeting of 'some bishops and many clerks':

> If it happens (God forbid!) that the archbishop should be killed in the cause of ecclesiastical freedom, shall we count him as a martyr? To be a martyr is to die for the faith.

Robert of Melun was distinguishing the cause of ecclesiastical freedom from the cause of faith. Becket's stand for the former would not suffice to make him a martyr. The faith was not in danger in England; so Robert implied. None of those present disagreed with him. Someone, however, took up the challenge and argued for Becket as a potential martyr on other grounds. Not one cause only, but many would make men martyrs: he listed St John the Baptist, the Maccabees, St Alfege, Abel and even the Roman Remus, as martyrs to various causes.[65] Fitzstephen does not say how the debate was concluded. He may have invented the story by anticipation;[66] but he probably records an opinion which Robert was thought to have held: one could be a martyr only if one died for the faith. That was vital, whereas ecclesiastical liberties were secondary. Robert's former teaching on St Paul should have led him to view Henry II as an offender against the Church; as such, on his own showing, Henry should have been excommunicated and disciplined. But there was an escape clause. An offending king should be allowed more delay than lesser men before the Church took action against him. Robert had also taught that the Church always judged rightly, if the canons and the decrees of the holy Fathers were observed. The bishop could have answered that the Church's judgement in Becket's case was not yet clear. It would have been difficult for him to have obeyed the papal mandate of 1165, ordering him to support Becket, while keeping his commission secret. So far, he could have justified himself.

The pinch came later when the conflict sharpened to such an

---

the spiritual exposition. If so, the original lectures have disappeared. Robert disapproved of the multiplication of glosses on Scripture; but he never said anything against homiletics.

[65] *Mat.* iii, 60–1.

[66] See below, p. 201.

extent that he had to take sides. Robert informed Henry through one of his clerks that he intended to answer Becket's summons to visit him abroad in 1167. The king replied that if he went he could not return to his bishopric in England. Robert tried to slip away secretly. Papal instructions turned him back at Southampton. He died later in the year, of grief according to Fitzstephen.[67] It is easy to believe that scruples troubled him. He could not have gone all the way with the Henricians without real inconsistency.

Both Robert Pullen and Robert of Melun taught more explicitly than their colleagues *in divina pagina* that the Church ought to resist a tyrannical ruler by spiritual means. Both masters dwelt on the role of the good prelate in their lectures. They will help us to understand Master Herbert of Bosham, though they were moderates and he was a natural exaggerator.

[67] ibid. vi, 74, 151, 173; iii, 87; Knowles, 106.

III

Herbert of Bosham

Master Herbert was a colourful character who enjoyed a scrap. He was also a gifted writer, an original thinker, an artist and the best Hebraist of his century. He figures large in my story for three reasons. First he acted as a channel through which Becket exposed himself to the teaching of the schools; second he presented his hero to the reading public through a scholar's eyes in his *Vita*; third, since 'a man is known by his friends', his friendship with Becket should tell us something of a man who had few intimates.

The murder broke Herbert's life and his career as an author into two parts. Each part is more interesting taken separately. To begin with the first stage: he was born at Bosham, an estuary port in Sussex, about 1120. The date can be deduced from his being called *senex*[1] by a friend writing 1173-6;[2] he would have been at least fifty by that time. He tells us that he had known his friend and patron Archbishop William of Sens ('William of the White Hands') when William was a little boy. William became bishop of Chartres in 1165 when he was barely thirty. Herbert must have been his senior by some years; otherwise he would have recalled that they were both children together.[3]

The first time that his name is recorded in a document is in a letter of Henry II, issued at Northampton in mid July, 1157. It comes rather late in his career; he already has the title of Master. The letter is worth dwelling on, since it gives important information on his experience. When Frederick Barbarossa became emperor in

[1] D.N.B. ix, 617.

[2] Glunz, 342, 346-7.

[3] ibid. Herbert also says that William has a debt to the English Church, whose breasts suckled him when he was a child; *Mat.* vii, 267. It is not known that William ever visited England as a child; but he may have. On William see R. R. Williams, 'William of the White Hands and Men of Letters', *Anniversary Essays in Medieval History presented to C. H. Haskins*, ed. C. H. Taylor (Boston, 1922) 365-87.

1152 he set about restoring the goods of his *Reich*. His lost treasures included a relic, the arm of St James the apostle. Contemporary devotion to St James can be gauged by the popularity of pilgrimage to his shrine at Compostella. The Empress Matilda, widow of the Emperor Henry V and daughter of King Henry I, had brought the relic to England on her return in 1126. Frederick wrote to Henry II asking that the arm of St James should be sent back to Germany. The request was embarrassing: Henry II wanted to keep on good terms with the emperor; but the arm had been given to Reading abbey and had begun to attract pilgrims. Henry could not despoil a royal foundation and site of royal tombs of a prized and profitable treasure. He met the difficulty by sending costly presents to Frederick; his embassy carried a letter full of flattering allusions to the emperor's superior status.[4] Its terms have been much discussed by historians of 'the imperial idea'. Flattery sugared the pill of Henry's 'no'. The arm of St James stayed at Reading. It was common practice in diplomacy to convey the essential matter orally through an accredited messenger, instead of putting it in writing. Henry's refusal is omitted from his letter and referred to obliquely at the end:

> We have given our answer concerning the hand of St James, about which you wrote to us, to be delivered by word of mouth by Master Herbert and William our clerk.

Thomas Becket witnessed the letter as chancellor. The two messengers had the awkward task of refusing Frederick's demand for the return of his property. Henry may have hoped that by sending a man with the respected title of Master he was showing proper deference.

---

[4] K. Leyser, 'England and the Empire in the Twelfth Century', T.R.H.S., 5th series, x (1960) 70. Rahewin describes the embassy and supplies a copy of Henry's letter under the year 1157, *Ottonis et Rahewini gesta Frederici I. Imperatoris*, ed. G. Waitz (M.G.H. SS ad usum schol., 1912) 171–2. Waitz identified Master Herbert with Herbert of Bosham. Henry II held a council at Northampton on 17 July 1157; see Eyton, 27. On the letter see H. Mayer, 'Staufische Weltherrschaft? Zum Brief Heinrichs II. von England an Friedrich Barbarossa von 1157', *Festschrift Karl Pivec* ed. A. Haidacher and H. Mayer (Innsbrucker Beiträge zur Kulturwissenschaft xii, 1966) 265–78. On Reading Abbey see G. Constable, 'An Unpublished Letter by Abbot Hugh II of Reading concerning Archbishop Hubert Walter', *Essays in Medieval History presented to Bertie Wilkinson*, ed. T. A. Sandquist and M. R. Powicke (Toronto, 1969) 22–3; see also G.F.L.C. 389–90.

We can safely identify this Master Herbert with Herbert of Bosham. It was not a common Christian name and he is called 'Master' in references to him from 1157 onwards. The identification clears up some problems in his career. It explains how Becket got to know him, since he served Henry while Becket was chancellor. It is not certain that Herbert was in permanent royal service, but it seems quite likely. Becket brought a number of his chancery clerks with him to Canterbury when he was promoted to the archbishopric; Herbert may have been among them.[5] His service to Henry would explain why the king came to hate him later on. Henry must have judged him to be able and trustworthy enough to send on a delicate mission: it made him all the angrier when Herbert changed sides; he was a Becket in miniature. A minor point: a visit to the imperial court in 1157 would explain why Herbert affected a German style in dress.[6]

He begins to record Becket's life as an eye-witness immediately after the election, when the new archbishop travelled from London to Canterbury for his ordination and consecration, 2–3 June 1162.[7] Fitzstephen, Gervase of Canterbury and Herbert himself all agree that he served Becket as secretary and as 'master of the holy page'.[8] Becket felt the need for instruction in theology to equip him for his new duties. The best was good enough for him in any office he held. Herbert was a qualified teacher of unimpeachable orthodoxy. He had a guarantee of that, in having been a pupil of Peter Lombard at Paris; he cherished the Lombard's memory throughout his life.[9] The Lombard's *Sentences* became the standard book on theology in the schools; his expansion of the Anselmian *Gloss* on the Psalter and the Pauline epistles into commentaries known as the *Great*

---

[5] See below, p. 163.

[6] See below, p. 63.

[7] *Mat.* iii, 185–6.

[8] ibid. 58; below, p. 73, n. 56. Herbert describes how he instructed Becket, *Mat.* iii, 204–5. Dom David Knowles suggests that Herbert may have been 'one of Hilary of Chichester's young men'; he pointed out that three members of Becket's archiepiscopal household came from Chichester and that Bosham was in the Chichester diocese; see *Episcopal Colleagues*, 26. Dr Henry Mayr-Harting tells me that he cannot find any evidence for Herbert's having been a protégé of Bishop Hilary of Chichester in the records he has studied.

[9] On Herbert's edition of his master's commentareis see below, p. 82. He refers to the Lombard as 'magistri mei suavis recordationis Petri Parisienisis episcopi'; P.L. cxc, 1418.

Gloss became the equivalent in exegesis. He died as bishop of Paris in 1159. Herbert probably studied under him about 1150.[10] A connection with the abbey of St Victor would have enhanced Herbert's prestige. He was an admirer and perhaps a pupil of Master Andrew of St Victor, an Old Testament scholar, a pupil of Hugh of St Victor and later abbot of Wigmore. Herbert could have attended Andrew's lectures at St Victor before 1147 or after 1154-5.[11] Peter Lombard had such good relations with the Victorines that it would have been natural for his pupil to study there.[12] Herbert had learnt rhetoric in the *Artes*, which qualified him to act as secretary and diplomat. The two gaps in his education were the Latin classics and civil and canon law. He could bring out the odd tag and look up a law text, but neither discipline had influenced him: he had the theologian's professional jealousy of lawyers.[13] Becket could dispense with these skills in Herbert: John of Salisbury was a classicist and lawyers worked in the Canterbury *familia*. The archbishop employed Herbert as theologian and publicist. It was a fatal choice. Herbert held extreme views on the relations between *regnum* and *sacerdotium*. He had learnt them at Paris, though not from the cautious Lombard; they were 'in the air'. He may have put them into storage for the time being when he entered into royal service, probably before 1157. They came out fresh when there was a chance to impress them on Becket. As a publicist, Herbert let his tongue and his pen run away with him.

His career is inseparable from Becket's from the moment of his joining the household staff until the murder. Every history of the

[10] On the Lombard's teaching period at Paris, see Brady, 'Peter Lombard', 277-95. Fr. Brady will publish his evidence for a revised dating of the Lombard's works in his *Prolegomena* to his new edition of the *Sentences*. Herbert enters into the puzzle on account of his edition of the Lombard's commentaries on the Psalter and St Paul. Fr. Brady kindly tells me that *c.* 1150 is the most likely date for Herbert's studies under the Lombard. The tentative attribution of a group of theological works of 1155-65 to Herbert made by P. Glorieux, 'Essai sur les "Quaestiones in epistolas Pauli"', R.T.A.M. xix (1952) 59, must now be rejected. Herbert left Paris too early to have composed them, since he was serving Henry II by 1157 and probably several years earlier.

[11] For Herbert's connection with Andrew, see below, p. 74, n. 62. On Andrew's dates see *Study of the Bible*, 112-15; G.E.L.C., 181.

[12] J. de Ghellinck, 'La carrière de Pierre Lombard', R.H.E. xxvii (1931) 804-5, 823.

[13] See his attack on them, *Mat.* iii, 207.

conflict tells how he sat at his master's feet at the council of Northampton; they whispered together and Herbert rashly advised Becket
to excommunicate his enemies. Becket sent Herbert on ahead to prepare for his coming, when he decided to escape overseas. The two
stayed together for most of the exile, at Sens, at the French court,
and 'among the rocks and monks' at Pontigny. Herbert went on
errands which brought him into touch with Louis VII, the counts
of Flanders and Champagne, and many French prelates.[14] We have
accounts of two confrontations with Henry II. Fitzstephen describes
a meeting at Angers in May 1166; Henry asked some of the archbishop's clerks to give their views on the questions in dispute.[15]
John of Salisbury came first. He gave a modest but firm answer.
Herbert was called in next. 'Now you'll see a proud fellow', said
the king to his entourage. Master Herbert of Bosham entered, tall
and handsome and splendidly dressed in a tunic and cloak of green
cloth of Auxerre, hanging down from his shoulders to his heels in
the German fashion. He refused to swear an oath of loyalty to his
king, unless Henry undertook to keep his archbishop by his side to
correct him when he did wrong. That was the only true kind of
loyalty, Herbert said. He showed what he meant by wrong-doing
when he went straight on to attack the Constitutions of Clarendon.
He granted to Henry that other kingdoms had bad customs as well
as England; but so long as they remained unwritten there was
hope; they might die out with time. Specifying some bad customs
in Germany, he refused the imperial title to Frederick I. Henry
protested sharply against this insult to his ally. 'He's just king of
Germany,' Herbert replied, 'though he writes his title as *Imperator
Romanorum, semper Augustus*'. It was a flick on the raw: Henry
was threatening to recognize Frederick's anti-pope; Herbert implied
that no schismatic could be truly an emperor. The king cried out in
fury that this 'son of a priest' was disturbing the peace of his realm.
Herbert denied being the son of a priest. His father had taken
orders only after his birth. Nor, he added, 'is a man the son of a
king, unless his father was king before his birth.' It was a rude
answer to Henry, son of a count of Anjou. One of the barons sitting
round admired Herbert's cheek: 'Well, son of whomsoever he be,
I'd give half my lands to have him as mine!' Fitzstephen gives

---

[14] The mission to the count of Flanders, otherwise unrecorded, is mentioned
in Herbert's letter to the abbot of St Crispin at Soissons, P.L. cxc, 1456–8.

[15] *Mat.* iii, 98–101.

the baron's name as Jordan of Taisun (or Tesson). He came of a wealthy family whose lands centred on middle Normandy. Jordan attended Henry's court when it met on the continent as a regular thing, from 1150–51, before Henry became king of England, until he died in 1178, and gave Henry military support. He was strong and loyal enough to crack his joke at the king's expense. Jordan of Tesson lacked neither lands nor sons in 1166; he had two sons by then, who grew to manhood.[16] It speaks for Herbert's unclerical character that Jordan would have liked to have fathered him. Clerk though he was, Herbert dressed like a gentleman, ignoring the rule that clergy should avoid bright colours and secular fashions.[17] Further, he stood up for himself and gave as good as he got.

Herbert referred in a letter to his proud and abusive words, spoken to the king at Angers 'last year'. They were held against him, but he does not seem to regret them, and cannot call to mind just what he said.[18] He had to abide their consequences. He had a narrow escape from arrest and capture, when Henry caught a papal messenger at Rouen in November 1166; the latter confessed that the letters had been handed to him by Master Herbert.[19] Herbert's property

---

[16] On the Tesson family see D. C. Douglas, *William the Conqueror* (London, 1964) 48, 112, 115, 144, 381; L. Delisle, *Histoire du Château et des Sires de Saint Sauveur-le-Vicomte* (Paris, 1867) 31–8. Jordan married in 1145 or earlier. His son and heir Ralph witnessed a charter with his brother Roger in 1174; hence they must have been born before 1166. On Jordan's constant attendance at Henry's court see *Receuil des Actes de Henri II*, ed. Delisle and Berger, i and ii, *passim*. Ralph de Tesson served King John and held the office of seneschal of Normandy in 1201. He went over to Philip Augustus in 1203; his lands in England were confiscated the following year; see F. M. Powicke, *The Loss of Normandy*, 2nd edn (Manchester, 1961) 146, 173, 352–3. The family had a long record of loyal service, which was rewarded by their lords.

[17] See *Thomae de Chobham Summa Confessorum*, ed. F. Broomfield (Analecta Mediaevalia Namurcensia xxv, 1968) 83: . . . non licet clerico habere pannos viridos vel rubeos nec capas manicatas . . . et cetera huiusmodi. The *Summa Confessorum* was probably written soon after 1215, but the author had earlier precedents in canon law; see liv–lv. Clerks were forbidden to offend 'inhonesta varietate colorum', by a canon of the Council of Rheims, 1148; Mansi, *Sacr. Concil. nova et ampliss. coll.* xxi, 714.

[18] P.L. cxc, 1422: . . . et me (nuntii domini regis) . . . linguis suis ubique consectantur, obicientes mihi quod anno praeterito domino regi Angliae nescio quae Andegavis in superbia et abusione locutus fuerim, quae tamen illa fuerint, credo me tibi . . . fideliter retulisse.

[19] *Mat.* vi, 73; Eyton, 100.

in England was confiscated with that of the other exiles. He saw no chance of returning to England during Henry's reign, having made himself more odious than anyone else.[20] The second confrontation with Henry comes as no surprise. Herbert went with John of Salisbury to discuss restitution of property before Becket's return to Canterbury in 1170. The king pointedly ignored him, and addressed his words to John of Salisbury alone.[21]

Again like his master, Herbert never reconciled himself to the hardship which followed logically on his behaviour. He complained to the count of Champagne of living in poverty and obscurity.[22] He scrounged. A begging letter to the bishop of Bayeux threatens that the writer will become a monk unless he gets the means to live as a clerk, a threat which nobody who knew Herbert would have taken seriously.[23] The pope, doubtless acting on a petition, tried to set him up in a provostship at Troyes, vacated in 1167; he recommended Herbert as 'famous for learning and worth'.[24] The canons of Troyes took no notice.[25] Herbert really had a reputation for learning. The abbot of St Crispin at Soissons, a close friend, wrote to say that he needed some sermons urgently for a near occasion when he would have to preach; he reminded his friend of an unfulfilled promise to send or bring his *De synodis et ad populum sermones* (that is, specimen sermons to be preached to clergy and people).

[20] *Mat.* v, 334: . . . in me tamen prae caeteris confirmatae sunt irae et Anglorum regis irruit furor, qui me in meo iam confirmavit exilio, et eo regnum agente omnem mihi spem reversionis ademit.

[21] *Mat.* iii, 468

[22] P.L. cxc, 1422. On this letter see below, p. 81.

[23] This letter has not been printed in full. The text is in MS C.C.C. Cambridge 123, fol. 44rb: Proinde, clemens pater, necesse est ut tu filium tuum operies, nisi forte negans habitum clerici monachalem habitum, cuius michi nunc copia est (me) assumere velis.

On Henry bishop of Bayeux see G.F.L.C., 530. He was dean of Salisbury 1155–65, when he was elected bishop of Bayeux. Herbert addresses him 'in novitate electionis eius', therefore in 1165 or soon after, from Pontigny, where he was among monks. He would have known Henry in England. Herbert here overdoes the rhetorical rule that a petitioner must show his need.

[24] *Mat.* v, 241.

[25] William of Champagne on his election to the bishopric of Chartres agreed to renounce his *praepositura* at Troyes in return for an annual rent; Troyes Arch. Dep. G. 1252, foll. 4–4v. He had no successor, and the office was suppressed at Troyes. There is no evidence in the Troyes archives that Herbert held any other benefice there. I owe this information to the kindness of Melle d'Alverny and Dr J. Ramackers.

Herbert put him off with the sort of excuses that a would-be borrower knows only too well: he was too busy working for the archbishop; he was living in the country at Pontigny (which had a splendid library); so he sent just a few scribbles *pro tem*.[26] The request proves that he had renown as a writer of sermons, though none have survived.[27] The abbot of Vézelay wrote to ask his advice on the procedure to be adopted in dealing with local heretics in 1167.[28] But fame was inadequate as a lever for benefices.

Becket relied on him to the end. He sent him to England on a commission to take seizin of restored possessions in July 1170.[29] Later in the year he returned again to England with the archbishop, and missed the murder only because Becket sent him back to France on 26 December on an embassy to the king of France and the archbishop of Sens. It was a pretext to get him out of the way; Becket realized that Henry regarded Herbert as the worst suspect.[30] Herbert regretted afterwards that he had not stayed with his master, while admitting frankly that perhaps it had been as well. He might have turned coward and hidden himself.[31]

His literary output in this period consists of letters, written either for Becket or on his own behalf. I choose one as a sample of his arguments and his rhetoric. He writes for Becket to Alexander III in 1166, putting Becket's case against his enemies and pleading for papal support. It may represent a draft of a letter which was never sent; but it illustrates his ideas.[32] To read it in the *Materials* is to see a tragic actor stalk into drawing-room comedy. Herbert rants and raves in the old-fashioned actor's way. It is an exciting perform-

[26] P.L. cxc, 1456-7. Herbert would have met the abbot when Becket and his followers stayed at Soissons on first reaching France; *Mat*. iii, 339. The abbot's letter and Herbert's reply show that they were on familiar terms.

[27] The library of St Crispin's abbey may have had a transcript of Herbert's notes or sermons, if he sent them; but it was burnt and suffered other damage during the Anglo-French wars and was sacked by the Huguenots in 1567; see P. Gasnault, 'L'abbaye de Saint-Crépin-le-Grand de Soissons en 1379', *Revue Mabillon* xlix (1959) 69–76; Jean Elie's history of the abbey, MS Paris. B.N. fr. 1877, fol. 20–20v.

[28] See below, p. 69.

[29] *Mat*. vii, 342, Becket to Ralph of Serres: . . . quia igitur amico vestro amicissimo et in omnibus voluntati nostrae devoto, magistro Hereberto legatio haec iniuncta est . . .; Eyton, 142.

[30] *Mat*. iii, 485–6.   [31] P.L. cxc, 1466.

[32] *Mat*. v, 285–94. At least one of the letters written by Herbert for Becket represents a draft only; see G.F.L.C., 219.

ance. His voice rises above intrigue, caution or mere peevishness; his diction has the plangency of the Latin Vulgate, which echoes through his phrases.

Writing early in the conflict, Herbert already presents it as a drama enacted on a cosmic stage. 'The world cries out, even should I keep silence', he makes Becket say. Christ's passion is renewed. Christ in the person of the clergy is judged by Pilate. Henry II and Frederick I have made a pact to destroy ecclesiastical liberties. Becket alone has stood up for the Church. Though bred in the palace, fellow-pupil of princes, he alone has shouldered the burden of pastoral care. He alone tries to ward off injuries to Christ. He alone confesses Christ's name on earth: *And so I have trodden the wine-press alone* (Isa. lxiii, 3). Herbert implies blame of all other prelates by repeating *alone*. Becket chooses to die in exile rather than to accept the spoiling of the widow's dower and of the patrimony of Christ crucified. Herbert means that Becket has refused to agree to anything less than full restitution of church property, confiscated by the king. The rhetor's task was to provoke pity and anger; he must also persuade. Herbert tries to persuade the pope that both duty and interest dictate full support for Becket. Having softened him up by bombast, Herbert resorts to argument. Henry II's policy touches the apostolic office directly and bids fair to pull it down. The pope's fear of Henry, however, is not justified by the current trend of events. His pact with the emperor is wearing thin. The great schismatic (Frederick), who seeks to rule the world, is disappointed in his ally. Henry himself is abashed and confounded: all his might has not sufficed to defeat the poor, ragged, unbreechered Welshmen. Herbert refers to Henry's campaign of 1165 against the Welsh princes, when he had to withdraw his army and fleet without engaging the enemy.[33] The picture of waning royal power clashes with a later argument, where it suited him to present Henry as a fierce, cunning lion; he waits to trap the archbishop into returning without safeguards, and will then spring out on him.

Herbert now outlines the papal role in the conflict, as it should be. The pope is Christ's vicar; let him prove it in deed, lest God should judge his shortcomings. Herbert's God is the Old Testament Jehovah, as we hear in his counsel to Alexander:

As you are father of mercies, so too be lord of vengeance. Be

[33] J. E. Lloyd, *History of Wales from the Earliest Times to the Edwardian Conquest* ii (London, 1911) 518.

F

judge, strong and righteous, terrible and *who taketh away the spirit of princes, terrible to the kings of the earth* (Ps. lxxv, 12–13).

Neglect advice to temporise as mere worldly wisdom. Do not sheathe your sword. Act now while the fight is on, lest the hosts of heaven reproach you. As a line of action, Herbert makes a fantastic suggestion, unparalleled elsewhere in the *Materials*. Becket seems to be advising Alexander to excommunicate Henry, absolve subjects from their oath of allegiance, and hope that the ensuing rebellion will bring the king to his knees:

> Come forth, prince of the Christian host, sheathe not your sword, but draw it out, especially as he is threatened by the other sword, not of the word, but of steel. Thus both swords shall serve the Church. . . . Rise, my lord, in your wrath. Repay the proud. . . .

The marginal caption in the Rolls Series, 'exhortation to vigorous action' lends a touch of bathos by understatement. Herbert had little hope that Alexander would act vigorously. He goes on to make Becket ask the pope to let him be a martyr if he wants to:

> The Lord's hand has touched me and stretches over me; so leave me alone to drink the cup of my sorrow.

Finally he tries to shame Alexander by pointing to the bolder policy of his predecessors: 'Adrian, Anastasius, Eugenius, Peter and Paul' would not have failed him. Herbert contrasts the wealth and feebleness of the Curia to the severity of the primitive Church:

> How happy were the times when the apostles wore neither purple nor gold nor shone with jewels. . . . They knew that they went naked. They knew that man is born to misery and toil, not to rank and glory.

Let the pope acknowledge himself, in spite of his splendid dress, as the heir of poor outcasts and fishermen.

Herbert quite realized that he was urging desperate measures. Only by throwing caution to the winds could Alexander have followed the examples of St Peter and St Paul, as he proposed. The English bishops made a sarcastic comment on his influence on Becket. Writing to the archbishop to complain of his intransigence and ask him to make peace, they added:

But high-minded men about you perhaps will not let you take this path.[34]

It reads as a clear reference to his hot-headed secretary.

Herbert's personal letters express the same ideas. Becket 'fights against the world on the stage of the world, as a spectacle for men and for angels'.[35] He saw the conflict between *regnum* and *sacerdotium* as insoluble as long as Henry reigned:

The king's peace which we seek and our justice which we cherish, his rule and our priesthood, cannot meet.

He wrote this to Archbishop William of Sens in 1170, telling him how Henry had refused to give Becket the kiss of peace. Herbert regretted his foresight, but he could not lie.[36] Two other letters outline his views on the Church's function. Herbert had all the theologian's horror at clerical participation in the shedding of blood. He warned the newly elected bishop of Bayeux against following the warlike example of one of his predecessors in the see, 'whom I neither name nor blame; he has gone to his judge'.[37] Herbert may have been referring to Philip of Harcourt, bishop of Bayeux 1142–63, a great litigant,[38] or he may have been harking back to the warrior bishop Odo of Bayeux. The second letter was a reply to the abbot of Vézelay, who had asked him how he ought to proceed against heretics. Procedure in heresy trials was still fluid and the abbot was puzzled. Herbert anticipated what would become standard practice in his advice: the abbot should hand over the heretics to 'the public power', in the person of the king of France, if they proved to be obdurate; he should not inflict the death penalty on them himself, even though he claimed to hold secular jurisdiction over Vézelay. It was consequent advice: Herbert believed that the secular sword should be wielded on the Church's behalf, but not

---

[34] G.F.L.C., 224: Sed qui penes uos alta sapiunt uos hac forte via progredi non permittunt.

[35] *Mat.* vi, 122.

[36] ibid. vii, 265–9.

[37] MS C.C.C., Cambridge, 123, fol. 43va: Corporalis (gladius) etsi pro ecclesia, non tamen ecclesie est. Ad nutum quidem eius debet esse, sed ad usum nequaquam, ut aliquis decessorum tuorum fecisse memoratur, quem tamen non nomino nec noto, utpote qui nunc habet iudicem suum.

[38] V. Bourrienne, *Un grand bâtisseur. Philippe de Harcourt évêque de Bayeux* (Paris, 1930).

by churchmen. The abbot did not take it. He kept the heretics for questioning for sixty days (long enough for him to have received Herbert's answer). Then he held a court, assisted by two bishops, appealed to the crowd for a verdict, and had the heretics burnt.[39]

The second stage of Herbert's career began with the murder. It knocked the bottom out of his world. He felt lost without his former friend and could hardly bear to shoulder his load alone.[40] Henceforth he lived on his memories and on the comfort of visions: the martyr appeared to him to console him in his sleep.[41] What else he lived on for the next fifteen years is unknown. Henry II forced an oath of loyalty on the rest of Becket's followers, but Herbert avoided it, since Becket had sent him abroad.[42] He refused to take it as a condition of ending his exile.[43] The pope sent him a kind letter of sympathy[44] and requested the papal legates to intercede with Henry in 1171. They did him no good. Herbert would not give in, although his friends tried to persuade him to.[45] He continued to accuse Henry of oppressing the Church, keeping sees vacant and abusing 'the temple furniture' like Balthasar. This occurs in a letter to the bishop of Durham, written before 1173, begging for help for the martyr's sake and complaining that he was still proscribed.[46] It was no wonder. So he remained in France.

Doubtless his patrons there looked after him. His old friend William of the White Hands, archbishop of Sens 1168–76 and then of Rheims 1176–1202, patronized scholars and had supported Becket; he was probably the lord referred to by Herbert, whose business

---

[39] P.L. cxc, 1462–3, 1468. On the Vézelay heretics and their punishment (one, a more doubtful case than the others, was whipped and banished instead of being burnt) see A. Borst, *Die Katharer* (Stuttgart, 1953) 103.

[40] P.L. cxc, 1466.

[41] Glunz, 348; he mentions a vision in a letter to John of Poitiers, not printed in full in *Mat.* vii, 513 or P.L. cxc, 1469. See MS C.C.C., Cambridge, 123, fol. 55rb: Adeo etiam quod proxime non modico unius noctis spatio astitit michi in visu, et consolatione quidem plus quam dici queat perfecta.

The letter to John of Poitiers was written before Becket's canonization, Feb. 21, 1173.

[42] *Mat.* vii, 576–7, a letter to Alexander III, 1177.

[43] P.L. cxc, 1463–7.

[44] *Mat.* vii, 529–30.

[45] He says so in his letter to John of Poitiers, fol. 55va–vb.

[46] ibid. fol. 58vb–59rb. Henry II arranged for six English sees to be filled at a meeting in London, 1173; see Poole, 220.

kept him from returning to England.[47] William's brother Henry the Liberal, count of Champagne, was also a patron of scholars; he had used the Becket conflict to pay off old scores against Henry II.[48] Herbert had written a letter in Count Henry's name during his first exile, 1166–7. He may have worked for the count again. Then he suddenly turns up at Paris. We find him acting as assessor in a judgement pronounced by the papal legate Cardinal Peter of Pavia sometime between June–July 1174 and August 1178[49] on a dispute between the abbot of St Geneviève and some of his tenants. Herbert comes last on the list of assessors, below two other *magistri*, Gerard la Pucelle and Simon of Tournai, which may reflect his lack of status. At about the same time Alexander III wrote to Richard, archbishop of Canterbury and papal legate, ordering him to allot Master Herbert of Bosham his revenues for three years, since Herbert wished to teach theology and should be helped to do so. The letter is undated, but it must have been sent to Archbishop Richard after he had received the papal legateship, 28 April 1174.[50] Herbert, therefore, was planning to open a school of theology. There is no record of his teaching, and the archbishop would have found it difficult to allot him revenues from his property in England, if it was still confiscated. Perhaps his plan never materialized. He certainly visited the abbey of St Denis near Paris during the rule of Abbot William le Mire 1172–3 to 1186;[51] he may have stayed there as a guest. However he supported himself, his stay in or near Paris from about 1174 for an unspecified period gave him a chance to

---

[47] *Mat.* vii, 512.

[48] G. V. Scammel, *Hugh du Puiset Bishop of Durham* (Cambridge, 1956) 33–5; J. F. Benton, 'The Court of Champagne as a Literary Centre', *Speculum* xxxvi (1961) 551–91.

[49] R. de Lasteyrie, *Cartulaire générale de Paris* i (Paris, 1887) no. 519, p. 429.

[50] S. Loewenfeld, *Epistolae pontificum romanorum ineditae*, p. 207, no. 347: Cum dilectus noster magister H. de Boseham de suo et aliorum profectu sollicitus vacare desideret auditoribus in theologie scientia instruendis, dignum est, ut propositum eius benigne prosequamur affectu et ad ipsum implendum favorem et auxilium impendamus. Inde est quod fraternitati tue per apostolica scripta mandamus, quatinus ei redditus suos triennio in scolis pro reverentia mandati nostri et consideratione sui ipsius facias contradictione et appellatione remota cum integritate conferri, ita quod litteras nostras sibi profuisse letetur et nos caritatem tuam merito possimus, cum audieremus, commendare.
Loewenfeld dated the letter 1178–81, the year of Alexander's death. He gave no reason for 1178 as a *terminus post quem*. It was probably earlier.

[51] Glunz, 346–7.

brush up his theology and to continue his Hebrew studies, as we know that he did.

Later on, when the dust had cleared, he had an interview with Henry II; he does not say when or where. He accused Henry point blank of responsibility for the murder. The king answered without turning a hair that it was done *for him*, alas, but not *by him*. Herbert reserved judgement, while accepting Henry's penitence as genuine.[52] Henry allowed his old enemy to return to England and made at least partial restitution or compensation. We know that Herbert held property, since the Pipe Roll for Essex, 1187, records a fine of one mark owed by Herbert of Bosham. It was evidently for a forest offence.[53] Royal forest covered the whole county of Essex during Henry II's reign. Herbert may have been poaching; but there were other ways in which one could offend against the forest laws. The fine remained unpaid. It was re-entered regularly on the Pipe Rolls until 1194.[54] In spite of Henry's concession, Herbert still felt that the royal anger dogged his path. A hopeful visit to Canterbury in 1184 brought no promotion. He found veneration enough for the martyr in death, but none for his most faithful followers in life. The English prelates shunned Herbert, who thought that the king's anger had frightened them off.[55] Perhaps so; but they must have found him a bore, with his stories of the martyr and his exhortations to tread in the martyr's footsteps. We see him at Canterbury again in 1187, this time through the friendly eyes of the monk Gervase. Herbert visited the convent out of special affection to advise the monks on their lawsuit against the reigning archbishop. He made an eloquent speech, but defeatist in tone, urging them to submit the case to the archbishop's decision. He put forward what seemed to him irrefutable reasons. These included the inconstancy of the Roman Curia and the might of the royal power; he pointed to Henry's chronic ill-will against the rights and liberties of the church of Canterbury. Herbert may have grown sadder

[52] P.L. cxc, 1312–15, 1323.

[53] *Pipe Roll* H. II, 34, 1187–8, p. 38: De placitis Galfridi filii Petri in Essexa. Oratius presbiter debet dim.m. pro transgressione assise. Herbertus de Boseham debet l m. pro eodem.

Professor J. C. Holt kindly tells me that 'pro transgressione assise' would refer to a forest offence in the context.

[54] ibid. R.I., 1, 1189–90, p. 26; 2, Mich. 1190, p. 107; 3, 1191, p. 27; 4, 1192, p. 169; 5, 1193, p. 3; 6, 1194, p. 31.

[55] P.L. cxc, 1403–4.

and wiser. The sub-prior, however, answered that the monks would stand up for their rights none the less. Herbert marvelled at their steadfastness and unity. 'In that case', he said, 'you must yield shamefully or resist manfully.'[56] It was a flash of his old spirit.

Employment and patronage came at last from a surprising quarter. Herbert's new master was William Longchamp, bishop of Ely and royal chancellor from the accession of Richard I, 1189. This ugly little man seems an odd successor to St Thomas as a patron; but he did take an interest in scholars.[57] Moreover, Henry II's disfavour would have presented no obstacle to Longchamp, a protégé of Richard I, given Richard's bad relations with his father. As Longchamp served Richard as his chancellor for Aquitaine before Richard succeeded to Henry, Herbert may perhaps have entered Longchamp's chancery even before 1189.[58] Our only evidence for their connection is a letter to Herbert from Longchamp, which Herbert preserved. It can be dated between June 1190 and March 1191 by the writer's references to political events. Longchamp antagonized the English bishops and barons while Richard was on crusade and lost his chancellorship in consequence. He confides his troubles to Herbert in general terms: his king is absent and the storm clouds are gathering. It appears from the letter that Herbert has already left him. Longchamp closes with the wish that his former protégé may soon finish the commentary on the *Hebraica* (St Jerome's

---

[56] *Chronica* (ed. W. Stubbs, Rolls Series) i, 393–4: Herebertus etiam de Boseham, gloriosi pontificis et martyris Thomae magister et clericus, quasi ex speciali dilectione Cantuariam accessit, eleganti quo pollebat eloquio venerabilem et decora dignum memoria Gaufridum suppriorem inducere cupiens, ut totam ecclesiae causam . . . archiepiscopi committeret arbitrio. . . . Proposuit enim, invincibili, ut putabat, ratione, enormes litigandi difficultates . . . de Romanae curiae mutabilitate, de potentia regis Anglorum, quam totam fere ad libitum archiepiscopi effundebat, praeter illam cotidianam et inveteratam malitiam qua Cantuariensis ecclesiae libertates et iura confundere nitebatur. . . . Haec itaque cum audisset Herebertus miratur constantiam, tantaeque congregationis obstupescit unanimitatem. 'Ergo', inquit, 'si ita est, aut cedendum est turpiter, aut standum viriliter.'

[57] E. Rathbone, 'Roman Law in the Anglo-Norman Realm', *Studia Gratiana* xi (1967) 261–2. According to Ralph of Diss he had studied the liberal arts; see *Op. hist.* ed. W. Stubbs (RS) ii, 177.

[58] On Longchamp see W. Stubbs, *Historical Introduction to the Rolls Series* (London, 1902) 214–59; H. G. Richardson, 'William of Ely', T.R.H.S. (new series) xv (1932) 46.

translation of the Psalter), which he has begun, so that he may have time for a visit.[59]

The story ended there until Mr N. R. Ker raised the curtain on Herbert's last years by discovering a copy of the commentary mentioned in Longchamp's letter. The library of St Paul's cathedral possesses the only known surviving copy of Herbert on the *Hebraica*.[60] The author begins with a dedicatory letter to Peter, bishop of Arras (1184–1203). Peter had been abbot of Pontigny and later abbot of Cîteaux; Herbert would have known him ever since the days of exile at Pontigny. The Cistercian bishop was in close touch with English church affairs; both sides in the dispute between Archbishop Baldwin of Ford and the monks of Christchurch tried to win his moral support and wrote to him frequently, 1186–9.[61] He seems to have been acting as Herbert's spiritual director.

Herbert writes in his letter that he has withdrawn from the restless atmosphere of the court (presumably the chancellor's household) to the Cistercian abbey of Ourscamp, in the diocese of Arras. His retreat to Ourscamp would explain why the only early copy of Herbert's writings on Becket belonged to this abbey; he would have brought them as a gift to the monks. To continue on his letter to Peter of Arras: the bishop has given Herbert three alternatives to choose from. He must become a monk himself or else occupy his time by teaching or writing. The implication is that he must not hang about as a parlour boarder. Herbert had no vocation for the religious life, even in his old age; he lacked the energy to teach; so he chose to write; hence his commentary on the *Hebraica*.[62] We hear nothing more of him. The disappearance of his debt from the Essex Pipe Rolls after 1194 suggests that he died about that time.

There is a local and unverifiable tradition that he was buried in the church at Bosham.[63] The tomb assigned to him is set into the

[59] P.L. cxc, 1474.

[60] *Medieval Manuscripts in British Libraries* i (Oxford, 1969) 241.

[61] *Ep. Cant.*, 15, 26, 74, 226.

[62] See B. Smalley, 'A Commentary on the *Hebraica* by Herbert of Bosham', R.T.A.M. xviii (1951) 29–65.

[63] D.N.B. ix, 618. F. Cristofori, copying older lists, makes Herbert a cardinal in 1178 with a query, *Storia dei cardinali di Santa Romana Chiesa* (Rome, 1888), 285. It is a mistake. Herbert was not a member of the sacred college; see J. M. Brixius, *Die Mitglieder des Kardinalkollegiums von 1130–1181* (Berlin, 1912); K. Ganzer, *Die Entwicklung des auswärtigen Kardina-*

wall beside the south doorway. It has no effigy or inscription and this part of the church was added in the thirteenth century. However, it seems possible that the builders might have transferred his coffin to the outer wall when they made the enlargement. In any case, he is still remembered there.

Herbert had more time for writing in the second stage of his career. We have a few letters, most of them intended to hasten the martyr's canonization. He appeals to the pope on familiar lines: you have the power; use it![64] Otherwise he devoted himself to making propaganda in the martyr's cause and to works of pure scholarship. His best known effort is his *Life* of St Thomas, written 1184–1186.[65] It is independent of the common tradition of the other *Lives*. Herbert drew on his own memories and he touched them up. This is clear from his account of the argument at Sens between Becket on the one side and the pope and cardinals on the other. Herbert presents the debate as an exercise in *Gloss* punching.[66] We should do well to read it as an exposé of all the reasons and authorities put forward by either side for the whole period of Becket's exile. Herbert's prolixity may repel his readers; but he had an unusual flare for self-revelation. Like many biographers, he tells us more about himself than about his hero. His digressions hide some odd flashes of originality.

A case in point is his long apology for Becket's mode of saying Mass when he became archbishop. He said it quickly instead of dragging it out.[67] Herbert explains that speed countered distraction; hence he is led to describe his restless questioning and wandering thoughts. While hearing Mass, he used to doubt the truth of the Christian religion. Suppose, he wondered, that the Jews were right in rejecting Jesus as no true Messiah and in still awaiting the fulfilment of the Old Testament promises? The Christian faith would then be unfounded. If that were so, then what would God make of it? Would he count our belief as of no avail? Herbert comforted himself with the hope that God would accept it as sincere, though mistaken. The Christian sacrifice of the Mass was purer and cleaner

lats in hohen Mittelalter (Bibliothek des deutschen historischen Instituts in Rom xxvi, 1963). [64] See for instance *Mat.* vii, 529.

[65] An allusion to the death of Henry II, 1189, must have been added later, perhaps by Herbert himself, since he lived on into the 1190s.

[66] *Mat.* iii, 352–9. See below, chap. VI, p. 158.

[67] *Mat.* iii, 211–19.

than the blood sacrifices of the Old Testament at least. His speculations resulted in a nightmare: he saw the consecrated Host whirling
round in the chalice. He confided in the archbishop in secret;
Becket interpreted the nightmare as signifying Herbert's restless
fancies and advised self-control. The biographer does not say how
much of his doubt he told to Becket: it would have been upsetting to
have one's master of the holy page admit to doubting the truth of
the Gospel *in toto*. However, Herbert took the advice. Henceforward his faith in the sacrament of the altar grew firmer.

It was exceptional for a Christian to commit his doubts to writing.
Herbert's confession deserves to have a place beside the famous
account of his temptations by the eleventh-century monk, Otloh
of St Emmeran. Their source in Herbert's mind was probably his
Hebrew studies and his consultations with rabbis. Judaism appealed
to some Christians, even in an age of pogroms;[68] pastors found that
their flocks needed to be convinced that the doctrine of transub-
stantiation was true.[69] But we hear of doubting mainly from those
who had a duty to preach against it.

The devil, expelled on one front, will always attack on another.
Having ceased to speculate, Herbert began to daydream. He describes
his wandering thoughts in an equally uninhibited way. He imagines
travels and battles:

I fly east and west through streets and byeways, through cities
and camps. I travel without cost or trouble to myself or to others.
I mount wars as the spirit moves me, where no blood is shed. I

[68] B. Z. Wacholder, 'Cases of Proselytising in the Tosafist Responsa',
Jewish Quarterly Review li (1960–61) 288–315; W. Giese, 'In Iudaismum
lapsus est', *Hist. Jarhrbuch* lxxxviii (1968) 407–18; B. Smalley, 'Ralph of
Flaix on Leviticus', R.T.A.M. xxxv (1968) 53–5.

[69] See for instance an exemplum recorded of Master Robert *de Camera*,
bishop of Amiens (1165–9), Baldwin, *Masters*, i, 154, ii, 106–7. Baldwin, abbot
of Ford 1175, bishop of Worcester 1180, archbishop of Canterbury
1184–90, to whom Herbert dedicated the *Life*, inserted a long dissuasion
from doubt on the Eucharist in his *De sacramento Eucharistiae*; he is distressed
by the prevalence of *impia dubitatio* and writes that he who doubts is almost
as bad as an infidel; P.L. cciv, 408–9. The chronology of Baldwin's works
cannot be fixed with any precision; see J. Leclercq in his foreword to
Baudouin de Ford 'Le sacrement de l'autel', ed. J. Morson and E. de Solms
with translation (Paris, 1963) i, 9. For other reported evidence on doubts,
see M. E. Thomas, *Medieval Skepticism and Chaucer* (New York, 1950 17–
20, 22. On Otloh see P.L. cxlvi, 30–50.

tell myself idle tales. And so I come and go; I act and I talk to myself.

There is an echo of this distraction in *Liber melorum*. Herbert writes that inability to concentrate is the worst result of man's fall. Man is a Protean monster, divided against himself and having too many thoughts and wishes, as Herbert knows from experience.[70] The mutability of the human heart was a *topos*;[71] writers would accuse themselves of having distractions at prayer.[72] It was less usual to specify what form they took. Here again, Herbert recalls an earlier scholar, Ratheri of Verona; but Ratheri used to turn over past scenes and events, whereas Herbert invented new ones.[73]

His story in the *Vita* raised the problem of conflicting values. Herbert admired the archbishop's new religious mood, though he did so from afar. Secular virtues appealed to him. Becket's conversion made him ask whether they could be reconciled with religious. He solved the problem ingeniously.[74] Before his conversion Becket had the virtue of *benignitas*. That is an urbane, civilized virtue, which makes its possessor a good companion. But *bonitas* is needed before one can achieve holiness. Herbert paints a repellent picture of the man who has *bonitas* without *benignitas;* he is holy indeed, but boorish and disagreeable. After his conversion, Becket combined the two virtues of *benignitas* and *bonitas*. They figure in scholastic *quaestiones* on the fruits of the Holy Spirit (Gal. v, 22); hence the discussion has a theological background. Herbert brings its abstractions to life in his account of the courteous prelate, whose *agréments* mellowed his sanctity.

These are fringe matters: the main purpose of the biographer is to propagate his cause. Herbert dedicated his *Life* to Archbishop Baldwin, hoping that it would persuade him to show more zeal in fighting for the liberties of the Church. We read the story as Herbert

---

[70] P.L. cxc, 1375.

[71] It goes back to St Augustine. Hugh of St Victor treats it amply in the prologue to *De arca Noe morali*, P.L. clxxvi, 617–18.

[72] See A. Squire, *Aelred of Rievaulx* (London, 1969) 68; Baldwin of Ford, *De dilectione Dei*, P.L. cciv, 420.

[73] *Excerptum ex dialogo confessionali*, P.L. cxxxvi, 398, 426–9; see G. Monticelli, *Raterio vescovo di Verona (890–974)* (Milan, 1938) 174–92; F. Weigle, 'Ratherius–Fragmente', *Quell. und. Forsch. aus Italien. Archiven und Bibliotheken* xxxii (1942) 238–42.

[74] *Mat.* iii, 163–5, 327.

believed that Becket lived and saw it. His *Life* amounts to a 'gospel according to Herbert'. Becket re-enacted the Passion of Christ. Herbert has the role of St John, the beloved disciple, doubling it with that of Becket's Green Eminence. The archbishop asks his advice at each crisis and he cries 'Forward!' He holds up to Becket the image of the good prelate; Becket practises what Herbert preaches. The teacher, proud and anxious, sees the Word of Scripture made flesh and submits to the dire consequences. It was part of the divine plan that one close witness should testify.[75] Other scholars get their due. Herbert's stress on learning gives his *Life* its unity of theme. The archbishop promoted learned men to be prelates. He surrounded himself with scholars and he consulted them. The *Life* ends appropriately with a list of the *eruditi sancti Thomae*. Herbert leads the chorus, but it sometimes speaks collectively: 'Your speech is of God, whose mouthpiece you are,' Becket tells his *eruditi* when bad news reaches Pontigny and he asks them what to do.[76] Herbert himself would hesitate to give advice in their absence.[77]

Why did Becket agree to accept the Constitutions of Clarendon, only to repent afterwards? Because, Herbert answers, he came to prelacy unprepared, not from the cloister or the schools, but from Caesar's court.[78] Lecturers on Scripture used to explain that the study of Scripture, and that alone, would equip the future prelate adequately to undertake the office of pastoral care and defence of the Church. The *Life* tells how Becket's *eruditi*, especially Herbert, supplied the defects in his education. Herbert describes his function as Becket's master of the holy page:

> *This is the disciple who giveth testimony of these things and hath written these things* (Io. xxi, 24). He was called by the master, called only, I say. He [Becket] admitted that he always feared to go astray in the dark deeps of the Scriptures, if he entered them without a guide, so that he needed a witness even to their literal understanding. Hence he always relied upon a witness to their plain and a guide to their darker meaning.

Herbert is telling us that he used to check or verify Becket's interpretation of the literal sense of the Bible, but guided him on the spiritual interpretation. The latter would include moralities on the

---

[75] ibid., 192.
[76] ibid., 362–3.
[77] ibid., 473.
[78] ibid. 289–90.

duties of the good prelate. When the lesson was over, Becket would dismiss his teacher in order to meditate on it alone.[79]

It has been claimed that St Anselm provides an important clue to Becket's change of heart after his elevation to Canterbury: he modelled himself on his holy predecessor. Herbert tells us that Becket used Anselm's prayers, and he 'made it one of his first objects to secure Anselm's canonization'.[80] But Herbert's Anselm differs from the gentle sage of his modern biographers: he was 'rod of heretics, hammer of tyrants, casket of the Scriptures, bugle of the Gospel and pillar of righteousness'.[81] The aggressive metaphors hang together. To be a 'casket of the Scriptures' meant beating heretics, hammering tyrants, proclaiming the Gospel and propping up the fabric of the Church, setting oneself 'as a wall to redeem Israel'. Seen in that light, Anselm's memory shone out like the perfect image of a good prelate, as Herbert proposed it to Becket.

Long as it is, the *Life* is a mere prelude to *Liber melorum*, 'The Book of Songs'. Herbert wrote it as an introductory hymn to be sung before the sacred concert in which he celebrated the martyr's trials and triumph. We hear martial music: St Thomas appears as a warrior of Christ; Herbert explains the symbolism of the warrior's arms, banner and equipment; he goes on and on. His collection closes with a homily intended to be delivered at Canterbury on the martyr's feast day: St Thomas returns to his cathedral church and displays his wounds.[82] An appendix contains the text of the Constitutions of Clarendon with annotations, to prove the justice of his cause.[83]

Liber melorum overlaps with Herbert's second kind of writing, 'pure scholarship'. Just at his most tedious, he embarks on a *summa theologiae*. It suddenly occurred to him when composing *Liber melorum* that there was no point in exalting a saint of the Church to readers who might doubt the existence of God: no God, no saints. He quotes the psalmist: *The fool hath said in his heart: there is no God* (Ps. xiii, 1, lii, 1). Then he brings forward every reason that he

---

[79] ibid. 204–5. Herbert stresses that he was 'called' (accitus) to witness and teach; he did not take the initiative.

[80] R. W. Southern, *Saint Anselm and his Biographer* (Cambridge, 1963) 337–8.

[81] *Mat.* iii, 210.

[82] P.L. cxc, 1403–14.

[83] See *Mat.* iii, 286–7.

can think of to refute the fool. Herbert had confessed to having had doubts himself on the truth of Christianity; perhaps he doubted God's very existence and felt the need to reassure himself.[84] His essay was personal and original. The problem of finding rational proofs for the existence of God barely figured in early scholastic theology. Serious discussion of it had to wait for the *Summa aurea* of William of Auxerre, 1222–5.[85] St Anselm had produced his famous ontological argument in order to refute the fool of the psalmist:[86] but Herbert had not read the *Monologion* and *Proslogion*; at least he shows no knowledge of them. Peter Lombard had ignored Anselm's works on theology in his *Sentences*; hence his pupils would not have been introduced to Anselm as a theologian.

Herbert collected a miscellaneous set of arguments to prove God's existence. 'The mighty heavens, a shining frame, their great original proclaim', as Addison put it; Herbert expatiated on the need for a First Cause to account for the wonders of nature. He also used arguments drawn from the *via negativa*. His source here was the mystical theology of Pseudo-Dionysius. The corpus of works ascribed to St Denis had a great vogue in the twelfth century in its Latin translations. The abbey of St Denis at Paris was a fountain-head of study. Herbert's contacts with the abbey kept him in touch. Theophany, or mystical experience of the divine, demonstrates that God exists. The word and the idea appealed to him: he used 'theophany' in his account of St Thomas's devotion at the altar,[87] and later in his commentary on the *Hebraica*. Typically, however, he admits to getting the idea at second hand and not from his own religious experience: he was too worldly and sinful to have theophanies. Another proof anticipates St Thomas Aquinas on the need for the

[84] P.L. cxc, 1355–62. I hope to edit and comment on this section of *Liber melorum* soon.

[85] C. Ottaviano, *Guglielmo d'Auxerre* († 1231) (Biblioteca di Filosofia e Scienze xii, undated); G. Grunwald, 'Geschichte der Gottesbeweise im Mittelalter bis zum Ausgang der Hochscholastik', B.G.P.T.M. vi, iii (1907) 4–61.

[86] See M. J. Charlesworth, *St Anselm's Proslogion with a reply on Behalf of the Fool by Gaunilo and the Author's Reply to Gaunilo translated with an Introduction and Commentary* (Oxford, 1965).

[87] P.L. cxc, 1369–73; *Mat.* iii, 217. On the Pseudo-Dionysian corpus see G. Théry, 'Documents concernant Jean Sarrazin', A.H.D.L.M.A. xviii (1951) 45–87; H. F. Dondaine, *Le Corpus Dionysien de l'Université de Paris au XIIIe siècle* (Rome. 1953) 11–68.

cosmos to have a First Mover (not only a First Cause), to account for movement. Herbert probably found the argument in Aristotle's *Physics*. Latin translations of 'the new Aristotle' were reaching northern France in the second half of the twelfth century. The abbey of Saint-Michel possessed some; John of Salisbury was interested.[88] Herbert may have heard talk of Aristotle's *Physics*; he may even have read it. The concept would have been familiar to him in a tag from Boethius' *Consolation of Philosophy*, which was current in the schools: '... stabilisque manens das cuncta moveri'. Herbert quotes it in a variant found in Robert of Melun.[89] But Herbert shows a grasp of Aristotle's argument which shows that he had gone to the original and did not depend on the Boethian tag.

Having got into his stride, he goes on to discuss a christological problem, *De homine assumpto*. This was one of the most hotly debated questions in twelfth-century theology. Herbert's treatment of it is too technical to interest us; but it shows that he had advanced beyond dependence on Peter Lombard and that he knew what was being said at Paris. The sequence from God's existence to christology was quite logical; the addition of *De homine assumpto* suggests the torso of a *Summa*. It breaks off short and he returns to his 'St Thomas as *miles Christi*' theme.

Lastly, we must survey him as a biblical scholar. His interest in the literal, historical sense of Scripture, which flowered in his commentary on the *Hebraica*, went back to the days of his first exile and perhaps earlier. A letter addressed to his friend Count Henry the Liberal exposes the falsity of the fable of 'the triple marriage of St Anne'. Herbert took strong exception to it and records a discussion on the subject among the monks of St Denis when he was visiting the abbey. Scholarly opinion agreed with him, though it did not suffice to discredit a popular legend.[90]

A much longer work of biblical scholarship was editorial. He

---

[88] L. Minio-Paluello, 'Iacobus Veneticus Grecus', *Traditio* viii (1952) pp. 291–295 and n.56. The author kindly told me that *Physica* viii, 10, 266b, 25–267b, 7 would be the probable source of Herbert's argument. For recent discussion of St Thomas's use of the argument, see J. Owens, 'Aquinas and the Proof from the "Physics"', *Mediaeval Studies* xxviii (1966) 119–50.

[89] P. Courcelle, *La Consolation de Philosophie dans la tradition littéraire* (Paris, 1967) 179–89.

[90] On this letter see B. Smalley, 'A Commentary on the *Hebraica* by Herbert of Bosham', R.T.A.M. xviii (1951) 37–9; the edition in P.L. cxc, 1415–22, has to be supplemented from ms London, Brit. Mus. Royal 6.E. iii. fol. 50b.

began it during his stay at Pontigny at Becket's request and finished it after Becket's death. He was planning to edit the *Great Gloss* of his master Peter Lombard on the psalms and the Pauline Epistles. An edition was needed because the Lombard had never expected that his *Gloss* would become a set book in the schools. He died as bishop of Paris before he could put the *Gloss* into its final form. Becket ordered Herbert to carry out his plan: Herbert obeyed him. The whole edition, when finished, was dedicated to his patron Archbishop William of Sens, after the murder at the end of 1170 and before William was translated to the archbishopric of Rheims, 1176. Herbert prefaced his edition of the *Great Gloss* on St Paul by a letter from the Greek scholar William le Mire, abbot of St Denis from 1172–3. He had asked Abbot William to send him Latin translations of some Greek prologues to the Epistles, which he now adds to his edition. The work survives in four volumes, given by Herbert to Christchurch, a token of what Gervase of Canterbury called his 'special affection for the monks'. To edit a reference book by a dead scholar calls for patience, acumen and accuracy. The Lombard was lucky. Herbert took pains to see that the authors quoted in the commentary were correctly labelled and attached to the right words of the text, as far as he could judge. These magnificent volumes bring us to his place in the history of manuscript illumination. Their similarity to other glossed books of the Bible bequeathed by Becket to Christchurch suggests that Herbert supervised their preparation as well as that of his edition of the Lombard's *Great Gloss*.[91] The layout in all these books and their decoration shows the same care and skill. Text and glosses are arranged on the page so as to facilitate study and please the eye.

The four volumes of his edition of Peter Lombard have rich decoration in the form of illuminated and historiated initials. A tinted line-drawing at the beginning shows Archbishop Thomas ordering Herbert to undertake the task. Art historians sometimes classify as 'the Bosham style' both the decoration of Herbert's edi-

---

[91] See Glunz, 341–50 for transcript of prologues and description of manuscripts. The four volumes are now MSS B.5.4, 6, 7 of Trinity College Cambridge and Auct. E. inf. 6 of the Bodleian Library. For Becket's and Herbert's bequests of books to Christchurch, recorded in the catalogue compiled by Prior Henry of Eastry 1284–1331, see M. R. James, *Ancient Libraries of Canterbury and Dover* (Cambridge, 1903) xli–xlii, 82–5. Some of the glossed books given by Becket have been identified.

tion of the Lombard and that of the glossed books presented by Becket to Christchurch. They do look alike, both in the illuminations and in the layout of the glosses on the page. The difficulty is that Herbert must have supervised the making of his *de luxe* copy of the Lombard while he was still in exile in France, 1170-6, whereas at least one of Becket's glossed volumes was written by a scribe called Roger of Canterbury, and therefore presumably in England. English and North-French techniques of book production are not easily distinguishable at this period.[92] Wherever they originated, these copies of the Lombard on the Psalter and St Paul and of other glossed books of the Bible show that Herbert had an artist's eye for style and layout. The fierce little white lions set into the initials were not invented by him as a decorative motif, but they fit aptly to the taste of one who called his hero *leo noster evangelicus*, 'our gospel lion'.[93]

Last came the commentary on the *Hebraica*. Herbert chose to comment on this version in preference to those more generally used because it was closer to the original Hebrew of the psalms. He chose to expound the literal sense only and to omit the spiritual. That was a daring enterprise indeed. Andrew of St Victor had commented on the literal sense of the Octateuch, Ecclesiastes and the Prophets. He laid himself open to criticism for 'judaizing' in his interpre-

[92] See T. R. S. Boase, *English Art 1100-1216* (Oxford, 1953) 185-8; C. R. Dodwell, *The Canterbury School of Illumination* (Cambridge, 1954) 104-9; H. Swarzenski, 'Fragments from a Romanesque Bible', *Essais en l'honneur de Jean Porcher*, ed. O. Pächt (Paris, 1963) 71-80.

[93] The lions derive from Monte Cassino illumination of the eleventh century and are found in both French and English illumination. A fifth volume left by Herbert to Christchurch is recorded in the catalogue as 'Thomus' and has not been identified. Some art historians have suggested that it was a glossed copy of Gratian's *Decretum*, formerly in the Dyson Perrins Collection; see R. Schilling, 'The *Decretum Gratiani* formerly in the Dysons Perrins Collection', *Journal of the British Archaeological Association* 3rd series xxvi (1963) 27-39. The grounds for identification are that the illuminations are remarkably similar to those of Herbert's four volumes; some may even be by the hand of the same artist. The *Decretum* manuscript must also have been produced at about the same time, soon after 1178, on the evidence of the glosses. However, the *Decretum* manuscript has no medieval marks of ownership or provenance. The same artist, if it is the same, could have worked for two different patrons. Herbert took little interest in canon law, so far as our knowledge of him goes. Hence the suggested identification is interesting but by no means certain. 'Thomus' could refer to a volume of any kind.

G

tation of certain prophecies. No Latin scholar before Herbert had
tackled the literal exposition of the Psalter in isolation from the
spiritual. The Psalter was the very core of religious life. Its place in
the liturgy and in meditation, prayer and 'holy reading' set it apart
from other books of the Bible. One of Herbert's contemporaries,
Gebuin, chanter of Troyes and friend of St Bernard, put the current
view of the Psalter in an apt commonplace. Gebuin was writing
a sermon on the text *Why, O Lord, are they multiplied. . . .?* (Ps.
iii, 2). A curt reference to the literal sense explains that King David
was complaining of the rebellion of his son Absalom. Gebuin goes on:

> But if mere history is to be understood here, why are the words
> recited so often in church and made so much of? We must crack
> the nutshell and seek the moral meaning within.[94]

The nut within the shell signified the allegorical and moral or
spiritual interpretation. Herbert set himself to make a scientific study
of the despised nutshell. His reason was partly humility. To uncover
the spiritual sense of the Psalter called for religious experience,
'theophanies', based on asceticism and virtue. These were not for
him. He thought himself too worldly and sinful to aspire to the
spiritual interpretation. On the other hand, the difficulty of literal
interpretation offered a challenge, which excited him as it had excited
Andrew. The military metaphors in the prefatory letter to Bishop
Peter of Arras suggest an old warhorse snuffing battle.

To expound in the literal sense demanded linguistic skills and
knowledge of Old Testament history. What did the psalms mean to
David (traditionally their author) and to the Old Testament Jews,
who read and chanted them? This question raised another in acute
form. Which psalms should Christians take as messianic in the sense
that David was expressing a direct foreknowledge of Christ? In such
cases his prophecy would belong to the literal meaning. Which
psalms referred to Old Testament history only? These would be
interpreted as messianic according to the spiritual interpretation.
Previous commentators did not feel obliged to face the question,
since they saw the whole book as part of the Christian revelation:

[94] MS Paris, Bibl. nat. lat. 14937, fol. 104ra: Sed si pura hiis verbis intelligenda
est historia, quare totiens, quare tam magnifice habetur et recitatur in ecclesia? Frangenda ergo est cesta . . . querendus est moralis intellectus, quo hec
ad nos figurative relata inter catholicos pro instruendis simplicibus et habenda
et recitanda sunt in ecclesia.
On Gebuin see below, p. 114.

'Christ entire, head and members (that is Christ and his Church) is the subject of this book', wrote Gilbert of la Porrée at the opening of his commentary on the Psalter, which became a school text.[95] A commentator on the literal sense would have to tackle the problem head on.

Herbert surpassed his master Andrew in his approach to both difficulties. Andrew learned just enough biblical Hebrew to follow the text with his teachers' help; he never mastered rabbinic Hebrew, which is harder for beginners.[96] Herbert could read both biblical and rabbinic; he may even have known Aramaic.[97] Andrew depended on his Jewish teachers for his knowledge of rabbinic traditions and exegesis. Herbert seems to have had a copy of Rashi's standard commentary and other Hebrew aids to study on his desk, to consult at pleasure. He quotes Rabbi Salomon (Rashi) by name. Nicholas of Lyre, the fourteenth-century scholar, was supposed to have been the first Latin to do so; now we know better. Herbert showed more clarity and firmness than Andrew in trying to distinguish prophecies which should be interpreted christologically in their literal sense from those which need not be. Andrew, painfully aware of the problem, would take refuge in ambiguity; Herbert avoided any suspicion of 'judaizing', doubtless with his master in mind. He accepted some passages as christological in their literal sense and rejected others. It was thoughtful work. The discipline of commenting on a text kept him to the point and clipped his verbiage, so that his style is more controlled than formerly; but the psalms attracted him as poetry and sometimes inspired him to embroider in his old manner. His personality shows through his scholarship.

To sum up Herbert: he was a bundle of contradictions and he had a choppy career. Ambition drove him from the schools into royal service and then to become Becket's right-hand man. He sacrificed

[95] Christus integer, caput cum membris, est materia huius libri. . . See *Rep. Bibl.* no. 2511. This was known as the *Media glosatura* on account of its place between the *Gloss* of Anselm of Laon and the *Great Gloss* of Peter Lombard on the Psalter.

[96] My pupil Mrs G. Hadfield has established this in her doctoral thesis, *Andrew of St Victor, a Twelfth-Century Hebraist. An Investigation of his Works and Sources.* She will also deal fully with Andrew's interpretation of the Prophet Isaiah.

[97] On Herbert's Hebrew scholarship see R. Loewe, 'Herbert of Bosham's Commentary on Jerome's Hebrew Psalter', *Biblica* xxxiv (1953) 44–77, 159–92, 275–98. He claims in his prefatory letter to have studied Greek as well as Hebrew, but he does not seem to have made much progress in it.

ambition to principle, but did so grudgingly. He would not compromise, but he resented the consequences of his stand. He seems to have returned to the schools after Becket's death, but again he did not stay there. He found a powerful patron in William Longchamp, but he would not stay at court; he left some time before Longchamp's disgrace and withdrew to a Cistercian abbey, though not to become a monk. He was neither priest nor religious, neither professor nor courtier. He combined clerical learning and defence of clergy with an unclerical character, which he deplored or flaunted according to his mood. He doubted everything except the rightness of clerical immunity: on that he never wavered. 'The nearer the Church the farther from God': Herbert recalls the sixteenth-century proverb.[98] Intellectually he was a windbag and a meticulous scholar, quick to cotton on to new ideas. His writings conform to no pattern. He discussed theological or exegetical problems in rhetorical language, expressive of deep feeling. Writing at leisure outside the schools, he never let their dry, technical diction check his flow of words. What did contemporaries make of him? Henry II hated him, but forgave him when he could do no more harm. The English bishops disapproved of his influence on Becket and cold-shouldered him after the martyrdom. He was odd man out even in the exiled *familia*. He never won the freedom of John of Salisbury's pious circle of friends. John included one letter only addressed to Herbert in his collected correspondence. It is cool in tone, the letter of a colleague rather than an intimate.[99] The coolness was on John's side: Herbert wrote that a letter from John always did him good.[1] His brashness offended John's sober taste.

Why did Becket choose as his friend and teacher this daring person, questioning champion of one unquestioned idea? Herbert had sound qualifications as a theologian and secretary, but there must have been other suitable candidates. The answer may be that Herbert linked together the two halves of Becket's experience. He sympathized with the proud chancellor and the converted archbishop. Becket felt more at home with him than he ever could with John of Salisbury.

[98] M. P. Tilley, *A Dictionary of the Proverbs in England in the Sixteenth and Seventeenth Centuries* (Ann Arbor, Michigan, 1950) no. C. 380; B. Smalley, 'Which William of Nottingham?', M.A.R.S. iii (1954) 214.

[99] P.L. cxcix, 316–17. Webb noted it as a surprising omission, 147.

[1] P.L. cxc, 1476.

IV
John of Salisbury

John of Salisbury and Herbert of Bosham made an odd pair when they confronted Henry II. They differed in physique as much as in character. John was small and fragile. He suffered from bad health and fell into the doctors' hands so often that he dared not satirize them, as he satirized members of other professions. Noting with alarm that they disagreed with one another, he hoped that different cures might have the same effect.[1] He was a more respectable and clerical type than Herbert, worthy of a testimonial from St Bernard, who believed his monks' good report of the young scholar.[2] If John allowed his thoughts to wander, he would have imagined battles of the books, not real warfare. The Paris schools had formed both of them, but their education poses distinct problems. In John's case we should not ask how he influenced St Thomas: that cannot be gauged, although he gave advice in plenty. It is rather a question of John's dialogue with John. The Becket conflict broke into his career, as it did into Herbert's. Unlike Herbert, John had already made his name as scholar, author and secretary. His career before 1164 is much better documented. He had worked out a philosophy of life based on his study of books and on his experience of men and affairs. John was a 'humanist' in the strict sense of being a student of 'the humanities'. He resembled Italian Renaissance humanists in that he saw the art of rhetoric as bound up with service to the commonwealth: the rhetor worked as civil servant and adviser to governments. But John was a theologian as well as a humanist. He combined the two disciplines, liberal arts and theology, the handmaidens and their queen. The Becket conflict put him in a

---

[1] His nickname or surname was 'Parvus'; see Webb, 1. On the doctors see *Policr.* i, 168–9.

[2] Ep. ccclxi, P.L. clxxxii, 562, addressed to Archbishop Theobald of Canterbury: Testimonium enim bonum habet a bonis, quod non minus vita, quam litteratura promeruit. . .

dilemma; an ambivalence latent in his thought came out into the open. Would the handmaidens rise against their mistress? If so, would she quell them, or would John manage to patch up a compromise?

The tale of his twelve years' study abroad after 1135–6 has been reconstructed and told too often to need repeating.[3] Only a few notes on his theological studies need be added. These came towards the end of the twelve years, after he had sampled the teaching and labelled the methods of the best masters of the *Artes*. He heard Gilbert of la Porrée on logic and divinity until Gilbert retired to become bishop of Poitiers 'all too soon', 1142. Robert Pullen was John's second master of theology. He, too, was promoted and became a cardinal in 1144. Both masters impressed their pupil. John admired Gilbert as a philosopher, theologian and preacher;[4] but Gilbert did not discuss politics, except to disallow the right of resistance to an unjust ruler.[5] Robert did put forward opinions on the relationship between *regnum* and *sacerdotium*. John knew his teaching on the two swords in his *Sentences*[6] and may have attended some of his lectures, preserved as sermons, on the duties of good priests and prelates. Simon of Poissy, John's third master in theology, is the joker of the pack. John may have heard him lecture for two years, 1145–7. Master Simon held a prebend at Notre-Dame from 1145 to 1160.[7] Peter the Chanter in his *Verbum abbreviatum* (probably drafted 1191–2) lists him with Robert Pullen and others as one of the old masters whose reading of Scripture could be imitated with profit.[8] In *Policraticus* John mentions a dictum of 'Simon, our venerable teacher in divine law', on the corrupt practices of rural deans and archdeacons.[9] This must be Simon of Poissy; the fact that John quotes a text of the pslams (xxv, 10) in connection with the dictum suggests that he may have recalled it from lectures on the Psalter. John probably meant Simon of Poissy when he referred to

[3] Webb, 1–10, with corrections by Southern, 61–73. It is improbable that John studied at Chartres as well as at Paris.

[4] See above, p. 25.

[5] Affeldt, op. cit. 144–5.

[6] H. Liebeschütz, *Mediaeval Humanism in the Life and Writings of John of Salisbury* (London, 1950) 23–30.

[7] Brady, 'Peter Lombard', 289–90; Simon's brother Osmund was also a canon of Notre-Dame.

[8] Baldwin, *Masters*, i, 15, 95, ii, 66.

[9] i, 353.

a 'Simon of Paris', who shared with other eminent scholars the distinction of having been attacked by the Cornificians, professional critics of their elders and betters.[10] Simon of Poissy was 'a sound lecturer, but duller in disputation', according to John.[11] No record of his teaching has survived, apart from these few allusions to him. Both John's and the Chanter's go to show that Simon specialized in moralizing lectures on the holy page. John may perhaps have owed his facility in quoting moralized texts to Simon as much as to Robert Pullen.

John left the schools in 1147. He was serving Archbishop Theobald as a household clerk by 24 January 1148.[12] Theobald took him to the council of Rheims in March the same year. Henry II sent him on a mission to the Curia at Benevento, where he spent several months in the company of the English pope, Adrian IV, 1156. They struck up a friendship and conversed as intimates at table. Meanwhile John had risen to be Theobald's confidential secretary and envoy. Only one trouble clouded his sky: he incurred Henry's anger in 1156 and feared exile in consequence; but the storm blew over in a few months' time.[13] Nor did frustrated ambition worry him. John was no place-hunter, unlike most of his colleagues in the archbishop's household.[14] Becket as chancellor wondered at his lack of thrust.[15] All he wanted was modest comfort and an interesting job. Reading and writing are expensive hobbies; so he lived beyond his means. He also complained of overwork, especially when Theobald's illness laid a heavier burden on his shoulders.[16] It did not prevent him from pursuing his studies. He went on collecting and comparing various points of view, trying to understand them, as well as to judge and criticize. Three major works belong to this period: *Metalogicon*, its verse introduction *Entheticus de dogmate philosoph-*

[10] *Metal.*, 18.

[11] ibid. 82. Simon of Poissy cannot be identified with the Master Simon who wrote a *De sacramentis* 1145–60; see H. Weisweiler, *Maître Simon et son groupe: De sacramentis* (Spic. sac. Lov. xvii, 1937) lxxx–ccxiv.

[12] Saltman, 169–75. On John's early career see *Letters* i, xv–xxviii and Southern, 243–8; on the letter collection see Southern's review of *Letters*, E.H.R. lxxxii (1957) 943–7.

[13] *Letters*, i, 257–8.   [14] ibid. xxix.

[15] *Policr.* i, 13–14: Noli ergo mirari, quare aliquem gradum scalae, quae nunc sola nouit ascensum, prout quandoque monuisti, non ascendo. . . . John is addressing Becket as chancellor.

[16] *Letters*, i, xxix.

orum[17] and *Policraticus*. All three are dedicated to Becket as chancellor. References to the siege of Toulouse date their completion to between 24 June and 1 September 1159. They distil the wisdom which their author had drawn from his reading and observation.

John had a passion for getting and transmitting his learning. 'Filial care and industry's conquest of sloth' is his phrase for the process. The opposite, irreverent criticism and impatience, shocked and angered him.[18] Study, undertaken in a proper way, is man's pleasantest and most useful task, except for prayer and contemplation; these come rather as an afterthought.[19] The usefulness of study, as John saw it, comes out in *Policraticus*. In form, *Policraticus* represents a swollen version of the *Speculum* genre, a *Mirror for Princes* combined with a *Mirror for Society*. The author holds up a mirror of the good prince, contrasted with the tyrant, and does the same for all groups and classes of society, satirizing each so as to contrast what is with what should be. His advice, if taken, would ensure the right government of the commonwealth and lead its citizens to eternal bliss hereafter. *Metalogicon* and *Entheticus* deal more with philosophical doctrines; but, as John assigned a practical end to philosophy, all three books must be taken together. He used personal observation to make his points in all of them.

Two currents flowed from the springs of ancient wisdom: pagan poets, philosophers and historians, with Cicero in the foreground; the Bible and the Fathers. John distinguished the two traditions in order to make a synthesis. Yielding to none in his admiration for 'good pagans', he tempered it with criticism. The Christian scholar should quote them only when their teaching conformed to his own standards. Pagan authors and the *Artes* serve the 'holy page', which rules them.[20] John showed more discrimination than many later moralists in his praise of pagan virtues. He kept a sharp watch on his pagan sages to see where they went astray, finding fault with

---

[17] Mrs P. Barzillay analyses and summarises this piece, 'The *Entheticus de dogmate philosophorum* of John of Salisbury', *Medievalia et Humanistica* xvi (1964) 11–29.

[18] E.D.P., 2–4, *Metal.*, 8–23.

[19] *Policr.*, i, 13: Nullam in rebus humanis iocundiorem aut utiliorem occupationem inuenies, nisi forte diuinitus compuncta deuotio orando diuinis insistat colloquiis aut corde per caritatem dilatato Deum mente concipiat et magnalia eius apud se quasi quadam meditationis manu pertractat.

[20] ibid. 14, 17; *Policr.* ii, 415.

both Stoics and Epicureans.[21] Their values must be supplemented by Christian. Desire for fame has its roots in virtuous delight in good deeds, but must be subordinate to love of justice.[22] Suicide is both wrong and cowardly: it means choice of the greatest risk of all as against lesser risks: 'while there's life, there's hope'.[23] Neither Cicero nor Aristotle always practised what they preached.[24] Philosophy's true goal is love of God and charity towards one's neighbour; therefore it needs a Christian framework.[25] John was a perceptive, discriminating critic. He realized that Epicurus taught a different doctrine than that commonly ascribed to him by his alleged followers.[26] He avoided the temptation to christianize Boethius. By relying on reason alone, he wrote, Boethius gave his *Consolation of Philosophy* a wider appeal than if he had introduced the Christian revelation.[27]

Armed with these safeguards, John treated the pagans as his clients and servants. He wanted to show that the Bible and pagan philosophy (within its limits) reinforced each other. The Scriptures brim over with *civilia*, teaching on social behaviour; he instances the feast given to welcome the prodigal son's return to his family.[28] Both the poet Terence and Christ in the gospel teach us to show sympathy.[29] Good and bad characters from both pagan and Christian sources are paired. John's advice to princes hinges on the text of Deuteronomy xvii, 14-20: the king to be set over Israel must avoid extravagance and pride; he must guide his conduct by daily reading

---

[21] He reproves the Stoics for neglecting divine grace, ibid. ii, 101, and for their belief in necessity; the Epicureans believe in chance, E.D.P. 19-23. On uncritical use of pagan philosophers see B. Smalley, 'Moralists and philosophers in the 13th and 14th centuries', *Miscellanea mediavalia*, ed. P. Wilpert ii (Berlin, 1963) 60-7.

[22] *Policr*. ii, 246, 335. John's critique of pagan virtue has been noted as a sign of his independence; see R. A. Gautier, *Magnanimité*. *'L'idéal de la grandeur dans la philosophie païenne et dans la théologie chretienne* (Paris, 1951) 453 n.

[23] *Policr*. i, 360.

[24] E.P.D., 45.   [25] ibid. 11-12, *Policr*. ii, 136-7.

[26] ibid. ii, 154, 276, 294; E.D.P. 20-2. On the Fathers' uncritical use of 'Epicurean' as a smear word, see R. Jungkuntz ,'Fathers, Heretics and Epicureans', *Journal of Ecclesiastical History* xvii (1966) 3-10.

[27] *Policr*. ii, 155; see P. Courcelle, *La Consolation de Philosophie*, op. cit. 343; John is praised for his exceptional penetration.

[28] *Policr*. ii, 279.

[29] ibid. i, 170.

of God's Law.[30] Quotations from philosophers back up the biblical text. These include an apocryphal piece known as the *Institution of Trajan*: Plutarch is supposed to advise his pupil Trajan on the duties of a good emperor. Pseudo-Plutarch and Trajan made a bridge between profane and sacred teaching on statecraft, since Pope Gregory I had prayed for Trajan's release from hell[31] on account of his justice and mercy to a poor widow; so the story went. John has been suspected of forging the *Institution of Trajan* to suit his purpose. Not all of his quotations from ancient sources can be traced, however; it seems just as likely that he found the *Institution* in the course of his reading and that he believed it to be genuine.[32]

Cicero was his favourite author. He read what was available to him: *De officiis, De oratore, De inventione, De finibus*, the *Tusculanes* and a few of the *Epistulae ad Familiares*;[33] he had some knowledge of *De re publica* through intermediaries.[34] A mere list of quotations and reminiscences would not tell us the extent of Cicero's influence on John. What the philosopher statesman had written became as the experience of his own mind. *De officiis* delighted him. A christianized version lay ready to hand in St Ambrose's *De officiis ministrorum*. St Ambrose had adapted Cicero to his own ends and borrowed from him, making a serious effort to put a Christian content into the Roman's four cardinal virtues. Charity to all men, alms-giving, self-sacrifice and holy poverty, these gave a new direction to Stoic morals. Much of his book applied to secular office-holders, though Ambrose wrote mainly for the clergy.[35]

---

[30] H. Liebeschütz, 'Bibel und klassisches Altertum in englischen Hochmittelalter', *Festchrift für Leo Baeck* (undated offprint) 91–105.

[31] *Policr.* i, 315–22.

[32] H. Liebeschütz, *Mediaeval Humanism*, op. cit. 23–6. See A. D. Momigliano, 'Notes on Petrarch, John of Salisbury and the *Institutio Traiani*', *Contributo alla storia degli studi classici* (Rome, 1955) 377–9. For another lost source of John of Salisbury see L. Ruggini, 'Sulla cristianizzazione della cultura pagana', *Athenaeum* new series xliii (1965) 59–61.

[33] B. Munk-Olsen, 'L'humanisme de Jean de Salisbury, un Cicéronien au 12e siècle', *Entretiens sur la Renaissance du 12e siècle*, ed. M. de Gandillac and E. Jeauneau (Paris, 1968) 53–70; R. W. Hunt, 'The Deposit of the Latin Classics in the Twelfth-Century Renaissance', *Classical Influences on European Culture, A.D. 500–1500*, ed. R. R. Bolgar (Cambridge, 1971) 52–3.

[34] E. Heck, 'Die Bezeugung von Ciceros Schrift *De re publica*', *Spudasmata* iv (1966) 246–55.

[35] The latest study on this subject is L. Ruggini, *Economia e società nell 'Italia annonaria'* (Milan, 1961) 618 and *passim*.

De officiis ministrorum was a well-known book: there may have been a copy at Canterbury in the mid twelfth century and it was often quoted.[36] Yet John ignored it. His editor found only one quotation in *Policraticus*; since neither the author nor the title is mentioned, the assumption is that John did not know it directly.[37] It seems that he made a deliberate choice in preferring the original *De officiis* to a patristic rehash. The task of baptizing Cicero he would keep for himself. He bequeathed copies of *De officiis*, *De oratore* and *Policraticus* to the library of Chartres.[38] The three books symbolized his love of Cicero and his application of Cicero's teaching to his own times.

A consistent picture of the ideal gentleman, scholar and statesman emerges from the pages of *Policraticus*. To begin with the private virtues, the keynote is *honestas*. Our language has no one equivalent to the adjective *honestus*. It means grave, fitting, dignified and heroic, if the occasion should call for heroism:

> Such orderliness of conduct is to be observed that everything in the conduct of our life should balance and harmonize, as in a finished speech.[39]

'Disorderly', 'unbecoming', 'dishonourable' or 'craven' are the opposites. The outward marks of order, moderation and discretion show forth the inner virtue of *honestas*, which John prized the most.[40] He launches *Policraticus* on the world with the advice that it should manifest these virtues.[41] 'The dignity of man', *dignitas humana*, was a concept dear to his heart. He invokes and applies it.[42] Warfare in the sense of showy exploits does not become 'human dignity'. John had a poor opinion of King Alexander, hero of

---

[36] There were twelfth-century copies at Bury, Exeter and Rochester; see *Medieval Libraries*, 18, 83, 162. Hereford and Lincoln cathedral libraries still possess twelfth-century copies; Becket bequeathed a copy to Christchurch, Canterbury; see *Ancient Libraries* 83. It was quoted in Gregorian polemic extensively; see M.G.H. *Lib. de lite* i, 276–7, 327–8, 350, 508, ii, 264, iii, 516.

[37] *Policr.* i, 32; ii, 316–17.

[38] A. Molinier and A. Longnon, *Obituaires de la Province de Sens* iii (1906) 107.

[39] *De offic.* I, xl, 144, transl. W. Miller (London, 1956) 147.

[40] E.D.P. 13–14; *Policr.* i, 34, ii, 335 and *passim*.

[41] ibid. i, 9.

[42] *Metal.*, 23: Si ergo, uerbi et rationis usu aliorum animantium naturam humana dignitas antecedit. . . .

medieval romance. He tells the story that Alexander accepted a legal decision against himself from the philosopher Pythagoras with the comment:

> That's the most remarkable fact I have ever learnt of Alexander, whom public opinion calls 'the Great'. With due respect to those who prefer bravery to virtue, poor Pythagoras will always be greater than rich Alexander to me.[43]

Cicero, too, had held a low opinion of Alexander; the revival of interest in his legend belonged to late antiquity.[44] Patriotic warfare, waged in defence of one's country, was praiseworthy, but not mere adventure.

Similarly John held that neither hunting nor dicing became a gentleman. Medieval moralists would pair these two pastimes in an omnibus condemnation of secular pleasures. Young nobles with hawks on their wrists or sitting at the dice-board typify the worldly life in the iconography of the thirteenth-century *Bible moralisée*.[45] But John disapproved of them for other reasons; he was not a puritan. He blamed hunting as an ignoble sport because it brought out the beast in man. A hunter would come to resemble the centaur Chiron, half man and half brute, or else Esau, who sold his birthright to Jacob. Hunting stirred up passions which struck at the manly soul and shook the support of reason. It was right to go hunting only if the object was not pleasure, but food.[46] Again he had classical precedents. Hunting went out of fashion in the first century B.C., partly because slaves had come to be used to carry the risks, while their masters looked on: Sallust called it a 'sport fit for slaves', and John may have recalled his stricture.[47] 'Dicer' is a word of shame in *Catiline's Conspiracy*.[48] John condemned the game as an irrational abuse of the science of numbers.[49] The stress is always on reason.

John embroiders on the *topos* 'all the world's a stage' so as to

---

[43] *Policr.* i, 335.
[44] See Cicero, *De offic.* I, xxvi, 90; II, xxv, 53; L. Ruggini, op. cit. 3–4.
[45] A. de Laborde, *La Bible moralisée* i (Paris, 1911) plates 12, 15, 19, 20.
[46] *Policr.* i, 21–38.
[47] *Catil* iv; R. Syme, *Sallust* (Berkeley, 1964) 43–5. John admired Sallust as *historicorum inter Latinos potissimus*; *Policr.* i, 211.
[48] *Catil* xiv.
[49] *Policr.* i, 35–6.

join the threads of Christian and pagan morality. The honourable man should be on his mettle when acting before an august house of retired actors (the holy souls in heaven), the angels, and his fellow men:

> The actor (man on the stage of the world) should be ashamed to make unbecoming gestures and dishonour himself by pantomime in so blazing a light.[50]

'Nature' would guide man to live well. John took the idea from Cicero. *Policraticus* contains no less than seven quotations from *De amicitia*:

> ... some men are entitled to be called 'good' because, in so far as it is possible for man, they follow Nature, who is the best guide to good living.[51]

Nature, dwelling in reason, gives us wise counsel.[52] She has to be supplemented by grace, which, joined to nature, makes her fruitful. Use and training help her too; hence the importance of education.[53] St Augustine taught that man had two loves, one holy, the other defiled: one draws man to the common good for the sake of the heavenly city; the other is self-seeking.[54] This was the root of his

---

[50] ibid. i, 199. On John's use of this *topos*, see E. R. Curtius, *European Literature and the Latin Middle Ages*, trans. W. R. Trask (London, 1953) 138–40, and St Augustine, *De civitate Dei* xiv, 9: . . . in theatro huius mundi, cui spectaculum factus est angelis et hominibus, legitime magnum agonem certantem. . .
St Augustine sees the spectacle as a contest, John as a serious play.

[51] *De amic.* v, 19, trans. W. A. Falconer (Loeb Classical Library, 1923) 129. *Policr.* i, 35, 185, 235, 250, ii, 60, 358.

[52] E.D.P., 15.

[53] ibid. 9; *Metal.* 23. John quoted two other definitions of Nature, one from Victorinus, 'vis quedam genitiva, rebus omnibus insita, ex qua facere vel pati possunt' (*Metal.* 23–4) and as the will of God, from Plato (*Policr.* i, 85–86). But the Stoic view, which he found in Cicero, influenced him most. Natural law in twelfth-century theology was generally defined as 'the primitive law of humanity', antecedent to the Decalogue and to positive law; it was innate in man's heart, as dictated by reason, and taught him in general terms to do good and avoid evil; God was its author; see O. Lottin, *Le droit naturel chez Saint Thomas d'Aquin et ses prédécesseurs* (2nd ed. Bruges, 1931) 98–9. This hardly differed from John's view, except that he tended to give Nature a more positive role.

[54] *De Gen ad lit.* xi, 15, P.L. xxxiv, 437: Hii duo amores, quorum alter sanctus est, alter immundus; alter socialis, alter privatus, alter communi

teaching on the two cities, *civitas Dei* and *civitas terrena*. John toned it down: man has two natural affections, one for what is right and one for what pleases him, *appetitus commodi*. The former resides in man's will, the latter in his need. The former can never be excessive; the latter becomes vicious (only) when it leads man to take more than he needs.[55] *Appetitus commodi*, which is good when not abused, replaces St Augustine's *amor immundus*. John has washed the black into a neutral shade. He did not see men on earth as always 'mourning and weeping in this vale of tears'. True, philosophy teaches that all earthly goods appear contemptible in face of death. It is wholesome to meditate on the subject of death for that reason, but not to excess. The thought of death will bring real death, if carried too far.[56] Where is that medieval contempt of the world, which Dr Bultot describes for us with a pen sharpened by dislike?[57]

Honestum joins hands with *utile* in *De officiis* and in John's books. Cicero's attitude to public service was that of a Roman aristocrat. Office-holding offered a gentleman the most rewarding outlet for his talents; the State meant *us* not *them*, and to serve it represented an enlightened form of self-interest, though that is implied, not stated. One should regard office as a trust, not as a prize to be snatched at. On the other hand, to refuse to serve the State by withdrawal into private life, even for the sake of study, was an unenlightened sort of selfishness. Seclusion may be safer, since the private citizen has fewer temptations to wrong-doing; but he maims himself by refusing to be useful to society. Cicero assures his readers that public office will leave time for private study, which belongs to the gentleman's way of life. Philosopy indeed fertilized action and taught man his duties. With equal optimism, he tells us that the statesman need not lose his integrity. The right course of action is always the most expedient: *utile* and *honestum* can never clash. It followed that learning in general and the study of rhetoric in partic-

utilitati consulens propter supernam civitatem, alter etiam rem communem in potestatem propria redigens propter arrogantem dominationem.

[55] *Policr.* ii, 243–4.

[56] E.D.P., 17.

[57] R. Bultot, *Christianisme et valeurs humaines. La doctrine du mépris du monde en occident de S. Ambroise à Innocent III* iv, 1–2 (Louvain, 1963–1964). For brighter views see M. -D. Chenu, *La théologie au XIIe siècle* (Paris, 1957) 19–51; R. Sprandel, *Ivo von Chartres* (Pariser hist. Studien i, Stuttgart, 1962) 24.

ular should be harnessed to the *honestum* and *utile*. A good general education, culminating in rhetoric, ethics and philosophy, equipped the statesman for his career, in which he would have to take decisions on policy and persuade men to follow him.

John was an eager pupil. He harnessed all the learning at his command to teaching the right ways of life in *Policraticus*. That explains its encyclopaedic character, the abundance of *exempla* and the insistence on rhetoric as a means of communication. But he did not live in the past; nor did he re-create it for the sheer fun of the thing; he wanted to adapt its lessons to the present and to get things changed. Instead of merely satirizing, he suggested improvements of a practical kind in concrete problems of law and taxation. He hoped that rulers would follow his advice. And so we come to his political thought.

Professor Post has claimed for John that he anticipated the discovery of Aristotle's *Politics* by over a hundred years. He 'reveals an early maturity of the theory that man is by nature a political animal'. The early medieval theory on the origin of the State regarded its coercive power as a divine remedy for the sin of fallen man. Government had a repressive function; it was no creative activity, offering scope for social virtues, but a nasty chore. Men must submit to the ills of government or take part in government if necessary because it offered them the only alternative to anarchy. Post argues that this theory was not in sole possession of the field: classical sources and even some passages in the Fathers handed down a more positive view of the State. John of Salisbury out-paced his contemporaries by finding out and developing this more positive view. He saw the State organization as corresponding to the function of man's natural reason: 'The State is a work of art, which imitates nature.' Professor Post has made a good case,[58] so long as we realize that John never examined or rejected the common view of the State as a result of sin. He quotes St Augustine to the effect that rule over one's fellows has been arrogated or extorted, by man's iniquity, from God. Forgetting his praise of eloquence as a useful art, John writes that in the age of innocence man talked little, in a simple, untutored way; corruption has made him a chatter-box.[59] It does not quite hang together.

John's description of the body politic incorporates some new features, which show him as an observer as well as a participant in

---

[58] *Studies in Medieval Legal Thought* (Princeton, 1964) 513–21.
[59] *Policr.* ii, 346, 414–15; *Metal.* 5–7. See Augustine, *De civitate Dei* iv, 15.

government: the archbishop's secretary had a good understanding of bureaucracy. He represents the commonwealth as an organic whole: it has the prince as its head, the peasantry as its feet, and the other members all performed their respective functions.[60] We recognize the medieval hierarchy, but his metaphor allows for the increasing complexity of the Angevin governmental machine. Society has far outgrown the simple threefold division into men of war, men of prayer and men of work. Officialdom has come to stay. John's prince is more than a mere overlord or war leader; he acts as chief magistrate, guiding, controlling and directing his judges and tax collectors. John's rational approach comes out in his reason for disapproving of the forest laws. Just as he blamed hunting as a sport inconsistent with human dignity, so he blamed afforestation for the preservation of game as wasteful of natural resources, as indeed it was.[61] Other moralists objected to forest laws on the grounds that they infringed on man's natural rights to use wild beasts and birds, an illogical objection, which would have called all property rights in question had they followed it through.[62] They do not seem to have regarded the royal and seigneurial forests as economically wasteful.

The role of the prince as guardian of the public welfare may help to explain why John put forward his theory of tyrannicide. If the prince becomes a tyrant, ruling by will rather than law, and for his own pleasure rather than for the good of his subjects, then he is a public enemy rather than a public servant. Hence a subject would be justified in killing him. The assassin must choose dignified means; poison is ruled out as too base a weapon.[63] *De officiis* was John's source for the theory;[64] but he preferred to authenticate it by quotations from the Bible and the Fathers. He probably realized that they gave less support than Cicero to the slayer of a tyrant, and wanted to exploit what little he could find.[65] Justification of tyrannicide

[60] *Policr.* i, 298– ii, 77.
[61] ibid. i, 31.
[62] Baldwin, *Masters*, i, 245–6.
[63] *Policr.* ii, 341–412.
[64] *De offic.* I. xlv, III, iv and vi. The theme of the tyrant as enemy of the philosopher, who understands the principles of statecraft, and the misfortune of his people, goes back to Plato; see B. Giger, *Der Tyrann. Werden und Wesen des tyrannischen Menschen und des Staatstyrannen* (Immensee, 1940).
[65] Ph. Delhaye, 'Le bien suprême d'après le *Policraticus* de Jean de Salisbury', R.T.A.M. xx (1953) 219–21.

agreed with his picture of man in society. To submit slavishly to a tyrant would destroy human dignity. John also observed the contemporary scene and could devise no alternative. It would have been hard to suggest any legal or constitutional check on Angevin government towards 1160. If force were resorted to, a magnate revolt or a popular rising would have been messier than tyrannicide and less likely to succeed. We may object that removal of a tyrant leaves the machinery of his government intact and available to his heirs. But that would be unfair to John. Kingship was still very personal. The tyrant's successor might be better disposed and at least he would have had his warning.

It is impossible to knead out the inconsistencies in the thought of *Policraticus:* John also exalts the prince as God's viceroy on earth and he did not work out any clear distinction between ruler and office. We should not ask too much of him. Admitting the current trend towards more government, he wanted to instil a sense of duty and responsibility in civil servants, so that the system might work smoothly and equitably. Thomas Becket, his former colleague in the archbishop's household, had the king's ear as chancellor. He wielded more power and influence than any other subject. He was spoken of already as Theobald's successor at Canterbury.[66] The chancellor and potential archbishop, with John's volumes dedicated to him on his bedside table, what vistas of reform opened up here!

Thomas might succeed Theobald. We have run into the Church. John's opinions on the Church stand out in *Policraticus* like a rock in a quiet sea. His comparison between the commonwealth and a human body breaks down; his prince is not autonomous, but the Church's servant. The Church formed a universal hierarchy with the pope at its head. John had a deep devotion to the papacy, warmed by his personal friendship with Adrian IV and alerted by Adrian's rebuke to Theobald in 1156 for neglecting papal interests in England.[67] Dissenters from papal doctrine were heretics and schismatics.[68] The lay ruler holds his sword from the Church as her minister; he performs those functions which she judges unworthy of clerics. John demotes him to the role of butcher; he represses crime by means of physical force. Ministers of human law stand as far below ministers of divine law as human matters are below divine.[69] John dots the 'i's and crosses the 't's in the resistance

[66] E.D.P. 47.
[67] Southern, 244.
[68] *Policr.* ii, 70.
[69] ibid. i, 239–40.

H

theory put forward by Robert of Melun.[70] Robert allowed resistance to secular tyranny, but not to ecclesiastical. John admits that churchmen can and do tyrannize; bad bishops sit on the front bench of his shadow cabinet of the wicked, but they must not be resisted: who would presume to judge the pope or a canonically elected bishop?[71] Robert gave to the Church the right to judge lay offenders, including the prince, and to use spiritual discipline. John went further; he gave to the Church the right to judge whether the lay prince had become a tyrant. If the prince offends against God and the Church, he endangers the soul of the commonwealth.[72] At worst, if the prince refused to obey, then a good priest would resist him to the point of martyrdom. John painted the contemporary scene darkly. The royal officials hound one, if one offends the tyrant. Try putting forward some clerical privilege in one's defence; they cry in the words of the Jewish high priest: *What further need have we of witnesses? Behold you have heard the blasphemy* (Mt. xxvi, 65); *Whosoever shall say likewise speaks against Caesar* (Io. xix, 12). Should the judge try to shield the clerk who is accused, then they shout on all sides: *If thou release this man, thou art not Caesar's friend* (ibid.)[73] A priest must show courage and constancy. To feel fear is permissible; to give way in time of need is not so.[74] Already, by 1159, we have the setting for the conflict on privilege of clergy, with the archbishop as martyr for Christ and the bishop of London as the Jewish high priest and friend of Caesar. John hoped that the chancellor, if he were promoted to be archbishop, would implement his teaching on the relations between *regnum* and *sacerdotium* as well as his advice on the conduct of *regnum*. It was hardly consistent. John thought on different levels when he moved from one subject to the other in *Policraticus*.

He prescribes as detailed rules for the conduct of clergy as he does for the laity. Ecclesiastics should not hold office as courtiers or royal servants.[75] The practice was condemned at canon law, on the grounds that secular office involved shedding of blood. It did not occur to John that the ban would have prevented his prince from employing the most highly educated men available to him. John anticipated the objections put forward by Becket to the Constitutions of Clarendon. In the first place, ancient custom is invalid if it

[70] See above, p. 53.
[71] *Policr.* i, 240, ii. 357, 400, 405–6.
[72] ibid. 78–9.
[73] ibid. 6–7.
[74] ibid. 400.
[75] ibid. 182–90.

goes against divine law and the dictates of reason. Tyrants cite precedents for their evil deeds, when they thrust a royal servant into a church without due election, force the clergy to accept an unworthy candidate, commit simony, compel the primate to consecrate an unsuitable man as bishop, and drive good bishops into exile. Bad precedents are no excuse.[76] On benefit of clergy also he anticipated Becket. The only point of difference between them is that John defended priests against the secular courts, whereas Becket extended his defence to all clergy. Respect for the sacrament of holy orders, John argues, should protect a priest from subjection to secular judgement. Nor should a priest be subject to double punishment, which must always be avoided, though an unfrocked priest who raises bloodstained hands against the Church is subject to the lay power. It is notable that John quotes the text Nahum i, 9 against double punishment in this context.[77] Church property should be protected by special sanctions: knights should be unbelted if they committed sacrilege by robbing churches.[78]

John blamed the English government for the sad state of affairs which had arisen. The English Church had suffered from royal tyranny in the past.[79] Now her liberties were reduced to a shadow.[80] He himself was reproached for upholding the rights of Rome,[81] and indeed he had supported Adrian IV's claim to dominion over Ireland as part of his inheritance by the Donation of Constantine: according to this forgery, Constantine had granted lordship 'over all the isles' and therefore over Ireland, John argued, to Sylvester I.[82] Naturally he backed Alexander III as the true pope against Victor IV, the imperialist anti-pope, in the schism of 1159. Academic doubt and delay should have no place in the question of recognizing Alexander immediately.[83] The German claim to empire annoyed him.[84]

John packed his ideas into an untidy parcel, but the string seemed firm. He admitted secular values to a degree unusual in his day,

[76] ibid. 186–7; E.D.P. 54.
[77] *Policr.* ii, 364; see below, p. 124.
[78] *Policr.* ii, 36.
[79] E.D.P. 47–8.
[80] *Letters* i. 32.
[81] ibid.; see Southern, 247.
[82] *Metal.* 217–18; see Southern, 242–3; A. J. Otway-Ruthven, *A History of Medieval Ireland* (London, 1968) 47–8; D. Maffei, *La Donazione di Constantino nei giuristi medievali* (Milan, 1964) 31.
[83] *Letters*, i, 214. [84] ibid. 204–15.

while giving the Church over-riding control. A good prince would accept her guidance: all power to his elbow in that case; *regnum* and *sacerdotium* should co-operate.[85] If the prince tyrannized, then a lay subject might resort to tyrannicide and a good priest would submit to martyrdom. The tension came in his ethics: are *cultus honesti* and the golden mean conductive to heroism? Can one preserve Ciceronian virtues if one joins in party politics? Before the conflict, John wrote on politics and ethics in his spare time, taking a sheltered, indirect view for the most part. The conflict plunged him into politics up to the neck. He always insisted that principles should govern practice; as he wrote to a friend in 1167:

> Philosophical truth concerns itself with deeds, not words. You know that I've never liked an opinion which relates to words alone.[86]

So there was no way out.

The chance to stand by his principles came all too quickly. John kept his place in the archbishop's household when Thomas succeeded Theobald. Royal anger forced him abroad even before the quarrel came to a head. His revenues in England were sequestrated; Becket's flight destroyed any chance of regaining them. Poverty as a way of life never appealed to him:

> Nothing befits a philosopher so well as to profess the truth and . . . to love poverty *when necessary*.[87]

In exile he lacked ready cash; the resulting slights upset him. 'Exile for God and the liberty of the Church'[88] proved so irksome that he tried to wriggle out of it for over a year. He wrote to staunch king's men, the bishop of London and the dean of Salisbury, and to other friends, explaining his dilemma and begging for help.[89] Illusory hopes alternated with prescient fears in his reports on the political scene. But Henry's terms of reconciliation were too stiff. John wrote to the pope to ask whether he should take the oath demanded of him. The answer was 'no': it might give the wrong impression; wait for the king to cool down.[90] John resigned himself to the loss of his revenues and to being cut off from his family. He had well-wishers in France, beginning with King Louis VII. His lifelong

---

[85] ibid. i, 190.   [86] *Mat.* vi, 180.   [87] ibid. v, 264.
[88] ibid. 105.   [89] ibid. 212, 217, vi, 105–7; *Gilbert Foliot*, 94–5.
[90] *Mat.* v, 216.

friend, Abbot Peter of La Celle, gave him a home at Rheims. He could write to less fortunate sympathizers that he lacked for nothing, while continuing to beg from the wealthier.[91] His appetite for study and writing remained healthy. Business letters gave him the chance to ask correspondents to send him rare books and new translations.[92] As well as writing letters, both official and personal, he worked up his 'memoirs of the papal court' into the *Historia pontificalis* for Peter of La Celle, in 1164.[93]

That John suffered unwillingly does not prove that he dissented from Becket's cause. Historians have presented him as a moderate and contrasted him with the extremist Herbert of Bosham. The assumption has been that John was a good, sensible man, who praised moderation. His *Historia pontificalis* shows that he could see both sides of a controversy and do justice to both Gilbert of la Porrée and St Bernard. Presumably, therefore, he kept his sense of proportion and used his influence with Becket in the interests of peace. There is no evidence for this view of him. In 1165 he advised Becket to desist from studying canon law in order to prove his case against Henry and to take refuge in prayer and meditation instead. The advice has been quoted out of context. John wrote at a moment when the horizon looked black. He despaired of mortal allies; they were all falling away. Henry II had squared Louis VII's butler and Count Robert of Dreux. The countess was a prudent woman, who hoped that Henry II would arrange noble marriages for her many children. She had sent him three hundred ells of cloth of Rheims to make shirts, with other little presents. The archbishop of Rheims might go over too; he loved Count Robert and his children dearly. John's call for Christian resignation went with his bad news, but it has a surprising tailpiece. It is reported that certain English bishops are usurping the rights of Canterbury. Becket should safeguard the rights of his see by getting letters patent from the pope.[94] That part of the letter is not quoted.

Where John differed from Herbert was in his handling of 'public relations'. He wanted to put out a different image of the archbishop in exile. Herbert saw his master as a knight of Christ; John wanted him to seem Christlike. He would make a better impression and annoy the pope less if he turned the other cheek and showed willing. He should accept Henry's offer of talks and take with him just a

[91] ibid. vi, 108, 195, 329. [92] ibid. 109, 181, 260, 362; v, 367–8.
[93] *Hist. pontif.* xxiv–xxx. [94] *Mat.* v, 163–5.

few level-headed, cautious clerks to advise him, if he had any. The absence of his other clerks would make a good excuse for delaying tactics. If the talks came to nothing, as seemed only too likely, Becket would have shown his moderation by his willingness to treat.[95] Should he return to England without adequate safeguards? It would certainly look better. He had chosen the path of martyrdom; it would be logical to act accordingly and to count the cost:

> You say you aren't ready for martyrdom yet. But who is? Any one of us can die for the faith with God's help, if he has the will.[96]

John urged his master not to show vindictiveness to his enemies[97] or rudeness to the cardinal legates. One of those appointed to adjudicate, Cardinal William of Pavia, was suspected of being pro-Henry. Becket sent an undiplomatic letter of protest, which John deplored. If the legate was really an enemy, better wait until he showed himself in his true colours. John tried to counter the protest by writing a personal letter, a model of tact and deference, calculated to mollify any prince of the Church.[98] But this concerns tactics, not principles.

His tone grew sharper as the struggle went on. At first he had refrained from personal attacks on Henry. Now he began to refer to the king as a tyrant, while still admiring him.[99] Power fascinated John, as it does many intellectuals, even when used in the wrong way. And it *was* used wrongly: Henry had received his sword from the Church to protect, not to oppress her.[1] John denounced the Constitutions of Clarendon. They were 'a new gospel of human traditions', contrary to the divine law. The archbishop could not yield, since he was a Christian by his profession, not a Henrician.[2] His enemies persecuted not the man, but his principles, the Holy Spirit within him.[3] John reported the last stages of the quarrel with sympathy for Becket, and justified his conduct.[4]

Like Herbert, John aimed at pushing the Curia to support his cause more strongly. The *Historia pontificalis* shows that he suspected cardinals of taking bribes in the normal way;[5] but he could see other men's viewpoints, and he realized that Alexander III was in a quandary. The pope's problems led him to put policy before

[95] ibid. 424. [96] ibid. 442. [97] ibid. 446.
[98] ibid. 221. [99] ibid. vi, 96, 364, 367, 500. [1] ibid. vi, 64.
[2] ibid. v, 349, vi, 234, 64, 137–8. [3] ibid. vi, 102.
[4] ibid. 509, vii, 2. [5] cap. vi, 12, cap. xxxviii, 75.

religion.[6] John thought he was mistaken, however, and said so: there is plain speaking in one of his letters. He tells Alexander that his reputation as pope is in danger. The exiles, proscribed for upholding the privileges of the holy See, feel the pope's disgrace more keenly than their own sufferings. John refers to a rumour that Alexander has given a deanery with cure of souls to the Henrician John of Oxford, Henry's envoy to the schismatics. 'If the rumour be true', John wrote, 'then I do not see how you can be excused.' The pope had power to make new laws and to abrogate old ones, but he could not absolve an impenitent sinner; even St Peter had no power to do that. The letter ends with an apology for having gone too far; he had been provoked.[7] He used even stronger words in a letter to a cardinal legate: whosoever should advise the English clergy to bow to royal tyranny was a heretic and forerunner of antichrist, if not antichrist in person.[8]

A subtler method of propaganda was slanted reporting. John tried to present the pope's actions as more decisive than they were. He wrote to warn the sub-prior of Canterbury of the dangers of anathema. Alexander had followed the example of Gregory VII, who deposed the emperor Henry IV. He had excommunicated Frederick I and deprived him of his royal dignity.[9] Henceforward John referred to Frederick as *ex-augustus*.[10] This was gross exaggeration in 1167, when the letter was written. The pope had excommunicated Frederick at the beginning of the schism in 1160 and had absolved subjects from their oath of allegiance, but he stopped short of deposition. Such a step would have meant arranging for the election of an anti-king, which was not on the agenda. Nor did Alexander renew the ban in 1167. John is our sole authority for the statement.[11] However, it gave point to his warning, which he couples with a prophecy that the ex-emperor would never win victory or enjoy peace until he submitted to the Church. Disasters to his cause in Italy had followed on the ban immediately: Milan had been rebuilt; schismatic bishops had been expelled and Catholic

---

[6] *Mat.* vi, 20: Sed eius sunt necessitates tot et tantae . . . ut interdum utatur licentia potestatis, procuretque ex dispensatione quod reipublicae dicitur expedire, etsi non expediat religioni. . .

[7] ibid. 176–9.   [8] ibid. 367–8.   [9] ibid. 298–9.

[10] ibid. 239–40, 279, 369, 386.

[11] His statement is dismissed as propaganda or wishful thinking by W. von Giesebrecht, *Geschichte der deutschen Kaiserzeit*, ed. B. von Simson

bishops had returned to their Italian sees. John was misinformed, perhaps; but he could have verified his sources.

We may ask how his mentor Cicero fared in the storm. The philosopher comforted John in the first years of exile. When it became inevitable, John wrote that he suffered it for the sake of his honour, reputation and conscience: no longer would he act as a courtier; the alternative of giving in to Henry would have disgraced him.[12] He recalled Cicero's teaching that *utile* and *honestum* coincide; nothing can be called *utile* if it is not dictated by *honestum*.[13] That was written in the fourth year of exile. Prolonged suffering made him reconsider his views. He criticized the Stoic doctrine of apathy. He had found little fault in it when he compiled *Policraticus*: now it struck him as unchristian. The true Christian is not apathetic; he feels emotion; the plight of the Church excites his pity and grief:

> Dull is the member of Christ's body, or rather he is no member at all, who is not moved to pity by such bitter affliction. The Stoics preach apathy, which means 'insensibility' in Latin, but their opinion has been exploded by sound reason and better philosophers. The precepts and examples of Holy Scripture carry more weight. . . . Our Lord himself wept over Jerusalem, teaching us by his example that the faithful should do likewise.

John draws a parallel between Jerusalem, which groaned under the yoke of the scribes and pharisees, and the Church of his day, which is oppressed by wicked prelates.[14] The rejection of apathy as un-

---

(Leipzig, 1895) vi, 473, by J. Haller, *Das Papsstum Idee und Wirklichkeit* ii, 2 (Stuttgart, 1939) 566, and by Pacaut, 175-8.

[12] *Mat.* v, 217.

[13] ibid. vi, 134: Philosophia . . . praescribit enim quoniam utile et honestum se praedicatione mutua circumscribunt, ut nihil unius admittat nomen, quod non et alterius exigat rationem.

[14] ibid. 412-13 (ep. ccccx, dated 1168): Stupidum est, aut prorsus de corpore Christi non est membrum, quod tanti languoris acerbitate non movetur ad compatiendum. Apatheiam, quam Latinus insensibilitatem dicit, Stoici praedicant, sed eorum opinio explosa est fidelissima ratione et virtute rectius philosophantium et, quod potissimum est, sacrae Scripturae praeceptis et exemplis. Videns Dominus civitatem . . . flevit super illam . . . Exemplum ergo dedit fidelibus similiter faciendi. . . .

John's term *philosophantes* referred to theologians who used philosophy in the exercise of their office and is an early example of it; see E. Gilson, 'Les "Philosophantes"', A.H.D.L.M.A. xix (1953) 135-40; G. Post, 'Philosophantes and philosophi in Roman and Canon Law', ibid. xxi (1955) 135-8.

christian was not original. He could have read it in St Augustine's *City of God*. Aulus Gellius and Cicero himself criticized the concept of apathy from a pagan point of view and in a more muted way.[15] But John really felt the criticism. He was writing about his thoughts to two intimate friends. He expressed it in his own words without verbal quotation. Total commitment had brought the moment of truth. Tension resolved itself. The holy page reasserted her rule over the *Artes*. The Man of Sorrows overshadowed Cicero.

Return to England raised the unwelcome spectre of martyrdom. John tried to restrain Becket from provoking his murderers, urging him to take wise counsel before giving them an answer. The advice accords with the image he wished Becket to present to his public: he should not tarnish it by angry impatience. John was also afraid; it seems that he hid himself from the knights.[16]

The rest of John's career and writings need not keep us now. He wrote a *Life* of St Thomas, but it is derivative and impersonal. In this it resembles his *Life* of St Anselm, written earlier for Becket in order to forward Anselm's canonization. He warned readers of both *Lives* that they must seek fuller treatment elsewhere.[17] Hagiography did not suit John's talents; he composed the *Lives* as a duty to be performed. Moreover, friendship with Becket had never been woven into the texture of John's feelings, as it had into Herbert's. Now his material problems vanished; he succeeded in being reinstated in England. Finally his friend William of the White Hands, archbishop of Rheims, arranged for his election to the bishopric of Chartres, where he died in 1180. An extract from the Chartres obituary will serve as his epitaph. This 'learned and lovable pastor' bequeathed privileges to his church, as well as books:

> He gained for the church the privilege of manumitting her serfs for manifest advantage or need, without hindrance from the violence of secular power. It is added in this privilege that if we should be drawn before secular or ecclesiastical judges, none may impose on us trial by battle or by ordeal of hot iron or hot or cold water,

[15] *De civ. Dei* xiv, 9. Augustine quotes Cicero, *Tusc.* iii, 6. See also *Noct. Attic.* xix, 12. John knew this book well; see the index of authors, *Policr.* ii, 486. Augustine and Cicero use the word *stupor*, which may lie behind John's *stupidum*, but he uses *insensibilitas* in preference to their *immanitas*.

[16] Webb, 116–19.

[17] *Mat.* ii, 302; R. W. Southern, *Saint Anselm and his Biographer* (Cambridge, 1963) 338.

108 *John of Salisbury*

but that we should be let prove our case by two or three lawful witnesses instead.[18]

John cared for ecclesiastical privileges to the end.

The contrasts between John and Herbert merely underline the identity of their principles. John's gentler character and more Fabian tactics did not make him a 'moderate', that word so soothing to English ears. Both scholars were papalist, anti-imperialist high churchmen.

[18] A. Molinier and A. Longnon, op. cit. 106–7: . . . vir magne religionis totiusque scientie radiis illustratus, verbo, vita, moribus pastor amabilis. . . . Privilegium etiam adquisivit ut servos Carnotensis ecclesie possit pro necessitate vel manifesta utilitate sua manumittere, non impediente secularis violentia potestatis, in quo etiam additur, ut si quando pro iustitia nostra ante seculares vel ecclesiasticos iudices tracti fuerimus, nullus nobis duellum vel iudicium candentis ferri vel aque ferventis seu frigide imponat, sed iustitiam nostram liceat duobus vel tribus testibus legittimis comprobare.

V

Thomas Becket

Much has been written on Becket's character and he still eludes us. A thumbnail sketch by a contemporary seems to me to give the best impression of him. A certain deacon had a vision on the occasion of Becket's flight to France after the council of Northampton in 1164. He saw a hedgehog pursued by a royal hunting party and carrying 'the book of the Acts of the Apostles' on its back. On reaching the coast, it plunged into the sea and disappeared.[1] The hedgehog typified wild animals living in deserted places. We can see one in a carving on the façade of the west door of Rouen cathedral, trotting about among the ruins of Nineveh to illustrate the fulfilment of the prophecy: *the bittern and the urchin shall lodge in the threshold thereof* (Soph. ii, 14). The hedgehog's refuge was in the rock (Ps. ciii, 18); just so holy men take refuge in Christ. 'Like the spiky hedgehog, I hope to have Christ as my refuge,' wrote a friend to Becket in exile.[2] 'The book of the Acts of the Apostles' seen on its back signified that St Paul had set the example of fleeing from his persecutors, as Becket did. I cannot improve on this picture of the wild, spiky archbishop. My aim here is only to examine the influences which came to bear on him and his reactions to them.

He had a patchy education. First he went to the choir school of Merton Priory, then to a school in London, and then to Paris, where he studied in the Arts course, probably under Robert of Melun.[3] He could not have studied theology with Robert, who did not begin to teach it until towards 1142.[4] Becket had left Paris by that time:

[1] From the Vita of William of Canterbury, *Mat.* i, 40–2.

[2] *Mat.* vi, 27.

[3] See L. B. Radford, *Thomas of London before his Consecration* (Cambridge, 1894) 20–4.

[4] See above, p. 51.

he was serving a London relative as clerk and accountant towards the end of 1140. 'He did not stay long in the schools after learning grammar and the other arts', says his biographer Guernes de Pont Saint Maxime.[5] Thomas entered Archbishop Theobald's household as a clerk about 1143.[6] Theobald gave him study leave for a year, to learn law at Bologna and Auxerre. Bologna was the chief centre for canon and civil law studies. We know much less of Auxerre: Master Gilbert the Universal, who was a lawyer as well as a theologian, taught there *c.* 1110–20, and the chapter had a *lector* among its canons, who may have held a school, 1123–66.[7] The future archbishop therefore had spent short periods of study in the Arts and in law, without taking his degree in either. Herbert assures us that Becket never learnt Latin verse composition in the schools:[8] versifying belonged to an elementary stage in the study of grammar. Archbishop Theobald gathered brilliant young men about him, some very learned, witness John of Salisbury, and a number boasting the title of Master. Fitzstephen says that Becket was less learned than his colleagues.[9] That is rather damning. Of his two rivals for promotion in Theobald's household, Roger of Pont l'Evêque, who became archbishop of York in 1154 was given the title of Master and was said to be *legisperitus*;[10] John of Canterbury, treasurer of York from 1153, then bishop of Poitiers and finally archbishop of Lyons, is never

---

[5] *La vie de Saint Thomas Becket*, ed. E. Walberg – (Paris, 1936) 7. Guernes finished his *Life* towards the end of 1174; an earlier version of it survives in fragments only; see E. Walberg, *La tradition hagiographique de Saint Thomas avant la fin du XIIe siècle* (Paris, 1929) and M. D. Legge, *Anglo-Norman Literature and its Background* (Oxford, 1963). Guernes' source for Becket's short stay in the schools was William of Canterbury, *Mat.* i, 3.

[6] Saltman, 166–7.

[7] B. Smalley, 'Gilbertus Universalis', R.T.A.M. vii (1935) 237–9; J. Lebeuf, *Mémoires concernant l'histoire ecclésiastique et civile d'Auxerre* ii (Paris, 1743) 11, 18, 23: three men, John, Hugh and Robert, appear in the witness lists of charters, 1123, 1159 and 1166, respectively, as *lector*.

[8] *Mat.* iii, 461. Becket heard a voice prophesying the deaths of the two princes, Henry and Geoffrey, and of their father, in a hexameter. Herbert explains in order to authenticate it as a prophecy that Becket could not have composed it himself while awake, much less in his sleep; nec arbitretur quis versum hunc quasi a dormitante aliquo casu compositum, quem etiam vigilanter vigilans non componeret, utpote qui versificandi nec etiam sub scholari disciplina artem attigisset, vel in modico. Hoc autem scio, quod versum auditum sic in crastino retulit discipulo qui scripsit haec.

[9] ibid. 16.

[10] Saltman, 370 (a charter of 1147); G.F.L.C. (1145–8) 102; Draco 745.

called Master. According to John of Salisbury he was good at languages;[11] but his letters as included in the Becket dossier are short and almost wholly lacking in biblical quotations. It seems probable that he relied on his *scholasticus* at Poitiers, Master Raymond, to coach him in theology, much as Becket came to rely on Herbert.[12] Nor did the Canterbury household supply teaching in theology. It was not equipped with a *studium* like the papal court in the fourteenth century.

It provided training of a different kind: Becket learned expertise in secretarial and diplomatic work, with that knowledge of legal business which all administrators needed. The promotion of his two rivals to be treasurer and archbishop of York respectively in 1153–4 left him in charge of Theobald's staff. Henry II, it has been suggested, made Becket his chancellor as his 'reward to Theobald for his support of the Angevin cause in the last two years of Stephen's reign'.[13] The appointment may well have had a political reason, but Henry II had an eye for efficiency and knew what he wanted in his chancellor.

A few bits of evidence, seemingly conflicting, but really complementary, throw light on Becket's intellectual powers. The chronicler of Battle Abbey, recounting the course of a law suit, tells how Becket as chancellor answered on behalf of the abbey 'with fluent speech'. Becket is compared in an implied quotation to Musaeus, who stood head and shoulders above the other heroic shades in Virgil's Hades.[14] It is a notable tribute, even taking account of the fact that he was on the right side from the chronicler's

[11] *Policr.* ii, 271. On John of Canterbury see *Letters* i, xxviii, Saltman *passim*; Ph. Pouzet, *L'anglais Jean dit Bellemains* (Lyons, 1927).

[12] Master Raymond was a friend and correspondent of John of Salisbury; see *Mat.* v, 366, vi, 149, 260. Raymond appears as 'master of the schools' in Poitiers cathedral documents of March/April 1167; see D. P. de Monsabert, 'Chartes et documents pour servir à l'histoire de l'abbaye de Charroux', *Archives historiques du Poitou* xxxix (1910) 153–6.

[13] Saltman, 168.

[14] *Chronicon monasterii de Bello*, ed. *J. S. Brewer* (Anglia Christiana Societas, London, 1846) 98: . . . imposito responsionis sermone Thomae chancellario regis, omnibus audientibus, facunda oratione hoc modo ita reddidit heros.

From Aen. vi, 672: responsum paucis ita reddidit heros.

On this chronicle see H. W. C. Davis, 'The Chronicle of Battle Abbey', *E.H.R.* xxix (1914) 426–34; H. Mayr-Harting, 'Hilary, Bishop of Chichester (1147–1169) and Henry II', ibid. lxxviii (1963) 209–24.

point of view. To set against it, we have the description of Thomas as archbishop at the council of Tours in 1163, given by Stephen of Rouen in *Draco Normannicus*. The author of the poem, a monk of Bec, was implacably hostile to the archbishop. According to the *Draco*, he kept silence at the council because he did not know enough Latin to speak:

> ut minus edoctus verba latina loqui.[15]

Stephen of Rouen was unscrupulously inaccurate and his slur on Becket has been dismissed as a nasty piece of spite,[16] but the context makes it sound plausible. The author dwells on the role of speech-ifying in elegant, biblical Latin at the council. Alexander III, 'polite in the Roman way', 'set forth David's words'; the imperialist pope, Victor IV, had already taken refuge in Germany 'supported by his rhetors'. Bishop Arnulf of Lisieux poured forth such a torrent of eloquence that the pope could hardly stop him.[17] The newly installed archbishop of Canterbury may well have distrusted his ability to compete in a tournament of ecclesiastical rhetoric, full of scriptural allusions and classical tags; it called for the kind of training that he lacked. Lastly, John of Salisbury's dedication of his books to the chancellor must be reckoned with. His praise of Becket's talents may be soft soap; but he must have hoped that the chancellor and potential primate would at least have parts of them read to him or ponder some pages himself and digest their teaching. John must have seen his friend as a clever and receptive amateur. He judged rightly. The chancellor liked to show his magnificence as a patron of scholars, as well as in other ways. He entertained the Paris scholars sumptuously during his embassy to France. He persuaded the king to recall poor Englishmen from abroad and to reward their learning with benefices.[18] As archbishop he was instrumental in getting Robert of Melun elected to the bishopric of Hereford, 1163.[19] There was continuity in his attitude here. The chancellor was a scholar *de dimanche*.

[15] *Draco*, 744.   [16] Foreville, 241–4.

[17] *Draco*, 744–5: Primus Alexander, Romano more politus, / Incipit, eloquium fluminis instar adest: / Dicta David pandens, sanctos quos congregat illi / Summo, multiplici verba tenore regit.

On Victor IV, 728: stipatus sociis rhetoricisque viris . . . On Arnulf of Lisieux, 744.

[18] *Mat.* iii, 32, 24.   [19] Knowles, 9, 28–30.

Contemporaries, and historians following them, have remarked on the change in Becket's habits, outlook and policy when he became archbishop. The chancellor disappointed Theobald's hopes that he would use his influence on behalf of ecclesiastical liberties; he passed over wholly to the royal side; he was Henry's boon companion and led a secular life to the point of equipping and leading troops. But the evidence suggests prodromal symptoms of his conversion. The stories told by his biographers of his secret devotions and asceticism need not be true. His correspondence with Abbot Peter of la Celle proves that he did not feel pleased with himself; he wanted to have it both ways. Peter of la Celle had studied at Paris in his youth; he may have had John of Salisbury as his tutor. He was abbot of la Celle near Troyes 1145–62 and then of Saint Rémi at Rheims; he died as bishop of Chartres in 1183. Peter cultivated a circle of pious and learned friends, who exchanged edifying letters. To receive a letter of spiritual direction from him conferred a certificate of piety.[20] He expected his friends to live up to his standards. The abbot of St Crispin near Soissons wrote to Peter of la Celle in high glee: he had been invited to an important function in Champagne. It had been a good party and the countess had singled him out for special favour. Peter's reply poured cold water. The abbot of St Crispin used to have a good reputation; it was finished now. He had lost his sense of values. Instead of going to the party, he would have done better to make peace between the archbishop and chapter of Rheims.[21] John of Salisbury belonged to Peter's inner circle. Herbert did not. Typically, he was on the friendliest terms with the backsliding abbot of St Crispin.[22] Becket aspired to be a pen-friend of Peter of la Celle. His dossier includes a letter from Peter, refusing his request. Peter wrote that he was too humble to become an intimate of so important a person as the chancellor: 'Who does not know that you come second to the king in four kingdoms? I can be a casual acquaintance only. Give me such friendship as you keep for your acquaintances, and I shall be grateful enough.'[23] It was a polite and cruel snub: *Procul, O procul profani*. The chancellor was unworthy. He made the grade as archbishop in exile, when

---

[20] J. Leclercq, *La spiritualité de Pierre de la Celle (1115–1183)* (Paris, 1946). On Peter and John of Salisbury, *Letters* ix–x.

[21] P.L. ccii, 551–2.

[22] Above, p. 65.

[23] *Mat.* v, 3–4, and P.L. ccii, 426: . . . Nullo igitur modo ad ingressum

Abbot Peter wrote to congratulate him in glowing terms for defying Henry in defence of the Church's freedom.[24]

Peter's first letter tells us something more of Becket's wish to contact the spiritual élite. Correspondents used to ask the abbot to send them books for devotional reading. Accordingly, Becket had asked him for the sermons of a 'Master G.'. Peter promised to look for them, and to send copies as soon as possible. That would be a better gift than his friendship. Reading between the lines, we gather that he would be glad to help Thomas improve himself spiritually. A similar request to Abbot Peter, made by John of Salisbury in 1157, identifies 'Master G.' as Gebuin, chanter of the cathedral of Troyes and holder of other offices, who died before 1161.[25] The chancellor may have heard of the sermons from John of Salisbury. Why did he want them? Master Gebuin was a friend and imitator of St Bernard: 'il a fait du Saint Bernard', as Dom Leclercq puts it. As chanter of Troyes, he addressed his sermons to secular clerks, probably those of his cathedral church. He provided 'St Bernard without tears', borrowing the saint's unctuous language, but avoiding his mystical flights.[26] Bernardine phrases made plain Christian doctrine sound exotic and exciting. Becket had had an opportunity to see and hear Gebuin's great model at the council of Rheims, which he attended as a member of Archbishop Theobald's staff.[27] Most of St Bernard's hearers, like Bernard himself, believed that the Holy Spirit spoke through his mouth. Gebuin's sermons would bring a beginner in the spiritual life as close to the holy of holies as he could get. If Peter of la Celle acted on his promise to send them, and Becket read them, he might have picked out a passage inviting him to martyrdom. Gebuin exhorts his hearers and readers to choose death rather than deny Christ. Three types of constancy are required for martyrdom: spurn riches; despise the power of office; suffer torments willingly. Such a man is a second St John the Baptist.[28]

---

amicitiae manum porrigo. Sed si vel de grege accidentalium amicorum fuero, bene mecum fecisse dignitatem vestram aestimabo.

[24] P.L. ccii, 563–5. He also wrote to Alexander III urging him to support the archbishop's cause; ibid. 532.

[25] *Letters*, 51, 54.

[26] *Recueil d'études sur Saint Bernard et ses écrits* i (Rome, 1962) 83–93; see also Schneyer, 236, 321, 367, 405.

[27] *Hist. pontif*, cap. viii, 17.

[28] MS Paris, B.N. lat. 14937, fol. 107rb (on *Mat*. iii, 1): Sequitur constantia in morte. . . Si igitur contigerit vel Christum negare, vel mori optare, potius

The sermons also taught the old lesson on the responsibilities of the good prelate: 'The prelate's badge is the blossom of piety, the subject's load the blossom of obedience.'[29]

Becket's conversion was predictable, given his temperament and circumstances. The sources point to a theatrical streak in him; but it is not play-acting to take ideas seriously. Two fixed ideas obtained in his milieu. Seculars, including secular clerks, were judged by lower standards than religious or prelates. Becket became a clerk because the Church offered better prospects of promotion;[30] that was normal. He did not study divinity while leading a secular life;[31] that was normal too. A clerk holding secular office could not be holy; he exposed himself to too many temptations; officials always took bribes and oppressed the poor. But certain virtues, chiefly 'magnificence', suited the status of a highly placed official. Secondly, it was thought that a prelate of the Church ought to aim at sanctity. He was not supposed to succumb to temptations. A royal chancellor, raised to the primacy of the English Church, had to cross the line. Becket's biographers mark the duality of standards by a change of style, when they describe his crossing. Herbert devotes a whole chapter to warning his readers that a change will be needed to mark the end of a gay success story and the beginning of hagiography.[32] Fitzstephen, a more concise writer than Herbert, makes the break abruptly. Classical allusions struck him as the right *décor* for his memoirs of Becket as chancellor. He makes only one reference to Scripture in this section; Becket was as rich as Solomon. Hannibal follows at once: the chancellor was so wealthy that he hoped to bribe the Romans, just as Hannibal did.[33] A torrent of biblical texts sweeps in with the story of Becket's conversion. Then Fitzstephen settles down to a roughly equal distribution of classical and biblical allusions. A tale had to vary its dress according to the

---

eligendum est mori quam Christum non confiteri. Fit autem constantia tribus qua prediximus (modis) in unum concurrentibus, videlicet cum quis in necessitate negandi positus divitias spreverit, honoris potentiam contempserit, tormenta libens pertulerit. . . . Ecce alter Ioannes baptista. . .

[29] ibid., fol. 114rb: Flos vero pietatis insigne est prelati; flos obedientie gestamen est subditi.

[30] According to his biographer Grim, *Mat.* ii, 361.

[31] Herbert, *Homilia*, P.L. cxc, 1410.

[32] *Mat.* iii, 189–92.

[33] ibid. 32. Hannibal is Fitzstephen's mistake for Jugurtha; see Sallust, *De bello Iugurthino* xxviii, 1.

I

subject matter. The Scriptures were laced into hagiography because the lives and passions of holy men prolonged the Gospels without any break in continuity.[34] Secular biography had different traditions. The division cut deep in literature and could influence men's behaviour.

The aspirant to greatness in any sphere where greatness could be conceived of would model himself on an admired predecessor. One chose Constantine or Charlemagne, St Gregory, St Antony or St Martin, St Jerome or Cicero. Similarly a writer would copy from an earlier work in preference to using his own words unless his theme gave him no alternative. The model could be near-contemporary as well as ancient. None of the models available was an exact fit for Becket on his election: 'He was in many respect an exceedingly eccentric figure to become archbishop of Canterbury. Since the Norman Conquest, the see had been dominated by the Benedictine monasticism of the Continent.' Only one of the five archbishops elected since the Conquest 'had not been a monk, William of Corbeil, an Austin Canon'.[35] The last civil servant and secular to hold the see had been Stigand, deposed in 1070, a discouraging example, especially as Anglo-Norman tradition had blackened the Late Old English Church. Lanfranc, Anselm and Theobald all got their training in monastic theology at Bec, and Ralph d'Escures at Séez. Ralph, 'undistinguished' and sick as he was during much of his pontificate, 1114–22, belonged to the Anselmian circle and left homilies of his own composition to Christchurch.[36] William of Corbeil, 1123–36, was elected as a compromise:[37] the bishops wanted a secular; the monastic chapter at Christchurch would have preferred another Benedictine as their archbishop. William had entered the Order of Canons Regular; but he too had contacts with Anselm's friends and pupils. Moreover, he had studied

[34] J. Leclercq, 'L'Ecriture sainte dans l'hagiographie monastique du haut moyen âge'; B. Smalley, 'L'exégèse biblique dans la littérature latine', *La Bibbia nell' alto medioevo* (Settimane di studio del Centro Italiano di studi sull' alto medioevo, x, Spoleto, 1965) 103–28, 631–55.

[35] R.. Franklin, 'Thomas Becket and the Church', *Canterbury Cathedral Chronicle* lxv (1970) 22–3.

[36] R. W. Southern, *Saint Anselm and his Biographer* (Cambridge, 1963) 235–7; A. Wilmart, 'Les homélies attribuées à Saint Anselme', A.H.D.L.M.A ii (1927) 16–23.

[37] D. Bethel, 'William of Corbeil and the Canterbury–York Dispute', *Journal of Ecclesiastical History* xix (1968) 145–9.

at Laon, probably 1107–9: Laon focused the study of theology on its school in the decades around 1100 and acted as a training ground for bishops. Henry I rewarded his civil servants with sees; but the primacy had escaped hitherto. Henry II's chancellor had to face a new situation. Perhaps he looked abroad as well as backwards to Canterbury. His rivals at York would hardly have pleased him as exemplars. The Continent was more promising. The species 'good prelate', though rare, existed in life as well as in lectures and sermons and in the pages of *Policraticus*. Becket had a paradigm before his eyes in the person of Geoffrey Loroux, archbishop of Bordeaux 1136–58. They both attended the council of Rheims and must have met and talked in a more familiar way in 1156–7, since they both witnessed charters (Thomas as chancellor) issued by Henry II when he visited the province of Bordeaux.[38] Geoffrey Loroux, known as Babion, 'the Stammerer', taught in the cathedral school of Angers from about 1103 to 1110.[39] He had most success with duller pupils; his stammer made him speak so slowly that they could take in what he said. As archbishop he was a great preacher: over seventy manuscript copies of his sermons survive, witnessing to their popularity. He used up material from the lectures he had given in the schools, just as Pullen did. He denounced the wickedness of secular princes who molested God's priests and who wanted to lord it over bishops. '*Our* master is Peter', he says to his clergy; '*our* lord is his vicar, the pope;' the pope must be visited and consulted on doubtful cases.[40] A reformer and friend of reformers, and supporter of Gilbert of la Porrée too, zealous for the liberties of his church, he contrasted sharply with those curial bishops who flourished under Angevin rule. Henry II had found him firmly entrenched at Bordeaux when he married Eleanor of Aquitaine, and left the old man alone until his death in 1158. Geoffrey seems to have spent some time living as a hermit in religious seclusion before he became archbishop. He therefore combined the study and teaching of the holy page with the religious life as a preparation for prelacy. He had less glitter than St Anselm, but Becket knew him personally and not only on hearsay.

[38] *Hist. pontif.* cap. viii, p. 17; L. Delisle and E. Berger, *Recueil des Actes de Henri II* (Paris, 1909–27) i, 121, 133, ii, 432.

[39] J. P. Bonnes, 'Un des plus grands prédicateurs du XIIe siècle: Geoffroy du Loroux, dit Geoffroy Babion', *Revue Bénédictine* lvi (1946) 174–215, Schneyer, 579 (index).

[40] Bonnes, op. cit., 202; P.L. clxxi, 792–6.

Could Becket have broken with tradition and looked forward to Hubert Walter, who served the crown first as justiciar and then as chancellor while he was archbishop, 1193–1205?[41] Walter drove tandem efficiently; loyalty to Richard I and John did not prevent him from keeping on good terms with the popes. Even so he drew the fire of righteous indignation from moralists. Hubert epitomized the type of prelate who had received his training at court instead of in the schools and who therefore entered on his office unprepared for the burden of pastoral care. Becket would have caused more scandal in 1162 than Hubert Walter did over thirty years later, if he had not mended his ways. 'The Voice of Paris' would have blamed him. We are still in the early summer of the reform movement. Becket also had to reckon with the irreproachable Gilbert Foliot. The bishop of London had studied and taught theology in the schools before becoming a monk at Cluny. He was a spiritual writer and director. Every qualification which was preached as desirable in a prelate marked him as the right successor to Theobald.

The new archbishop tried to meet both requirements. He made himself an honorary monk: he could lead the religious life in person. His theology had to be second-hand; but he could absorb its lessons and practise its precepts. A model needs adapting to the times. The holy page, as interpreted by Herbert of Bosham, held lessons which did not figure on the syllabus of monastic studies. Political theory, centred on the relationship between *regnum* and *sacerdotium*, came up for exposition, and Becket had chosen an 'ultra' for his master. Still, he might perhaps have compromised. The establishment ran on compromise, in practice, though not in academic theory. It was to the interest of all rulers to combine in defence of order so as to secure their revenues. But would Henry let him?

Henry wanted him to continue as chancellor. Canon law forbade bishops to hold secular office and the ban was renewed at the Lateran council of 1179. But Alexander III made exceptions to the rule. He allowed, even encouraged, Louis VII's chancellor, Hugh of Champfleury, to retain his office after his election to the bishopric of Soissons in 1159. The pope was hoping that Hugh would use his influence with Louis, who was planning to have talks with the emperor concerning the schism in 1162, the date of Alexander's letter

[41] C. R. Cheney, *Hubert Walter* (London, 1967).

to the bishop-chancellor. Henry and Becket must have known of the arrangement in France. It was unlikely that Alexander III would raise serious objections to a similar request for England, given the need to concililate Henry II. The empire opened up a prospect which appealed to Henry even more. Conrad III's chancellor had been archbishop of Mainz. Frederick I continued the practice: the archbishop of Mainz served him as arch-chancellor in Germany from 1153; he gave the archbishopric of Cologne to Rainald of Dassel, who held the same office for Italy.[42] Ralph of Diss, the dean of St Paul's,[43] tells us that Henry II had heard of this and that he liked the idea: an archbishop held the pastoral staff in his right hand; in his left was the imperial seal. His double office advanced both the welfare of the empire and the peace of the Church.[44] Ralph of Diss made a plausible guess, if he was guessing. Henry's close relations with the empire at the beginning of his reign may well have suggested imperial practice as a useful parallel. It would have frightened Becket. Rainald of Dassel acted as Frederick's publicist in chief and helped him to foster the schism. To say that Rainald stood for the Hubert Walter type of 'bad' or inadequate prelate would be putting it weakly: he looked more like an agent of antichrist. Faced by a choice of absolutes, Becket resigned the chancellorship.

That left him with both hands free to defend the liberties of the Church. The latest research on ecclesiastical history has proved that the Church in England was losing her liberties fast. The sharp divisions between the reigns of Henry I, Stephen and Henry II have broken down. It seems that the last years of Henry I's reign,

---

[42] *Ottonis et Rahewini Gesta Frederici imperatoris*, ed. G. Waitz (M.G.H., SS. in usum scholarium, Hanover, 1912) 90, 110, 176, 335. On Frederick's control over episcopal elections and *regalia* in Germany see R. L. Benson, *The Bishop-Elect. A Study in Medieval Ecclesiastical Office* (Princeton, 1968) 284–91.

[43] 'Diss' is the correct form of his name; see C. Duggan, *Twelfth-Century Decretal Collections* (London, 1963) 10–11.

[44] *Ymagines historiarum*, in *Opera historica*, ed. W. Stubbs (Rolls Series, 1876) i, 308: Audierat namque quod Maguntinus archiepiscopus in Theutonica sub rege, quod Coloniensis archiepiscopus in Italia sub imperatore, nomen sibi vendicent archicancellarii. Nec promiscuis actibus aestimant turbari rerum officia, si gestant in dextera baculum pastoralem, et ad expediendas regni vel imperii necessitates et pacem ecclesie procurandum propensius accinguntur, dummodo cancellarius curiae sinistro lateri sigillum allateret nunc regis, nunc imperatoris.

corresponding to the pontificate of William of Corbeil, 1123–36, brought the English Church into closer relations with Rome. The civil wars of Stephen's reign accelerated the change. But Stephen always struggled to keep control of the Church, and did so to some purpose after defeating Matilda: he had the name of 'tyrant' in John of Salisbury's circle. Henry II went straight on where his predecessor had left off, and he was more masterful. He did not wait for the death of Theobald, who had performed a heroic balancing act in trying to help his king and to obey the pope.[45] The schism of 1159 spotlighted the dangers of the situation. Henry II recognized Alexander III as the true pope, as his prelates wished, but he took his time.[46] Across the Channel Henry tightened his grip. He interfered in the election of a successor to Geoffrey Loroux at Bordeaux in 1158–9.[47] His policy towards the bishops and chapters of Anjou was 'masterful, if not violent,' and succeeded better as the years went by.[48] The bishops of Normandy generally supported their duke: Bayeux in particular performed signal services.[49] The case of Avranches is interesting: Henry refused to authorize the canonical election of Abbot Achard of St Victor to Sées in 1157, putting in his chaplain Froger instead; he allowed Achard to become bishop of Avranches in 1161. In spite of his Victorine background, Achard seems to have kept quiet during the Becket conflict.[50] Ducal control over Normandy was firm.

Becket deduced from observation that he could not serve two masters. He chose to serve God and changed his way of life to

[45] On royal control of ecclesiastical jurisdiction, finance, elections and recourse to Rome, see D. Bethel, op. cit.; Saltman, 37–9, 124; M. Howell, *Regalian Right in Medieval England* (London, 1962) 29–33; H. Mayr-Harting, op. cit. 214–24; *Letters of Arnulf of Lisieux*, lv, 21.

[46] See M. G. Cheney, 'The recognition of Pope Alexander III: some neglected evidence', E.H.R. lxxxiv (1969) 474–97.

[47] *Historia pontificum et comitum engolismensium*, ed. J. Boussard (Paris, 1957) 44–6.

[48] J. Boussard, *Le comté d'Anjou sous Henri Plantagênet* (B.E.H.E. cclxxi, 1938) 97–102.

[49] S. E. Gleason, *An Ecclesiastical Barony of the Middle Ages* (Cambridge, Mass., 1936) 26–38. For a general survey of Henry's control of the Church in his continental possessions see I. P. Shaw, 'The Ecclesiastical Policy of Henry II on the Continent, 1154–1189', *Church Quarterly Review* cli (1951) 137–55.

[50] J. Châtillon, *Théologie, spiritualité et métaphysique dans l'oeuvre oratoire d'Achard de Saint-Victor* (Paris, 1969) 87–111. Achard died 1170–1.

signify his break with his earthly lord. It was total commitment. He would defend the liberties of the Church, great or small, and the cause of Rome; he would rebuke Henry as John the Baptist rebuked King Herod. It infuriated Henry when his former crony spoke to him as a spiritual father. It dismayed former friends when the archbishop 'was not amused' by mealtime jokes against St Bernard.[51] The blast of Paris teaching drove him forward.

Herbert of Bosham describes how Becket surrounded himself with learned men to be his companions at the table of Holy Scripture; the list of Becket's *eruditi* corresponds to *the names of the valiant men of David* (II Reg. xxiii, 8).[52] Herbert saw Scripture as an armoury of weapons: it followed that what David's men were in arms, that Thomas's men would be in scriptural argument. Hostile propaganda supported Herbert's view of them. A friend of Becket's, Brother Nicholas of Rouen, wrote to tell him so in the winter of 1164:

> From the beginning of your primacy, your critics say, you have gathered to yourself not religious men, but noble scholars, whom they call by such unsavoury names that it is better not to repeat them.[53]

The *litteratos nobiles* is striking. Most scholars had middle-class origins, but Herbert dressed and looked like a noble;[54] he may have had imitators. It is true that Becket chose Robert prior of Merton as his private chaplain. Robert counted as a religious, since he was an Austin canon; but his Order encouraged study in the cloister and attracted scholars; Merton Priory was a centre of learning.[55]

---

[51] Walter Map, *De nugis curialium*, ed. M. R. James (Oxford, 1914) 38–9.
[52] *Mat.* iii, 207.
[53] ibid. v, 146.
[54] See above, p. 63.
[55] See J. C. Dickinson, *The Origins of the Austin Canons and their Introduction into England* (London, 1950) 116–18, 254; J. R. L. Highfield, *The Early Rolls of Merton College* (Oxford Historical Society, 1964) 9. A canon of Merton called 'Ricardus medicus' witnessed charters of Archbishop Theobald, 1157–61; see Saltman, 307–8. John of Salisbury's brother, Master Richard, became a canon of Merton, and he, like John, was a protégé of Peter of la Celle, who wrote his *De disciplina claustralium* at Richard's request; see *Letters* i, *passim*; J. Leclercq, *La spiritualité*, op. cit. 15–23; on Robert of Merton see Knowles, 75.

The Constitutions of Claredon set an acid test: would Becket follow the teaching of his *eruditi* in resisting an attack on ecclesiastical liberties or would he give way to Henry II? It is difficult to know just what Henry intended when he drew up the Constitutions. He always said that they gave a true account of the customs of his forebears, which could have meant almost anything. He certainly had no idea of separating England from the Roman Church. The Curia was too useful to a medieval king for him to contemplate such a step, even if it occurred to him. Popes could grant dispensations, privileges and other benefits. Henry II had already been obliged by Adrian IV in 1156; the pope released him from his oath, taken in 1151, to allow his younger brother Geoffrey to succeed to the county of Anjou, which would have cut off Normandy from his southern possessions in France. That is one example of what papal favour could do.[56] The same applied to papal control over bishops. A docile, co-operative episcopate, whose obedience the pope would reinforce, when and as the king asked him to, would have suited Henry. Clause 9 of the Constitutions forbade appeals to proceed further than the archbishop's court 'without the assent of the lord king'. In spite of its trenchancy, this clause must be seen in the light of a brilliant epigram on the purpose of prohibitions made by medieval governments: 'These ordinances merely introduced a licensing system which gave some measure of governmental control and brought in a considerable income.'[57] Clause 9 was deliberately provocative none the less. Henry threw out a challenge. Whatever might happen in practice, no orthodox churchman could agree in theory to a ban on recourse to Rome without royal permission. The same principle inhered in clause 4, which forbade 'archbishops, bishops and beneficed clergy of the realm to depart from the kingdom without the king's leave', and provided for their giving security on departure, if leave were granted.[58] The king would not normally refuse licence to visit the Curia, but he was putting travellers at the mercy of his policy or whim, and involving them in trouble and expense before ever they started.

[56] J. Boussard, *Le gouvernement d'Henri II Plantagénet* (Paris, 1956) 408.

[57] N. Denholm-Young, *Collected Papers on Medieval Subjects* (Oxford, 1946) 64–5.

[58] *English Historical Documents 1042–1189*, ed. D. C. Douglas and G. W. Greenaway (London, 1953) 720.

Clause 3 of the Constitutions, restricting clerical immunity, gave rise to most controversy, then as now:

> Clerks cited and accused of any matter shall, when summoned by the king's justice, come before the king's court to answer there concerning matters which shall seem to the king's court to be answerable there, and before the ecclesiastical court for what shall seem to be answerable there, but in such a way that the justice of the king shall send to the court of holy Church to see how the case is there tried. And if the clerk be convicted or shall confess, the Church ought no longer to protect him.

Henry was claiming that a clerk convicted of felony in a secular court should be brought before an ecclesiastical court, there to be punished by unfrocking; then he should be returned under guard to the secular court to be punished as a layman. Canon law did not allow ecclesiastical judges to inflict penalties which involved execution or mutilation. They imposed penances, imprisonment, pilgrimage or outlawry. The unfrocked clerk could no longer claim the protection of ecclesiastical courts for subsequent crimes.[59] Henry wanted to extend royal justice over him immediately, instead of letting him go free until he committed felony twice. Clause 3 belongs to my subject because modern historians have generally considered it in the context of canon law. They have asked whether Becket's objections to the clause had sufficient backing in Gratian's *Decretum* and in contemporary collections or comments on Gratian, or whether he went further than the claims which were currently made. Our sources make it difficult to decide what arguments were put forward at various stages of the discussion. Becket's biographers, writing after the event, would tend to draw up a dossier of the case for both sides irrespective of chronological order. Each one would choose the arguments that struck him as having the most cogency and authority. Canon law provided an arsenal of texts. William of Canterbury makes a long chain of canons to support Becket's rejection of the Constitutions, with special reference to clause 3;[60] Herbert and Fitzstephen both mention canon law, though in less detail.

---

[59] C. R. Cheney, 'The Punishment of Felonous Clerks', E.H.R. li (1936) 215 and n.

[60] *Mat.* i, 26–9.

It used to be thought that Becket and his advisers made a poor showing as canonists and that Henry had a better case for his demand that unfrocked clerks should be handed over to secular justice, since *traditio curiae* was conceded at canon law. Professor Duggan has reopened the question.[61] He defends Becket on the grounds that many canons forbade the subjection of clerks to secular justice without the consent of the Church. No judge might distrain or condemn clerks without the bishop's consent; no one might accuse a bishop or clerk before a secular magistrate. *Traditio curiae* had been contemplated, even favoured, but only in cases where the ecclesiastical authorities desired it for their own protection against a clerical offender. Professor Duggan admits that the canons were still confused and discordant in the mid-twelfth century: Henry had some minority support; his interpretation, though a more novel concept, was 'winning wider recognition at that time'. Becket's firmest and most famous objection to *traditio curiae* hinged on the text: *God will not judge twice for the same offence*, the Septuagint version of Nahum i, 9. Henry's demand would involve the infliction of double punishment on the unfrocked clerk, since he would suffer first degradation from his orders and secondly whatever penalty the secular judge might exact from him.[62] Curiously enough, the canonists never quoted this crucial text on *traditio curiae*. They applied it only to punishments inflicted within the Church. For instance, exclusion from communion ought not to be added to the penalty of degradation; otherwise the text would be flouted. It would be easy to infer that if double punishment for the same offence must be avoided by the ecclesiastical courts, much more should *traditio curiae* be forbidden. Perhaps Becket made the inference himself. If so, he took a bold step forward. Canon law offered no precedent for his use of the text against Henry.

He had a precedent elsewhere. Professor Duggan points to *Policraticus*:

But the material sword may not be wielded against a priest, even if he should tyrannise, for reverence to the sacrament (of his holy orders), unless perhaps, after being unfrocked, he should lay his blood-stained hands upon the Church of God. Even so, the

[61] 'The Becket Dispute and Criminous Clerks', *Bulletin of the Institute of Historical Research* xxxv (1962) 1–28.
[62] *Mat.* i, 28–9; ii, 388; iii, 281.

rule must always be observed that he does not suffer double punishment for the same offence.[63]

John of Salisbury brought together 'the long-established use of the scriptural maxim and the problem of criminous clerks'. But we have moved into a theological context. John cites no canon law authority to support his application of the scriptural maxim. Hugh of St Victor had defended privilege of clergy.[64] Canon law and theology were sister disciplines, whose teachers did not always see eye to eye.[65] Becket's theological advisers may have run ahead of the canonists on the subject of *traditio curiae*. Becket's use of the Nahum text had a background in the teaching of theology in the schools.

St Jerome handed down the LXX version of Nahum i, 9 in his standard commentary on the Twelve Prophets. His translation from the Hebrew became known as the Latin Vulgate; but the LXX continued to be venerated. Seventy translators were supposed to have reached the same result separately by divine inspiration when they translated the Hebrew into Greek. Medieval scholars used the LXX in a Latin translation where it struck them as preferable to St Jerome's:

> The Seventy translators put it more clearly, as though explaining, when they said: *God will not judge twice for the same offence*, where the Hebrew original has: *there shall not arise a double affliction*. And so the Seventy's version is customarily in all men's mouths.[66]

I quote from a commentary on the Twelve Prophets by Haimo of

---

[63] *Policr.* ii, 364: . . . in sacerdotem tamen, etsi tirannum induat, propter reuerentiam sacramenti gladium materialem exercere non licet, nisi forte, cum exauctoratus fuerit, in Ecclesiam Dei cruentam manum extendat; eo quidem perpetuo optinente ut ob eandem causam non consurgat in eum duplex tribulatio.

John quotes the Nahum text in the Vulgate, not the LXX version here.

[64] Above, p. 29.

[65] Y. Congar, 'Un témoignage des désaccords entre Canonistes et Théologiens', *Etudes d'histoire du droit canon dédiées à Gabriel Le Bras* ii (Paris, 1965) 861–84.

[66] P.L. cxvii, 170: Sane hoc quod in Hebraica veritate habetur, *Non consurget duplex tribulatio*, LXX apertius quasi exponentes dixerunt: *Non iudicabit Dominus bis in idipsum*, et sic usitatum versatur per ora omnium.

On medieval appreciation of the LXX version see B. Smalley, 'Ralph of Flaix on Leviticus', R.T.A.M. xxxv (1968) 55–6.

Auxerre, who was working about 840–55. It was much copied and reached the peak of its popularity in the eleventh and twelfth centuries.[67] Haimo tells us that the LXX version of the text had more currency than the Vulgate already in the mid ninth century. The allusion to double punishment made commentators reflect on the incidence of divine and human penalties. Does God sometimes punish his people for their sins in the present instead of in the life to come? Does an earthly judge usurp God's function when he sentences a man who will be punished in the hereafter? St Jerome raised and answered both questions.[68] The compiler of the *Gloss* on Nahum abridged him;[69] so the ban on double punishment already had a judicial application on the holy page, which included the *Gloss* as the school textbook on Scripture. Neither St Jerome nor the glossator considered the distinction between spiritual and secular jurisdiction; but it would occur to masters when the issue arose.

Theologians quoted the text on the question whether a felon condemned to death should be expected to make satisfaction to the Church by penance, although he was paying for his sin by his life. Ivo of Chartres, Peter Abelard and Robert Pullen discussed the problem. The Nahum text dictated the answer that the culprit need not make satisfaction to the Church; the temporal penalty would suffice, provided that he suffered patiently.[70] The same text reverberated through the schools in debates on 'the return of pardoned sins'. Suppose that the sinner after repentance and absolution 'returned to his vomit', as so often happened, would his relapse nullify the previous forgiveness, so as to make him still guilty of the sins committed previously? 'Whether sins, once forgiven, return afterwards' became a major topic of controversy. Hugh of St Victor

---

[67] R. Quadri, 'Aimone di Auxerre alla luce dei "Collectanea" di Heiric di Auxerre', *Italia medioevale e umanistica* vi (1963) 1–48.

[68] P.L. xxv, 1238.

[69] Gloss *ad loc.*: Scitote ideo pro peccatis punisse (Deus) ne in aeternum puniret, quia *non iudicabit Deus bis in idipsum*. Qui ergo puniti sunt sufficienter, post(ea) non punientur, alioqui(n) mentitur scriptura, quod nefas est dicere. Si fidelis in adulterio deprehensus decolletur, videtur non amplius puniendus, ne bis in idipsum iudicetur. Sed sciendum Deum sicut omnium rerum, ita suppliciorum quoque scire mensuram, nec praevenire sententiam iudicis, nec illi in peccatorem exercendae de hinc poenae auferri potestatem, et magnum peccatum diuturnis cruciatibus, sed levem culpam (levi) compensari supplicio.

[70] P. Anciaux, *La Théologie du Sacrement de Pénitence au XIIe siècle* (Louvain, 1949) 294.

upheld the opinion that they did return. The majority of Paris theologians shared his view. Peter Lombard would not commit himself in his *Sentences*, but agreed with Hugh of St Victor in his oral teaching. However, Abelard and some who were influenced by him denied the reviviscence of sins.[71] His followers included Roland Bandinelli, later Pope Alexander III, who refuted the doctrine in his *Sentences*, 1149–50.[72] *Non iudicabit Deus bis in idipsum* figured in the arguments. Those who taught the return of pardoned sins had to find a way round it. The contrary thesis eventually won through. It was bound to win in the long run, as the theology of penance became better established. The reviviscence of pardoned sins cast a slur on God's mercy and worked as a disincentive to recourse to the sacrament of penance. It may be noted that Gratian considered the question in his *Decretum*, but without quoting the Nahum text, so popular among theologians.[73]

Becket's theologians must have been aware of this controversy. If the text were used to argue against the return of pardoned sins *in foro interno*, as a matter between the penitent and his confessor, then it might be applied *in foro externo* too. Why should a clerk be judged in two courts and suffer double punishment for the same offence? It might be objected that Herbert of Bosham, as a pupil of Peter Lombard, would have inclined to the Lombardian and Victorine view. But his respect for the Lombard did not prevent Herbert from criticizing or differing from him on occasion.[74] Alexander III's rejection of the opinion would have carried weight. Privilege of clergy would call for the transfer of a text from scholastic debate to actual problems.

It is just as likely, therefore, that Becket drew his text from a

[71] A. M. Landgraf, *Dogmengeschichte der Frühscholastik* iv, 1 (Regensburg, 1955), 193–270; D. E. Luscombe, *The School of Peter Abelard* (Cambridge, 1969) 204, 219–21.

[72] ed. A. M. Gietl (Freiburg-im-Breisgau, 1891) 250: Item si Deus dimittit peccatum, et illud punitum, . . . si punitum est, amplius ergo non redit, qui si rediret, et iterum puniri debet. Sic ergo Deus bis aliquem puniret et pro eodem peccato, quod absonum est, praesertim cum dicat propheta: *non iudicabit Deus bis in idipsum.*
On the date of Master Roland's *Sentences* see Pacaut, 62–5.

[73] *Decretum* pars II, causa xxxiii, dist. 4; and see Luscombe op. cit. 221.

[74] B. Smalley, 'A Commentary on the *Hebraica* etc.', op. cit. 41. Herbert also differs from the Lombard in his discussion of the *De homine assumpto* problem in *Liber melorum*.

theological as from a canon law context. Subsequently he found his warmest defender on the issue of criminous clerks in the Paris theologian Peter the Chanter.[75] According to Edward Grim, a good witness, the archbishop set his objection to clause 3 of the Constitutions in a purely biblical framework. King Solomon deposed the priest Abiathar on account of his disobedience, but inflicted one penalty only; he exiled Abiathar, but did not mutilate him. Solomon's respect for Abiathar's priesthood had loomed large in Gregorian polemic. Now it served as ammunition against clause 3; Grim goes on to quote the Nahum text:

Hence it seems unfitting that mere man should exact a twofold vengeance for one single fault, when God, judge of all men, as it is written, judges no one twice for the same offence.[76]

According to Herbert, Becket did not think of the text as an objection until he saw the clause in writing for the first ime.[77] It is missing from the arguments which Herbert puts into Becket's mouth at the preceding council at Westminster. When he turned to the study of canon law at Pontigny, he may have felt that he had relied on theologians too heavily.

We find the same preference if we turn to the umbrella type of argument against the Constitutions. Fitzstephen puts forward the canon-law ruling that custom, however ancient and well attested, must give way to the teachings of reason and revelation. God orders us to keep his laws and threatens those who make bad ones; Christ never said: 'I am custom', but *I am the truth* (Io., xiv, 6).[78] Other-

---

[75] Baldwin, *Masters*, i, 145-7.

[76] *Mat.* ii, 388: . . . Indignum proinde videtur ut pro simplici commisso duplicem homo exigat ultionem, quum iudex omnium Dominus neminem, ut scriptum est, bis iudicet in idipsum.

Wenric of Trèves brought up Solomon's punishment of Abiathar and Manegold of Lautenbach replied to him; M.G.H. *Lib. de lit*, i, 289, 409.

[77] *Mat.* iii, 281.

[78] ibid. 47-8: . . . ne de antiquitate et usu potius quam de iure niteretur, rex, in illis spuriis statutis firmandis, attendere debuisset quia Dominus dicit *Leges meas custodite*. Item illud: *Vae qui condunt leges iniquas*. Item nusquam invenitur Dominus dixisse "Ego sum consuetudo"; sed dixit *Ego sum veritas*. Item, consuetudinis ususve longaevi non tanta est auctoritas aut ratio. . . . Immo revelatione facta aequitatis et veritatis, cedat usus rationi. . . .

On this argument see Duggan, op. cit. For its origin see G. B. Ladner, 'Two Gregorian Letters', S.G. v (1956) 225-35.

wise, if we believe Herbert, Becket's arguments at Westminster derived from theology.[79] First comes the theory of the two swords in its classic High-church form. Becket or Herbert for him uses the doctrine of *Policraticus* to defend privilege of clergy. There are two kings, Christ, king of heaven, and the kings of the earth, two laws, divine and human, two modes of enforcing them, spiritual and corporal, according to the text: *Behold, here are two swords. It is enough*, said the Lord (Lk. xxii, 38). The clergy, therefore, form a separate and peculiar people, directly subject to Christ their king.[80] They stand above earthly kings, who receive both the belt of knighthood and the sword of material power from them. Becket adds later that the two powers should co-operate, since the clergy may not participate in bloodshed: they wield 'the sword of the word'.[81] But he withdraws the power to enforce law on the clergy from the secular judge, on the ground of their superiority over all laymen in spiritual matters. His claim goes back to Gregory VII's case against Henry IV: a priest has power to bind and loose the soul; how much greater is this power than any which belongs to earthly rulers?[82] It follows for Becket that the dignity of their orders should protect clergy from the degradation of secular punishment. Clerical offenders can be sentenced only according to their own law. The practice of branding defaces God's image in man (Gen. i, 26). It insults the clergy in particular and is forbidden even by civil law as applied to laymen.[83] Henry had objected that penalties inflicted in the church

---

[79] *Mat.* iii, 268–72.

[80] ibid. 268. The concept of 'Christ the King' was well established; see J. Leclercq, *L'idée de la royauté du Christ au moyen âge* (Paris, 1959). There is an echo of Hugh of St Victor's *De sacramentis* I, viii, 11 and II, ii, 4, P.L. clxxvi, 312, 417–18, in Becket's argument.

[81] *Mat.* iii, 271.

[82] *Registrum*, ed. E. Caspar, M.G.H. Epistolae selectae II (1920) 448, 553, 556–7.

[83] *Mat.* iii, 269 . . . Adeo etiam quod ordinis privilegium excludat cauterium; quam tamen poenam communiter inter homines etiam ius forense damnat, ne videlicet in homine Dei imago deformetur.

Becket alludes to *Codex* IX, xlvii, 17, ed. P. Krueger (Berlin, 1954) 391: Si quis in metallum fuerit pro criminum deprehensorum qualitate damnatus, minime in eius facie scribatur . . . quo facies, quae ad similitudinem pulchritudinis caelestis est figurata, minime maculetur.

He may have been told of Justinian's prohibition through some intermediate source, and perhaps did not know that it referred to convicts sent to forced labour in mines or quarries.

courts were too light to act as deterrents. He also contested their right to impose exile: that right belonged to Caesar, who ruled over the land, not to the ecclesiastical authorities, who could only excommunicate and suspend from the altar.[84] Becket answered that the church courts did in fact discipline offenders by exile or imprisonment, and had the right to exercise discipline by these means. Finally, he claimed that if a clerical offender happened to escape due punishment, he should be left to the judgement of God. The status of clergy could hardly have been rated higher. He drew the logical consequence later, when he cried out that clause 3 meant a second judgement of Christ before Pilate:[85] clergy represented the person of their king in heaven.

The cogency of Becket's proof texts depends on their scholastic setting: take one of his arguments from the psalms:

> For the men of our service (the clergy), although 'weak, despised' and unwarlike, *shall bind the kings* 'of the nations' *with fetters and the nobles* 'of the earth' *with manacles of iron*, as a great king and prophet foretold of them.[86]

Herbert alludes to the *Great Gloss* on Ps. cxlix, 8 by his master, Peter Lombard, and applies it to the dispute. The subject of David's prophecy was *the children of Sion* (v.2). *Sion* stood for the church in medieval exegesis, and her *children* could stand for priests. According to the *Great Gloss*, they rejoice *in their king*,

> that is Christ, who is king and priest. *Two-edged swords* (v. 6), that is Christ's word, sharpened on the Old and New Testaments, *shall be in their hands*, that is in their power. . . . *With fetters*, that is God's precepts . . . *with manacles of iron*, that is God's commands, which are called *of iron* because they are hard and they cannot be loosened. *The kings* of the nations *and the nobles* of the earth shall be bound by the weak and despised of this

---

[84] *Mat.* iii, 267.

[85] ibid. 281.

[86] ibid. 268: Isti enim, etsi in saeculo 'infirmi, contemptibiles,' et imbelles nostri officii viri, tamen, iuxta quod de ipsis praenuntiavit rex quidam magnus et propheta, *alligant reges* 'gentium' *in compedibus et nobiles* 'saeculi' *in manicis ferris.*

I have put the verbal quotations from the *Great Gloss* in inverted commas.

world, whom the Lord has chosen that he may confound the strong.[87]

The prophecy plus its glosses plus Herbert exalts the power of the clergy over secular rulers. It strikes all the better at Henry in that David was a king as well as a prophet.

The archbishop could have quoted a verse of the Psalter from memory, untrained as he was; it is doubtful whether he could have quoted glosses with it. Herbert must have expanded the argument.[88] However, the gist of his narrative rings true, because he records two blunders on Becket's part. Firstly, some of his arguments in defence of clerical privilege were irrelevant, in that Henry did not claim jurisdiction over felonious clerks until after they had been degraded and lost their status. Hence the importance of the Nahum text, forbidding double punishment, which Becket did not advance until a later stage; he should have thought of it sooner. Secondly, Henry floored him by pointing to the Old Testament: the levites, Henry said, were subject to the corporal penalties of the Law of Moses like everyone else.[89] Ecclesiastical theorists made much of the dignity and privileges of the Old Testament priesthood, but Becket could not deny that the sons of Levi had no exemption from punishment. He answered weakly that he would say nothing about that for the present; Henry's advisers had scored a point. Becket took refuge in the New Testament for his authority:

> *The old things are passed away. Behold all things are made new* (II Cor. v, 17). We have a new king, a new law, a new flock, new sacraments, new sacrifices, new works and new duties, and thus new penalties and new modes of enforcement.[90]

[87] P.L. cxci, 1287-9: exsultent in rege suo, id est in Christo, qui est rex et sacerdos. ... *Et gladii ... ancipites,* vel bis acuti, ... id est sermo Christi, qui acutus est Veteri et Novo Testamento, *erunt in manibus,* id est in potestate eorum ... *compedibus,* id est praeceptis Dei ... *ferreis,* id est Dei mandatis, quae dicuntur vincula ferrea, quia dura sunt et insolubilia. ... His vinculis ligantur gentium reges et nobiles saecula ab infirmis et contemptibilibus huius mindi, quos elegit Dominus ut fortia confunderet.

[88] He claims to have heard the argument and to give the gist of it in his writing, though he does not vouch for the actual words: ... etsi non eadem verba hinc inde dicta, hinc inde tamen dictorum virtus et materia haec quae hic scripsi; *Mat.* iii, 272.

[89] ibid. 267.

[90] ibid. 272.

K

A master of the holy page would resort to allegory, when the literal sense of the Old Testament went against him. Becket could not be expected to have allegories at his fingertips: he gave up on the levites.

He made a readier use of Scripture when he saw the written Constitutions at Clarendon. Perhaps Herbert had coached him in the meantime. The text from the Psalmist with all its implications did duty again on clause 7, which forbade the excommunication of tenants-in-chief and officers of the crown without royal consent. *They shall bind ... the nobles with manacles of iron* had more point in this meeting. Becket reinforced it by stressing the power of the priest to bind and loose and to judge *between leprosy and leprosy* (Deut. xvii, 8).[91] The duty of the Old Testament priests to distinguish between various kinds of leprosy and to judge what precautions should be taken in each case had become a standard precedent and figure of penance under the New Law.[92] Lecturers on Scripture and writers of theological treatises used the word *leprosy* almost interchangeably with sin. A secular ruler had no business to interfere, though he was expected to enforce the ecclesiastical sentence. Clause 12 ordered that elections to vacant bishoprics and abbeys should take place in the royal chapel (so that royal influence might be brought to bear on the electors). Becket objected that the practice originated in tryannical usurpation rather than lawful institution, even if it had been known in England in former times.

He added arguments from various figures of elections, which we learn from ecclesiastical histories, following on the pages of both Testaments.

Secular princes never interfered in elections in the early Church. Changes have come with time. Hence the Church has now made rules for elections other than those which the early Church observed. These cannot safely be altered without the Church's authority. Here he appeals to 'the expanding Bible'.[93] Sacred history continues

[91] ibid. 282–3.

[92] Peter Lombard. *Sent.* IV, xviii, 6 (ed. Quaracchi, 1916) 863: Et in remittendis vel retinendis culpis id iuris et officii habent evangelici sacerdotes, quod olim sub Lege habebant legales in curandis leprosis. Hi ergo peccata dimittunt vel retinent, dum dimissa a Deo vel retenta iudicant et ostendunt. Ponunt enim sacerdotes *nomen Dei super filios Israel, sed ipse benedicit,* ut legitur in Numeris (vi, 27).
Many other examples could be cited.

[93] *Mat.* iii, 282–3.

unbroken from the Old and New Testaments to later periods. It includes canon law, because the canons make necessary adjustment possible, as Hugh of St Victor taught.[94] Becket's spirited protest against royal control of elections contrasts with his 'slightly passive resistance' to Henry's claim to draw the revenues of vacant sees and abbeys, put forward in the same clause. The claim should always be contested and thwarted and resisted as much as possible; it should never be agreed to, even if what cannot be corrected has to be borne. No authorities *contra* are quoted.[95] Becket had held vacant sees and abbacies in custody as chancellor. That may have embarrassed him, especially as Henry demanded an account of the income he had received from them. Another reason may be that definition of ecclesiastical rights during a vacancy belonged to canon-law territory.[96] Again, he seems to have been at a loss when his defence of the Church called for quotation of specific texts at canon law. Scripture could have supplied only general denunciations of wicked princes who oppressed the Church on the technical question of rights *sede vacante*; they would not have helped in this case. Still, he had Paris theology to back him on essentials.

It is puzzling that Becket should have drawn back and subscribed to the Constitutions, when he was so well briefed. Herbert traced his weakness to his curial training: a qualified theologian or religious would not have buckled under, as the ex-chancellor did.[97] Perhaps he realized for the first time the consequences that his stand on extremist doctrine would bring. He now gauged the full force of Henry's wrath on the one hand and the limits of his colleagues' backing on the other. It is by no means certain that the English bishops would have stayed firmly on his side, if he had not broken rank by giving way to Henry.[98] He made a moral and tactical error from his own point of view. Recognition of it added to his obstinacy afterwards.

---

[94] *Didascalicon* IV, ii, ed. C. H. Buttimer (Washington, 1937) 72: In tertio ordine (Novi Testamenti) primum locum habent Decretalia, quos canones, id est regulares appellamus, deinde sanctorum patrum et doctorum ecclesiae scripta.

Hugh assumes that Scripture requires later writings to complete it.

[95] *Mat.* iii, 283-4.

[96] M. Howell, op. cit. 32-4.

[97] *Mat.* iii, 289-90.

[98] See R. W. Southern, reviewing *Episcopal Colleagues*, E.H.R. lxvii (1952) 87-90.

Proceedings at Clarendon and Northampton reopened the question of relations between England and the Curia. Becket followed the logic of his argument on privilege of clergy. To quote Fitzstephen's comment:

> The archbishop is subject to the judgment of the pope alone; the pope to that of God alone.[99]

The clergy served Christ in heaven; the pope was Christ's vicar on earth. The change in the papal title from 'Vicar of St Peter' to 'Vicar of Christ', which took place in the second half of the twelfth century, reflects a change in both theory and practice at Rome. An earlier generation had used the title 'Vicar of Christ' for any prelate, instead of reserving it for the pope.[1] Now the Curia had more business on hand, as litigants and petitioners applied to it in greater numbers. Centralization and bureaucrcy increased. The pope needed a title to express his new function:

> Interpreted in the spirit of the new scholasticism it made a precise claim to universal sovereignty. The new formula showed that the popes no longer looked backwards, and were no longer primarily concerned to preserve an ancient tradition as the trustees of St Peter on earth. They were the deputies of Christ in all the fullness of his power.[2]

English churchmen were among the first to recognize the pope's dynamic role by calling him 'Vicar of Christ'. Gilbert Foliot used the title in a letter concerning an appeal to Rome 1154-7.[3] Mgr. Maccarrone has noted three instances where John of Salisbury and Becket addressed or referred to Alexander III as 'Vicar of Christ'.[4] The number can be enlarged in writings emanating from the Becket circle. John of Salisbury used the title in one other letter at least. It

---

[99] *Mat.* iii, 60.

[1] M. Maccarrone, *Vicarius Christi, storia del titolo papale* (Rome, 1952). On the earlier use, see Robert Pullen, P.L. clxxxvi, 950: Provideat ergo (praelatus) saluti animarum; nec corporalem negligat administrationem vicarius Christi.

Pullen is describing the duties of all prelates of the Church. Fitzstephen still gives the title to Becket as archbishop, *Mat.* iii, 60.

[2] R. W. Southern, *Western Society and the Church in the Middle Ages* (Pelican History of the Church ii, 1970) 105.

[3] G.F.L.C. 167.

[4] op. cit. 101, 103.

occurs frequently in Herbert's letters and in his *Life* of St Thomas.[5]
Herbert used it to shame the pope into supporting Becket:

> You are Christ's vicar. Let your actions prove it. . . . I beseech
> you, O Vicar of Christ, . . . conceal no longer the wrong done
> to Christ.[6]

The title highlighted the superiority of *sacerdotium* over *regnum*.

Becket drew both his inspiration and his arguments from the
schools. The story of his relations with the Curia belongs to the
next chapter. He provoked Henry at Northampton, appealed to
Rome and then escaped to France. Once he had bolted there was no
stopping him. It remains to be said that he returned to the place of
his martyrdom loaded with books. Fitzstephen adds, after telling us
that Becket was less learned than his colleagues in Theobald's household, that he became 'the most learned afterwards'.[7] He left his
library to Christchurch; Prior Henry Eastry listed the *libri Sancti
Thomae* in his catalogue of the cathedral library, drawn up in the
early fourteenth century. Some of the items have been identified; the
surviving manuscripts would make an interesting study as a group.[8]
The list bears out Fitzstephen's statement in showing that Becket
was methodical and discriminating as a book collector.

His method appears in the range of aids to study. The catalogue
begins with the Bible itself and nearly all the books of the Bible
glossed, plus the *Great Gloss* of Peter Lombard on the psalms and
the Pauline epistles. The few gaps were filled by an abridgement of
the Old Testament and Raban Maur's standard commentary on
Ecclesiasticus. Peter Lombard's *Sentences* provided doctrinal theology. The *De officiis* of St Isidore of Seville was to hand as a complete, though elementary, dictionary for the use of clergy. He had
collected the standard texts on civil and canon law and a comprehensive set of books on Latin grammar and composition, including
Martianus Capella's classic on the *Artes*. In patristics he was selective. There are eleven titles for St Ambrose. St Gregory is represented by his *Homilies* (on Ezechiel or the Gospels or perhaps on
both) and by the newest and largest set of extracts from Gregory,

---

[5] *Mat.* vi, 426 for John of Salisbury; iii, 348–9, v, 290, vi, 38–40, vii, 533
for Herbert and other secretaries.
[6] ibid. vi, 39.
[7] ibid. iii, 16.
[8] *Ancient Libraries*, 82–5; *Medieval Libraries*, 29–40.

made by Garnier of St Victor.[9] Becket had the letters of St Cyprian, a favourite book, and the *Liber apologeticus* of St Gregory of Nazianzas in translation.[10] St Jerome and St Augustine are conspicuous by their absence. Becket may have felt that the former was too erudite and the latter too deep for him. In any case, the glossators drew largely on Jerome and Augustine, but neglected Ambrose. The Ambrosiana in the list may have been intended to supplement the *Gloss*. Becket also had a strong preference for pastoral theology, which St Ambrose suited. It comes out in the long list of sermons and aids to preaching. Many of them are anonymous and cannot be identified by their incipits; but he had one by the much-copied St Peter of Ravenna and the sermons of the Cistercian abbot, Guerric of Igny (1138–57). Guerric was a mystic and a stylist like St Bernard, though less exalted.[11] The *De moribus ecclesiae* by Odo of Morimond, who died about 1161, another Cistercian, would have served as an aid to preaching.[12] So would the *Mariale*, a set of homilies or a treatise on St Mary; too many books were called *De laudibus Sanctae Mariae* to make Becket's identifiable. There are only two works by St Bernard: *De consideratione*, addressed to Pope Eugenius III, and *De amore Dei* (probably the *De dilectione Dei*). From St Victor, in addition to the *Gregorianum*, came two copies of Hugh of St Victor's standard commentary on Ecclesiastes, one of his treatises on the Noah's Ark and part of his *Didascalicon*, also Richard of St Victor's *De statu interioris hominis post lapsum*.[13] These are mainly religious and devotional works. Becket had acquired a world chronicle and a geography of the Holy Land. John of Salisbury's *Metalogicon* and *Policraticus* were probably presentation copies. Their author would have advised him on the Latin classical section. Becket had a fine collection of texts, including Livy, a rare author at the time. A copy of Cassiodorus' *Varia* brought it up to late antiquity.[14]

[9] *Rep. bibl.*, no. 2365.
[10] No. 2 of his *Discourses*; they were quite common in Rufinus' translation.
[11] See the introduction by J. Morson and H. Costello, *Guerric d'Igny: Sermons* i (Sources chrétiennes 166, Série des textes monastiques d'Occident, xxxi, Paris, 1970).
[12] J. Leclercq, 'A la découvert d'Odon de Morimond', *Collectanea Ordinis Cistercensium Reformatorum* xxiii (1961) 307–13; L. Grill, 'Odo Morimundensis', ibid. 314–53.
[13] P.L. cxcvi, 1117, listed here by its incipit *Omne capud languidum*.
[14] It goes under a current title *Epistolae regis Atheniensium*.

The archbishop had equipped himself with all the sacred and profane learning needed to carry out his duties, on a generous interpretation of the latter. He was more interested in the Bible and its glosses and commentaries than in theology proper; that may betray Herbert's influence. He specialized in works suitable for devotional reading and aids to preaching. He preached as archbishop. Herbert records a sermon to ordinands, preached in 1162. We have some general references to his preaching subsequently, as well as to the sermon he gave at Canterbury on his return from exile.[15] His library witnesses to efficiency and a taste for the best. It was very like him.

[15] *Mat.* i, 10, iii, 38, 238–41.

VI
Alexander III

Roland Bandinelli was an intellectual in politics. He came of a Siennese family and studied probably at Bologna, perhaps at Paris. He certainly taught both theology and canon law at Bologna, making a serious contribution to both subjects in his *Sentences* and in his *Summa* on the *Decretum*.[1] His official biographer Boso writes that he was eloquent and learned in sacred and profane letters and of tried experience in very subtle interpretation of their senses. He spoke with polished fluency as a man of learning. Boso's 'very subtle' strikes the keynote of Alexander's mentality, though it is a conventional phrase.[2] M. Pacaut in his sensitive study of Alexander suggests that the intellectual gave way to the politician, when the former professor became cardinal, papal chancellor and finally pope. It depends on one's definition of 'intellectual'. If it refers to a man who directs all his policies to the realization of an idea, who subordinates them to this one aim and who finds a theory to justify himself, then Alexander was an intellectual quite as much as a politician. We must follow the story of his practice and then of his theory to see how they were co-ordinated. What looks like the guile of a politician in desperate straits involved the development of a consistent theory. He used the second in order to justify the first.

His personality eludes us because he hid it behind his chancery *dictamen*. The language of papal letters, however formal, generally

---

[1] Pacaut, 52–62. On Master Roland as a theologian see D. E. Luscombe, *The School of Peter Abelard* (Cambridge, 1969) 15–17, 244–53.

[2] Pacaut points out (108) that Boso modelled his praise of Alexander on the *Life* of Leo II, but his words make it clear that he wrote with Alexander's personal gifts in mind. I have underlined the words taken from his source: *Erat enim vir eloquentissimus, in divinis atque humanis Scripturis sufficienter instructus et in earum sensibus* subtilissime exercitatione probatus (for 'subtilis et limatus'); vir quoque scholasticus et eloquentia polita facundus.

See *Liber pontificalis*, ed. L. Duchesne i (Paris, 1886) 359, ii (Paris, 1892) 377.

took some colour from the character of the reigning pope. Alexander's on the contrary are as colourless as they are correct. He put no warmth even into his letter to the English hermit Godric, sending his blessing and asking for the holy man's prayers.[3] He was reserved and cautious, as he had to be, given his disputed election and the schism. The strain never broke his sense of dignity. He is said to have reproved his cardinals for their open joy at the news of his rival's death.[4] The reproach was both decorous and politic, if he hoped for negotiations with the emperor.

It is natural to compare Alexander with Innocent III, who was a canonist and theologian too. Both were 'politely fluent in the Roman way', to quote the *Draco* on Alexander. But their politeness differed. Innocent had a way with petitioners: he could make them feel welcome and appreciated. Gerald of Wales describes how Innocent walked and chatted with him and how he kept Gerald's book by his bedside.[5] Less famous, but just as revealing, is the chronicle of a monk of Ardres from the Pas-de-Calais area, who visited the Curia on business of his abbey. He managed to push into the papal bedchamber, where Innocent was just finishing his siesta, in order to buttonhole him. If the pope felt cross, he did not show it, but promised his favour 'as far as right would allow' and added a personal reminiscence. He had once put up at the abbey in his student days, when he was making a pilgrimage from Paris to the shrine of St Thomas at Canterbury; he found the abbey in good order under the rule of a venerable old man, as far as he could judge.[6] Neither Gerald nor the monk of Ardres prospered in his lawsuit in consequence of the pope's kind words; but at least they had met with charming and tactful courtesy. A newly discovered

---

[3] W. Holtzmann, *Papsturkunden in England* (Abhandl. der Akad. der Wissensch. Göttingen, phil. hist. Klasse clxiii, 1952) 303. This letter was written *c.* 1168–9.

[4] *Mat.* v, 90–1.

[5] *De iure et statu Menevensis ecclesiae, Opera,* ed. J. S. Brewer (Rolls Series) iii, 176, 252–3, 336. Gerald ascribes a wisecrack on bishops' nepotism to Alexander III, *Gemma ecclesiastica,* ibid. iii, 304. It is unlikely to be authentic, since it comes into a collection of *exempla,* which were often attached to famous names.

[6] M.G.H., SS. xxiv, 737–8. The chronicle was written after 1226 (see 684) and places the visit in 1207. Quoted by M. Maccarrone, 'Innocenzo III prima del pontificato', *Archivio della R. deputazione romana di storia patria* lxvi (1943) 59–64.

eye-witness account of the Fourth Lateran Council records an instance of his 'highly personal and unceremonious manner of speech'; he joked and kept his temper when interrupted: 'You hear me now, and I'll hear you later.'[7] We have no such intimate glimpses of Alexander III. His path was rougher than Innocent's. A more human, relaxed attitude might have made it a little smoother.

Alexander's leading idea was the liberty of the Church, which he identified with the liberty of the Roman Church.[8] To uphold it he had to end the schism and to reinstate himself in Rome. The liberties of Canterbury and of other churches must take their places in the queue. Haller judged him as 'no fighter by nature'.[9] Perhaps not, but necessity made him a fighter on the home front. The Siennese formed quite another impression of him as promoter of the Lombard League, defender of the communes against imperial attack, and their fellow countryman too. The head of a Siennese embassy to the newly elected Pope Urban IV reported that no pope had been more energetic in word and deed or less influenced by those around him 'since Alexander III'. The report makes no mention of Innocent III, Gregory IX or Innocent IV.[10] Such was Alexander's reputation in Siena at least. The end of the schism and Frederick's submission in 1177 did not free his hands. Paradoxically, he had his work cut out to undo the effects of his alliance with the communes. He bent all his energies to prepare for the Lateran Council of 1179. It legislated for the whole of Christendom, but its main target was the anticlericalism of the communes and their protection of heretics: 'It was not the spectre of Becket which haunted the Council, but the living, present problem of the Italian cities.'[11] Alexander could still see no way to pursue any advantage that Becket's murder had given him in dealing with Henry II. Faced with less pressing problems, he acted on the proverb 'what can't be cured must be endured'.

His debt to the Paris schools put him in a false position from the start. Haller has pointed to the role of Paris masters, whether regent

---

[7] S. Kuttner and A. García y García, 'A New Eyewitness Account of the Fourth Lateran Council', *Traditio* xx (1964) 126, 128, 151, 158–9.

[8] Pacaut, 130–1.

[9] Haller, op. cit. 152–4.

[10] E. Jordan, *Les origines de la domination Angevine en Italie* (Paris, 1909) 296.

[11] G. de Vergottini, *Studi sulla legislazione imperiale di Federico II in Italia* (Milan, 1952) 8–12.

or retired, in supporting the Roman pope against the imperialist.[12] John of Salisbury and Arnulf of Lisieux illustrate the energy of Anglo-Norman intellectuals in making propaganda for Alexander. The clergy of England and of northern France backed him almost to a man. The brothers Archbishop William of Sens and the bishop of Auxerre received him at Sens before his election had been fully confirmed, as even kings and princes feared to do, according to the author of the *Gesta* of the bishops of Auxerre.[13] The core of opposition to his rival in the imperialist camp depended on former schoolmen. Conrad of Wittelsbach, archbishop of Mainz, had studied at Salzburg and Bologna. He lost his see on going over to Alexander's side, and stayed with the Roman pope or travelled on his service as cardinal until the end of the schism.[14] Becket wrote to Conrad as 'his dear friend and other self', a powerful ally at the Curia.[15] A common fate united the two exiled archbishops. Salzburg, where Conrad began his studies, was the chief centre of resistance to Frederick's ecclesiastical policy in Germany. Here, among the small fry, we find a Master Peter of Vienna, who had studied in France and was a disciple of Gilbert of la Porrée. He held the post of *scholasticus* at Vienna, but lost it because he recognized Alexander as pope.[16] Master Peter makes another link between the Roman pope and the Paris schools in the fight against the schismatics.

[12] op. cit. 145–7.

[13] ed. L.–M. Duru (Bibliothèque historique de l'Yonne i, Paris, 1850) 421: Huius consilio et providentia, universali ecclesia fere fluctuante et schismate seviente, prenominatus archiepiscopus frater eius, immo ipse recepit et Senonis addixit beate recordationis Alexandrum papam tertium, nondum plene confirmatum, quod etiam reges et principes facere formidabant; in qua receptione, et quamdiu apud eos morata est curia, quam laudabiliter se utrimque habuit non est facile dictu.

The passage comes in a notice of a bishop of Auxerre who was brother to Archbishop William of Sens (1167–81). On the *Gesta episcoporum Autissiodorensium* see R.–H. Bautier, 'L'historiographie de la France de l'Ouest aux Xe et XIe siècles', *La storiographia altomedievale* (Settimane di studio del Centro Italiano di studi sull 'alto medioevo XVII) ii (Spoleto, 1970) 811–12.

[14] Ganzer, op. cit. 104–14. Conrad was a fellow pupil of Peter of Blois at Bologna; see ep. cxliii, P.L. ccvii, 429, quoted by Southern, 108.

[15] *Mat.* v, 389; vi, 51, 162, 211, 471.

[16] For the latest studies on him see P. Classen, *Gerhoch von Reichersberg* (Wiesbaden, 1960) 162–3.

The support of scholars cut two ways. It helped Alexander to win recognition. On the other hand, his supporters looked to him to defend ecclesiastical liberties against secular princes, wherever they threatened the Church's interests. Frederick was the worst culprit, being a schismatic; but there were local tyrants, hardly better than Frederick or Henry II. The Becket conflict and the schism have stolen the limelight from many good causes, whose champions bombarded Alexander with demands and exhortations. A letter from Peter of la Celle sets the tone. A secular lord is oppressing a monastery in Abbot Peter's charge. The pope has the means to free it, if only he will exert himself:

> The whole of God's Church, venerable Father, has recourse to St Peter's see and yours in grave questions, just as recourse was had to Moses in ancient times. The common care of all churches now devolves on *you*, since it was said to Peter, separately and in particular, so it seems: *And thou, being once converted, confirm thy brethren* (Lc. xxii, 31). . . . . Say the word, St Peter, and your Church shall be healed. . . . Catch that fox which is destroying our vineyard.[17]

Abbot Peter felt entitled to lecture the pope on the corruption of his Curia, just as St Bernard had lectured Eugenius III.[18] Peter's letter to Alexander urging stronger action in favour of Becket[19] was but one of many cries for help. His office obliged Alexander to put up a show of curing the evils brought to his notice. He pretended to bear them with sorrowful patience, when the cure failed. It did not pacify the clamourers; but he could at least make use of unwelcome pressures, as when he wrote to Henry in May 1169:

> . . . we grieve and sorrow when many great men and almost the whole Church raise frequent complaint at our lukewarmness and our neglect of our duty. We know that many men blame us for letting our patience be abused.[20]

If he could not take action against Henry, he could threaten that he was being forced into action by public opinion.

[17] P.L. ccii, 405–6, 526.
[18] ibid. 529–30, written in answer to a summons to attend the Council of 1179.
[19] ibid. 532.   [20] *Mat.* vi, 566.

Alexander wanted to foster study, even though scholars could be tiresome. He sacrificed regular discipline to academic interests by granting dispensations to cathedral clergy and Canons Regular to attend the schools as non-residents: 'The schools flourished, but the cloisters were left deserted.'[21] Some of his many dispensations resulted from his political needs. It was a matter of reciprocal profit, as he wrote to the canons of Tours; he was asking them to allocate a prebend to a certain master for two years to meet his expenses while he stayed in the schools:

> If you comply out of reverence to the Roman Church and to our prayers, Master Theobald will be bound to you by closer affection, and we should hope to be all the more ready and anxious to seek the good of you and your church.[22]

The pope was setting an example to bishops to grant dispensations for non-residence, which they followed.

Learning had its due in promotions to the sacred college. Analysis of his appointments shows that in rewarding learning he preferred canonists to theologians.[23] Eight men who had pursued legal studies were raised to the cardinalate during his reign: Conrad of Wittelsbach, who deserved promotion for political reasons too (he had lost his see in consequence of his opposition to the emperor), the papal notary Master Herman, Master Gratian *utriusque iuris peritus*, Master Laborans, Master Lombard, Peter of Pavia,[24] Master Rainer of Pavia,[25] and Master Vivian, who was an advocate at the Curia[26] and archdeacon of Orvieto. A ninth lawyer may be added if we can believe Gerald of Wales; he says that Alexander summoned Master Matthew of Angers, who had taught canon law at Paris, to the Lateran Council of 1179, in order to make him a cardinal.[27]

[21] Maccarrone, 'I Papi', 381–8.

[22] ed. Loewenfeld, op. cit. 199–200.

[23] For dates, titles and biographical details see Ganzer and Brixius, op. cit. Notices on those who left works on canon law will be found in *Dictionnaire de droit canonique*, ed. R. Naz (Paris, 1935–6).

[24] P. H. Delehaye, 'Pierre de Pavie légat du pape Alexandre III', *Revue des questions historiques* xxv (1891) N.S. v, 9–10, proves that Peter originated in Pavia and suggests that he may have been a fellow student or colleague of Stephen of Tournai at Bologna; there is no proof that he studied at Paris.

[25] It is not known where or what Master Rainer the Less of Pavia studied; see Brixius, op. cit. 125. It seems safe to suppose that he was a lawyer.

[26] According to John of Salisbury, *Mat.* vii, 31.

[27] *De rebus a se gestis, Opera* (op. cit.) i, 48. Gerald says that he heard

Theological learning seems to have been incidental as a qualification. Alexander promoted monks of Montecassino, who would have
had some theological training; the key position of their abbey on
the border of the kingdom of Naples and Sicily made them useful
in another way. St Galdin of Milan was 'instructed in sacred letters
from his childhood' in the cathedral school, according to his biographer;[28] but Milan formed the centre of resistance to Barbarossa
in Lombardy. William, archbishop of Sens and then of Rheims, was
a learned man and a patron of scholars; but his services to the pope
in exile and his key position in the French kingdom are quite enough
to account for his promotion. Hence accident rather than design
explains the presence of theologians in the Curia.

Concentration of legal business made canonists indispensable from
a practical point of view. They forwarded papal claims as eagerly
as theologians, but showed more tact in application. The only member of Becket's circle to reach the heights was a canonist: Master
Lombard came from Piacenza and won fame as a teacher of canon
law; Alexander summoned him to the Curia soon after the murder;
he subscribed as cardinal on 3 April 1171, being already a sub-
deacon of the Roman Church. Alexander made him archbishop of
Benevento, another key place in papal politics, in the same year.[29]
Master Vivian, later cardinal, mentions the Lombard in a letter to
Becket, written in 1169. Vivian was serving on a papal commission
to reconcile king and archbishop; he invites Becket to attend a
conference with the kings of England and France:

> We hope that Master Lombard, our dear colleague, may show
> his good sense in this business, as is the custom of his people.[30]

It sounds like an implied contrast between a prudent canonist from

Master Matthew of Angers lecture on laws and decretals at Paris. On a
summons from Pope Alexander to go to the Lateran Council to be made a
cardinal, Master Matthew recommended Gerald as his successor in his chair.
Matthew is not known to have subscribed any document as cardinal. Gerald
may have been mistaken or embroidered to make himself important.

[28] *Acta sanctorum*, April, ii, 594.

[29] Ganzer, 121–3. The Lombard resigned his see before 27 April 1179. He
was probably too old or ill to continue in his post, since he stayed on in
Benevento as a pensioner of his church.

[30] *Mat.* vii, 152: Optamus ut charissimus socius noster magister Lombardus,
more sue gentis, in hoc negotio prudenter sapiat.
The editor rightly amends the ms *Longinus* to Lombardus.

Lombardy and English theologians in the exiled household. Master Vivian had more confidence in the former.

Alexander's handling of the Becket crisis depended on the shifts and turns imposed on him by the schism of 1159. He began by bribing Henry II to recognize him by granting a dispensation for the marriage between Henry's son and Louis VII's daughter, although both children were under age. Henry could therefore claim instant legal possession of the bride's dowry. It included the Vexin castles, seized by Louis before Henry's accession, a strategic key to his Norman border. It is doubtful whether Henry could have brought his clergy to recognize the imperial pope instead of Alexander either then or later; but he could have postponed his decision, refusing his subjects recourse to either claimant in the meantime. Alexander dared not call Henry's bluff at that stage. Both Henry and Louis agreed to recognize him at a council held at Beauvais towards the end of July 1160.[31] So far, so good. But he had slighted Louis and ran the risk that he might therefore negotiate with the schismatics. The queen of France, Adelaide of Champagne, and Count Henry of Troyes had ties of kinship with Victor IV.[32] They persuaded Louis to treat with the emperor for the summoning of a general council to end the schism. It was to meet at a spot on the river Saône on the border of France and Germany. If either claimant refused to attend, then his cause would go by default. Alexander, now in exile at Sens, agreed to be represented, though not to come in person. The plan had fallen through by the end of September 1162. The French bishops stood firm for Alexander; Louis lost his nerve; the count of Troyes deserted his imperial ally. Alexander's patient waiting tactics had worked.[33]

Louis needed lesser bribes than Henry to keep him sweet, but Alexander accommodated him as far as possible. The case of Hugh of Champfleury will show how he did so at Hugh's expense. Hugh was a master of Paris, though not certainly a theologian.[34] Louis VII made him royal chancellor in 1150. He was elected to the bishopric

---

[31] M. G. Cheney, 'The recognition of Pope Alexander III: some neglected evidence', E.H.R. lxxxiv (1969) 474–97.

[32] P. Kehr, 'Zur Geschichte Viktors IV.', *Neues Archiv* xlvi (1925–6) 53–85.

[33] W. Heinemeyer, 'Die Verhandlungen an der Saône im Jahre 1162', *Deutsches Archiv* xx (1964) 155–89.

[34] L. Minio-Paluello, 'The *Ars Disserendi* of Adam of Balsham "Parvipontanus"', M.A.R.S. iii (1954) 119, 159–60.

of Soissons in 1159, while already archdeacon of Arras and canon of Paris, Soissons and Orleans.[35] Alexander relied on him as an ally at court and wrote asking him for money and good offices in the papal cause.[36] Hugh seems to have consulted him on the propriety of holding a bishopric together with the chancellorship. The pope reassured him in a letter of 2 September 1162, commending his devotion to the Roman Church and promising that nobody should induce him to lessen Hugh's dignity.[37] The chancellor's influence mattered to Alexander at a time when Louis was still negotiating with the emperor. Later, in 1172, Hugh fell into disgrace with his king for unknown reasons. Alexander, now sure of Louis's adhesion, wrote to the archbishop of Rheims telling him to order Hugh to resign from being chancellor and to content himself with his bishopric: Hugh could not administer both offices together, since each was a full-time job; let him devote himself to the church and people committed to his care. The pope grounded his order on his wish to see pastoral charge performed by a bishop undistracted by secular office.[38] Alexander first conciliated Louis by allowing him to keep his chancellor after election to a bishopric, and then rewarded him for his services by helping to disgrace a former favourite, when Hugh had no further importance. Nor did the pope neglect his opportunity to state the principle that bishops should not hold secular office, although he had made an exception and a promise in Hugh's case.

[35] M. Pacaut, *Louis VII et son royaume* (Paris, 1964) 110–11, 173.

[36] P.L. cc, 107–8, 137, 164.

[37] ibid. cc, 263–4: Nec quisquam, volente Domino, ad hoc nos inducere poterit, quod collata tibi dignitas seu officium per nos minui debeat vel auferri; sed potius augere volentes, consilium tibi et auxilium in quibus honeste poterimus, libenti animo curabimus impertiri, ut et devotionis tuae integritas meritum habeat, et recipiat praemium quod magnis sacerdotibus et iustitiae cultoribus promissum est.

[38] ibid. 790–1: . . . Caeterum quoniam venerabilis noster Suessionensis episcopus cancellariae officium et pontificalis administrationis sollicitudinem non potest simul et congrue exercere, cum utrumque officium totam non divisam desideret habere personam, ei mandavimus ut, relicta cancellaria, curae et administrationi iniunctae sibi sollicitudinis diligenter et studiose intendat et super custodiam Ecclesiae et populi sibi commissi vigil et intentus existat...

The archbishops of Sens and Rheims would have supported the pope, had he chosen to protect Hugh of Champfleury; see A. Duchesne. *Historia Francorum* iv (Paris, 1641) 570, 575.

Further afield he conciliated the rulers of Hungary and Sicily by restricting the liberties of local churches for the rulers' benefit.[39] The history of the abbey of Vézelay in Burgundy will illustrate his tactics in miniature. He sacrificed its liberties to the count of Nevers, who was accused of usurping rights of the abbey. Alexander displayed all his diplomatic skill in bringing over Frederick's allies in this border area.[40] The count of Nevers had a key position there. Hugh the Notary, writing on the liberties of Vézelay, put Alexander's motives clearly:

> Alexander considered the schism, which was weakening the Church. He feared that graver scandal would afflict her if he took a harder line against secular princes. He therefore merely admonished the count in plain writing to cease from oppressing the church of Vézelay, a daughter of St Peter and allod of the Roman Church.[41]

'He merely admonished in writing' for fear of a graver scandal. What chance had Canterbury against the gravest scandal of all?

The Becket crisis and the consequent appeals to Rome threatened Alexander's hard-won gains.[42] Now it was Henry who negotiated with the schismatics; his nerve was less likely to fail. Political interests and connections encouraged Henry to make a German alliance.[43] We shall never know just how serious or how feasible was his threat to recognize the anti-pope. It served as a lever in two ways: it frightened Alexander and it provided the English bishops

[39] W. Holtzmann, 'Papst Alexander III. und Ungarn', *Ungarische Jahrbücher* vi (1926) 397–426.

[40] G. Duby, *La société au XIe et XIIe dans la région mâconnaise* (Paris, 1953) 538–42. For Frederick's efforts to win recognition for his antipopes in Burgundy see J. Y. Mariotte, 'Une lettre de Frédéric Barberousse au sujet de l'abbaye de Baume les Messieurs en Franche-Comté', *Archiv für Diplomatik* vii (1961) 204–13.

[41] M.G.H. SS. xxvi, 149 (s.a. 1164): Alexander quoque recognitans scisma, quo infirmabatur aecclesia, et veritus, ne forte, si aliquantulum durius erga saeculi principes procederet, graviori scandalo aecclesia affligeretur, simplici tantum scripto commonuit comitem, ut a gravaminibus aecclesiae Veziliensis, quae filia beati Petri et alodium Romanae aecclesiae existebat, desisteret.

On the special relationship between Vézelay and Rome see H. E. J. Cowdrey *The Cluniacs and the Gregorian Reform* (Oxford, 1970) 13–14, 85–7.

[42] On the appeals see Knowles 95–101.

[43] A. L. Poole, *From Domesday Book to Magna Carta* (Oxford, 1951) 326–329.

L

with an excuse to plead the dangers which might follow on their resistance to the royal will. Finance entered into the problem: Alexander needed Peter's Pence during his exile more than ever. He pledged it to creditors several years in advance. No wonder that his letters early in the quarrel sometimes suggest that he was more anxious to have it collected and dispatched than to get Becket reinstated.[44] Henry put him between Scylla and Charybdis, as William of Canterbury noted.[45] 'Those accursed evil customs', as Master Vivian called the Constitutions of Clarendon in a letter to Alexander,[46] loomed on one side: on the other side he saw incalculable risks and certain losses. If Becket had persisted in accepting the Constitutions instead of withdrawing consent, he would have received a letter of reproof from the Curia, written more in sorrow than in wrath, and beautifully drafted; the matter would have rested there for the time being. The crisis came too early from Becket's point of view. He would have stood more chance of support after Frederick's defeat at Legnano in 1176. Did he fail to understand the pope's difficulties during the schism, as has been suggested? He was not so stupid. He realized that Alexander would give in to Henry unless his hand were forced; and forced it should be. Becket was not the first or the last Catholic to think that he knew better than the pope what was good for the Church, though few have acted more obstinately on their belief. Shifty as Alexander was, the exiles feared that the cardinals might elect an even weaker man to succeed him.[47]

Alexander played for time. He advised Becket to regain Henry's favour, lest Henry should turn against both pope and archbishop.[48] He fielded Becket's anathemas, though some got through. He flattered Henry and reproached him gently.[49] He thanked persons who entertained the exiles in France and urged them to show even more hospitality.[50] His cardinals were divided; some took bribes from Henry, or so it was said. Alexander appointed commissions to reconcile the antagonists, weighting them with men who were not hostile to Henry, to put it mildly, such as Cardinal William of

[44] W. E. Lunt, *Financial Relations of the Papacy with England to 1327* (Cambridge, Mass., 1939) 48–54. See *Mat.* v, 177, 202, 295, G.F.C.L. 251.

[45] *Mat.* i, 65.   [46] ibid. vii, 167–9.

[47] ibid. vi, 70, 153. For criticism of the Curia by Becket and his friends, including Archbishop William of Sens, see ibid. v, 92, 335, 439, vi, 132, 216.

[48] ibid. v, 86.   [49] ibid. vi, 377.

[50] ibid. v, 172, 198, 242, 244.

Pavia and the archbishop of Rouen. But he expected them to keep up an appearance of impartiality. The pope becomes almost human in his dismay when rumours reach him that his envoys are supposed to have made a deal with Henry and that they plan to decide against Becket.[51]

Incapable of blowing hot and cold, he blew warm and cool. Changing fortunes in Italy decided which it should be. His return to Rome in 1165 brought some pro-Becket gestures. Alexander annulled the Northampton sentence against Becket on his way back to Italy at Clermont and authorized the censure of invaders of church property early in 1166. He made Becket papal legate for the province of Canterbury in a bull issued from the Lateran on 2 May the same year. In June he ratified some of the Vézelay sentences.[52] Frederick's capture of Rome in 1167 brought a second period of marking time. Then plague wiped out the imperial army and forced Frederick to withdraw. He would strike again; but the formation of the Lombard League was now well under way. Alexander began to threaten Henry in May 1168, and wrote that his affection for the archbishop was increasing.[53] Henry provoked him in a way that could not be ignored by making more stringent decrees on recourse to Rome in the autumn of 1169.[54] In 1170 Alexander told the archbishop of Sens that he regarded Becket's cause as his own. Becket now had papal support, if not full support.[55] Alexander authorized the archbishop's excommunications of his enemies, but allowed him to return to England without receiving the kiss of peace, contenting himself with exhortation on that vital point.[56]

His attitude to the Constitutions was ambiguous. He refused Henry's initial request for approval, but he did not issue a public condemnation. None of the *Lives* tells us so. William of Canterbury, Grim and Fitzstephen agree that Alexander condemned some of the clauses either before or after his talk with Becket at Sens at the beginning of the exile. Herbert, who was present at the talk, says that the pope condemned the more obnoxious clauses in the hearing of his cardinals. Even Herbert does not claim that the ban

[51] ibid. vi, 200.

[52] ibid. v, 178, 316–17, 328–9, 386–92; W. Holtzmann, op. cit. F. 3, xiv–xv (1935–6) 312.

[53] *Mat.* vi, 437, 440, 461.   [54] Knowles, *Becket*, 124–5.

[55] *Mat.* vii, 299.   [56] ibid. 189, 345.

was made public.[57] The letters are as reticent as the *Lives*. Becket condemned certain clauses of the Constitutions at Vézelay, June 1166.[58] John of Salisbury reported to the bishop of Exeter that the archbishop acted *de consilio Romanae ecclesiae*.[59] It reads like another example of John's slanted reporting. Becket wrote to Alexander begging him to ratify the Vézelay censures; he followed it up by writing to friends at the Curia begging them to use their influence with the pope to make him grant the request.[60] This démarche would have been unnecessary if he already had papal approval for his condemnation. All he had, it seems, was a papal promise that Henry's demand for ratification of the Constitutions had not been granted, a negative sort of assurance.[61] Alexander responded to Becket's plea that he should confirm the censures issued at Vézelay by ratifying the archbishop's sentences against Richard of Ilchester, John of Oxford and all other perverters of God's Church: that was all.[62] His letters to English bishops imply that he had never publicly condemned the Constitutions. He ordered the bishops of London and Hereford to warn Henry not to impede recourse to the Curia in 1165.[63] In September 1170, when he felt stronger, or perhaps more constrained to brave Henry's wrath, he lectured some of the bishops in writing on their cowardice in swearing to 'those evil customs'; he explained why he had waited so long to deprive them of office in consequence.[64] Even then, he did not blame them for disobedience to his express command. His refusal to issue a public, official ban would account, at least partly, for the face-saving compromise at Avranches after Becket's murder. The pope had not left himself elbow-room to exploit the martyrdom, even if he wanted to. Perhaps he did not. The settlement at Avranches left Henry almost as free as before.[65] Henry's conquest of Ireland and the reform of the Irish church made his goodwill less expendable than ever from Alexander's point of view.

The pope's theories on the relationship between *regnum* and

---

[57] *Mat.* iii, 340–3; ii, 404; iii, 49. Becket stated that Alexander absolved him at Sens from his guilt in agreeing to the Constitutions and from his obligations to observe them; vi, 512. The Becket dossier would have included a public ban if it had ever been issued.

[58] ibid. v, 384. [59] ibid.

[60] ibid. 387–8, 391. [61] ibid. 85–7.

[62] ibid. [63] ibid. 176. [64] ibid. vii, 360–70.

[65] H. Mayr-Harting, 'Henry II and the Papacy, 1170–1189', *Journal of Ecclesiastical History* xvi (1965) 39–53.

sacerdotium show the same caution as his diplomacy. His statements are refined and inconclusive. We may begin with his teaching as a professor of canon law; his theological *Sentences* do not touch on political theory. In his *Summa* on the *Decretum* he answers the question 'whether a clerk should be brought before a secular judge', that he should not be in a criminal case, unless the bishop has first deprived him of his orders.[66] On the question whether confession may be forced by torture, he answers that such confessions are invalid, adducing as a parallel the invalidity of oaths made under duress; he adds that the pope can absolve even from oaths of fidelity (taken by vassals). Here he is expounding Gratian. He does not draw the consequence that papal absolution from oaths of fidelity may lead to the deposition of the ruler.[67] The question whether a clerk corrected by his bishop may leave his office and resort to a secular judge brings Master Roland on to more controversial ground. He answers that, according to St Paul: *No man, being a soldier to God, entangleth himself with secular business* (II Tim. ii, 4), and elsewhere: *If therefore you have judgments of things pertaining to this world, set them to judge who are the most despised in the church*, that is laymen (I Cor. vi, 4). But from the time of Constantine, he continues, it is agreed that examination of secular matters too has been transferred to the pope; and 'Louis' solemnly confirmed it. His conclusion is that no clerk may resort to a secular judge in spiritual matters. In secular matters, if he accuses a layman, he may go before a civil judge; if he is accused, however, he may not presume to do so.[68] Is this a reference to the forged Donation of Constantine, according to which the emperor transferred imperial power in the west to Pope Sylvester, and to its supposed confirmation by Louis the Pious? If so, the reference is oblique, since Roland does not mention or quote the text of the Donation.[69] Again he fails to draw consequences: even though the pope has power to act as judge in secular matters as well as in spiritual, a clerk may accuse a layman in a secular court. It is not suggested that secular justice should be subject to spiritual in secular matters or that there should be a right of appeal to the pope. The canonist Paucapalea, working 1140–48, added the text of the Donation to the *Decretum* and com-

[66] Thaner, 25.   [67] ibid. 35. See *Decr.* I, Causa XV, q. vi, c.2.
[68] ibid. 79–80.
[69] D. Maffei, *La Donazione di Constantino nei giuristi medievali* (Milan, 1964) 32.

mented on it. Hence Roland, working before 1148, would not have had the text in his copy; Gratian mentioned only *donaria*, gifts made by Constantine and other emperors to the Church.[70] The list of *distinctiones* or titles at the beginning of Roland's *Summa* includes two 'hierocratic' statements:

> Laymen have no power to dispose of clergy or things pertaining to the Church and the emperor ought not to judge the actions of bishops; the pope may transfer the realm and depose the emperor.

The next *distinctio* underlines the emperor's subordinate role and the papal dignity:

> The emperor is wont to help the Church in trouble at the pope's command; the Roman Church is not wont to receive an embassy without due credentials.[71]

The claim that the pope may transfer rule and depose an emperor rests on inferences from existing canon law sources. It hints at the theory of *translatio imperii*: the pope had in the past transferred rule over the empire from the Greeks to the Romans, from the Romans to the Franks and from the Franks to the Germans. It would follow that the empire was in his gift.[72] Roland leaves his readers or pupils to make their own deductions. He does not explain how his statement is to be applied. Historians have suggested that Roland withdrew from his hierocratic position when he became pope.[73] There was little to withdraw from. The claims that the pope may judge in secular as well as spiritual matters and that he may absolve subjects from oaths of allegiance do not occur in an anti-imperial context in either case. The provocative *distinctiones* are not discussed, but left open.

As cardinal and papal chancellor Roland had to work for the militant Pope Adrian IV. The episode of his legation to the emperor at Besançon, 1157, has often been told and commented on.[74] Adrian

---

[70] ibid. 27–9.   [71] Thaner, 11–12.

[72] P. A. Van den Baar, *Die Kirchliche Lehre der Translatio Imperii Romani bis zur Mitte des 13 Jahrhundert* (Analecta Gregoriana lxxviii, series facultatis historiae ecclesiasticae, sectio B (n. 12) Rome, 1956) 73–6.

[73] F. Kempf, 'Kanonistik und kuriale Politik im 12 Jahrhundert', *Archivum historiae Pontificiae* i (1963) 49.

[74] *Ottonis et Rahewini gesta Frederici*, op. cit. (above, p. 119) 172–7.

sent his chancellor and Cardinal Bernard with a letter to Frederick protesting at his failure to punish those who ill treated the archbishop of Lund when he passed through Germany on his way back from the Curia. Charging Frederick with ingratitude, Adrian recalled the favours bestowed on him, and added the words:

> . . . sed, si maiora beneficia excellentia tua de manu nostra suscepisset, si fieri posset, considerantes, quanta aecclesiae Dei et nobis per te incrementa possint et commoda provenire, non inmerito gauderemus.

The imperial chancellor Rainald of Dassel translated the word *beneficium* as 'fief', giving it to be understood that Adrian regarded the empire as a fief held from the papacy. There was an uproar; the meeting broke up in confusion. According to Rahewin it was reported (*ferunt*) that one of the legates added fuel to the flame by saying: 'From whom then does he have the empire, if not from the lord pope?' Historians have generally assumed without evidence both that Rahewin's report was correct and that the legate who put the question was Cardinal Roland and not his colleague Bernard.[75] They have provided adverbs at pleasure, beginning with Otto of St Blasien, writing after 1209, who added 'stolidissime' to his report of the question.[76] We do not know whether Adrian was trying it on when he used the ambiguous term *beneficium* or whether he meant it to refer to the papal right to crown emperors. In the latter case it implied that the pope had a right to withhold coronation rather than a duty to crown the candidate elected to empire, which ruffled German susceptibilities only a little less than the implication that the empire was held as a fief.[77] The pope explained later that he had not meant *beneficium* in the sense of fief.

To mark Roland's part in the proceedings, it has been argued that he would have drafted and approved the letter to Frederick in his capacity as chancellor. That he drafted it is hardly in doubt. That he approved it depends on the question whether he always

---

[75] Rahewin's most recent editors disagree with the common assumption; see the *Gesta Frederici*, ed. with translation into German by A. Schmidt and F. J. Schmale (Ausgewählte Quellen zur deutschen Geschichte des Mittelalters xvii, Darmstadt, 1965) 417 n.

[76] *Chronica*, ed. A. Hofmeister (M.G.H., SS. ad usum schol. 1912) 9.

[77] See W. Ullmann, 'Cardinal Roland and the Diet of Besançon', *Miscellanea historiae pontificiae* xviii (1954) 107–79.

saw eye to eye with Adrian. The latter seems to have wished that Cardinal Bernard and not Roland should succeed him as pope; Bernard was seriously considered as a candidate at the ensuing election.[78] Both men adhered to the pro-Norman, anti-imperial faction in the Curia; but Adrian may have doubted Roland's determination to carry it through to the end. Whatever his role at Besançon and his relations with Adrian, it seems clear that the future Pope Alexander learnt his lesson, a congenial lesson in his case: never bluster; never stake a claim which may prove to be untenable. That would be his policy as pope.

His pronouncements as pope have been squeezed dry to extract the juice of his doctrine. The result is to show that advances from the more conservative tradition were marginal and minimal: he claimed more in Dalmatia and Spain than elsewhere. His harshest rebukes to Henry II turned on the unimpeachable argument that a secular ruler should not interfere in spiritual matters.[79] No one could quarrel with the principle, but only with its application. Alexander avoided committing himself to definition of his rights over the imperial crown in his negotiations with the Greek emperor Manuel. He aimed at aligning France, Sicily and Byzantium in an anti-German alliance. How far he really expected it to materialize and how far it was diplomatic bluff (Alexander could bluff as well as Henry II) is not clear. The negotiations raised delicate problems, since Manuel demanded the Roman imperial crown as his by right. Alexander put him off, while keeping the theory of *translatio imperii* well in the background.[80] If he made it a condition, as a Greek chonicler states, that Manuel should transfer his capital from Byzantium to Rome, he must have been asking the impossible of set purpose.[81] The plan lapsed after 1168. Stephen of Rouen in his *Draco Normannicus* reports in verse, or perhaps invents, a speech by Alexander supporting his claim to be recognized as the true pope against Victor IV. He summarizes the history of Rome from its foundation as a prelude to invoking the Donation of Constantine. 'The whole world' was subject to Pope Sylvester in consequence,

---

[78] S. Tengnagel, *Vetera monumenta contra schismaticos* (Ingolstadt, 1612) 391–2; G. Hödl, 'Die Admonter Briefsammlung', *Deutsches Archiv* xxv (1969) 347–470, xxvi (1970) 150–99.

[79] *Mat.* v, 157.   [80] Van den Baar, op. cit. 76–80.

[81] John Cinnamus; see *Cambridge Medieval History* IV, 1 (Cambridge, 1966) 231. Cinnamus was Manuel's secretary and wrote soon after his death; he was well placed to know.

but his successors suffered from tyrants until the Franks were called
in to protect them. Stephen of Rouen makes Alexander limit the
force of the Donation to Rome or to Italy at most, as was logical
when he was claiming to be the true Roman pope. He does not
claim the right of *translatio imperii*.[82] The *Draco* pictures Alexander
as arrogant and greedy; so it is interesting that his theory of his
rights remains within reasonable bounds even in an anti-papal poem.

He chose Master Rufinus, bishop of Assisi and former professor
of canon law at Bologna, to deliver the sermon which opened the
proceedings at the Lateran Council of 1179. His choice of preacher
and the sermon throw light on his mind, when the end of the schism
left him free to express himself. Rufinus in his *Summa* (1157–9)
demoted the emperor to the role of agent or steward of the papacy.
The old biblical metaphor of the two swords, one of which the
emperor received from the pope, lacked precision and depended on a
debatable interpretation of the gospel text. Rufinus argued for papal
superiority on new lines, using legal analysis and legal termin-
ology.[83] The honour conferred on him by Alexander, though it was
tacit approval, leads one to suppose that the pope did not repudiate
the political theory set forth in the *Summa*; but he did not adopt it in
his official pronouncements. His choice also indicates his preference
for canonists as against theologians. But there were other reasons.
Political theory forms a small part of Rufinus's comprehensive survey of canon law. Alexander's long reign had seen a rising tide of
inquiries from all quarters addressed to the Curia. Daily business
involved answers and often new decisions on routine questions concerning the canon law on marriage, inheritance, tithes and so on.
The pope published his decisions in decretal letters, which ecclesiastical dignitaries and their canon law advisers or the canonists of
their own accord assembled in compilations to supplement Gratian's
Decretum.[84] The volume of inquiries and answers witnessed to the
fact that contemporaries expected the pope to act as Christ's vicar in
an active, dynamic sense. The routine work of the papal chancery
made theories superfluous. A ruler who enjoys or carries the burden

---

[82] *Draco*, 746–50; Van den Baar, op. cit. 70–1.

[83] For recent discussion and bibliography see R. L. Benson, op. cit. 56–89.
The interesting treatise *De bono pacis*, which is almost certainly by Rufinus,
could not have influenced Alexander's choice, since it was not written until
after his death, 1181–2.

[84] C. Duggan, *Twelfth-Century Decretal Collections* (London, 1963).

of real power has less need to theorize on the subject than one who has to bolster up a shaky institution. Secular princes caused political difficulties; the true source of papal strength evaded them because it came from a longing for direction felt by the clergy in their realms. Canon law as the instrument of direction over the whole field of Christian life was honoured in the person of Master Rufinus.

The pope, his advisers and the preacher must have consulted on the text of the sermon. It would have to outline the programme of the council and set it against the background of Alexander's twenty years' pontificate. Each word would need scrutiny. Dom Morin, who discovered and edited the sermon, described it as 'assurément l'un des plus magnifiques documents qui existent sur la primauté et les droits du Saint-Siège apostolique de Rome'.[85] Rufinus praised Alexander as the sun rising out of the ocean of troubles; the beasts of the night have crept back to their lairs:

> How strongly he shouldered the weight of the tottering Church and what health he brought to our time ... the outer limits of all lands have learnt.[86]

Thus the schism and its problems are referred to in tactfully general phrases. The preacher puts the whole weight of his discourse on the primacy of the Roman Church over the hierarchy and over the other patriarchates. Rome has *monarchia*. The pope signifies the king, the cardinals patricians and peers, the archbishops consuls, and 'we bishops' the people; Rufinus preached as bishop of Assisi. In relation to the council it is stressed that the pope alone has power to summon a general assembly. This council is truly ecumenical. Rufinus expresses its legislative task by means of a biblical parallel: he compares Alexander to Josias, whose priests discovered the lost book of the Law, and who read it out to all the inhabitants of Jerusalem (II Paral. xxxiv): so the canons of the Lateran Council would renew and reinforce Christian law. The oration makes a fine epilogue to a laborious reign. It sets forth Alexander's leading idea, 'the primacy and rights of the apostolic see of Rome'. It says nothing of

---

[85] 'Le discours d'ouverture du Concile Générale de Latran (1179)', *Atti della Pontifica accademia romana di archeologia* 3rd series, Memorie ii (1928) 133.

[86] ibid. 119–20: Quam fortissimis et etiam humeris ruibundae ecclesiae molem iste fulciuerit, quantumve salutem saeculo nostro pepererit, ... terrarum omnium extrema nouerunt.

the relations between *regnum* and *sacerdotium*. Alexander had followed up his disputed election by summoning a council to be held at Tours, 1163. It could hardly be described as ecumenical. Moreover, he promised Henry II that his summons to the prelates in the Plantagenet realm should not prejudice the rights of the crown.[87] The council of 1179 made a pleasing contrast to the council of Tours; but the pope saw to it that he should never appear to be eating his words. He left it to others to raise him above the princes of the earth, and contented himself officially with his place above the princes of the Church. If consistency is a sign of being an intellectual in politics, then he had it to a high degree. He achieved it in a negative way, which brought dangers. They stretched his mental powers to the utmost.

Such dangers would have surprised Pope Gregory VII. He had to spur on his prelates, whereas Alexander had to rein them in. High-church doctrine had become so common that subordinates would cast it in his teeth, if he did not act on it as they wished. Becket in Herbert's story tells the pope at Sens:

> It is not only schismatics and heretics who disturb the peace of the Church, but often tyrants, her sons. . . . Ecclesiastical censure should be pronounced and St Peter's sword drawn against them, even in time of schism and heresy.[88]

Henry was a tyrant and should be disciplined.[89] A strict sentence imposed on his land overseas would soon break his obstinacy, Becket assured the pope in June 1166.[90] Becket would have liked to include Henry in his Vézelay censures, but did not quite dare to. He kept excommunication in reserve until the pope should be more amenable.[91] Alexander felt sure, for his part, that Henry would never yield to threats, which might do harm; mildness would do no harm and might even do good.

The Becket *Materials* bring out two points in papal theory. Alexander upheld his power to discipline secular rulers in principle.

---

[87] *Mat.* v, 33.   [88] ibid. iii, 348.

[89] ibid. v, 139, vi, 158–9, vii, 226.

[90] ibid, v, 391: Scimus antem et certum habemus quod obstinatio regis citissime frangeretur, si in terram eius cismarinam districta sententia poneretur.

Becket is asking Conrad of Mainz and two cardinals to put this view to Alexander.

[91] ibid. 388.

Henry must neither think nor believe that *the Lord* shall not *be awakened out of sleep* (Ps. lxxvii, 65); nor is St Peter's sword so rusty that it cannot inflict due punishment, as he instructed his commissioners to warn the king in 1168.[92] It was necessary therefore to excuse compromise and delay in drawing out his sword of spiritual censure. Alexander had a theory to hand. 'Inopportune' is the key word. He 'weighed up the dangerous times' in dealing with Henry. 'One must stoop to the desires of princes and temper their will,' he wrote to Becket in 1164.[93] The archbishop should refrain from censures, 'since the days are evil. Many things must be tolerated on account of the times.'[94] The Roman Church resembles a wise old mother or a skilled physician, who must try every cure on a mortally sick patient (Henry).[95] The Roman custom is to move slowly, incurring harm and loss thereby, rather than to sin by rashness.[96] He quoted a Pauline text at Becket: 'Remember how our elders redeemed *the time, because the days* were *evil*' (Eph. v, 16).[97] The text, carefully chosen, had a sting in its head and its tail. It follows the words: *See therefore, brethren, how you walk circumspectly: not as unwise, but as wise.* Becket does not walk circumspectly or behave wisely. Further, according to the *Great Gloss* on St Paul, *redeeming the time* meant attending quietly to one's devotions instead of engaging in lawsuits.[98] Not for nothing did Robert of Torigny call Alexander 'a very great teacher of the holy page'.[99] He could justify himself from the Scriptures and their glosses. Herbert of Bosham, who knew the *Great Gloss* like the back of his hand, felt the insult to Becket so keenly that he answered it in his *Life*. He gave his master the right of reply by anticipation, expounding the text and its gloss through Becket's mouth in his interview with Alexander at Sens. The apostle did not mean, as the pope supposed, that prelates should stand by idle, while the Church suffered. Becket had truly 'redeemed the time' in St Paul's meaning by giving up the temporalities of the see of Canterbury on account of the time. He had renounced its riches and dig-

[92] ibid. vi, 440.   [93] ibid. v, 86.   [94] ibid. v, 179, vi, 421.
[95] ibid. vi, 462.   [96] ibid. 484.   [97] ibid. 564.
[98] P.L. cxcii, 211–12: *Redimentes tempus*, id est praeparantes vobis opportunitatem serviendi Deo et vacandi divinis . . . Redimit ille tempus qui perdit, id est dat de suo ut vacet Deo non litibus. . . . Sic perdas de tuo, ut emas tibi quietem; hoc est tempus redimere . . . ut habeas quietum cor, ne perdas tempus vacandi Deo tuo, a quo vult te avocare damno et litibus.
[99] Quoted by Pacaut, 109.

nity on behalf of its liberty as entrusted to his care. That was Herbert's interpretation of the text. Alexander might have claimed that his own accorded better with the original intention of both St Paul and the glossator.[1]

He saw politics as the art of the possible. His estimate of the possible was pessimistic and practical: he did not look for miracles to pull him through, but trusted rather to the Lombard League and the goodwill of princes. His arguments for doing so amount to a negative, but recognizable theory of *raison d'état*. There is no question as yet of justifying crimes committed for the good of the commonwealth; but there is a theory that principles may be shelved and individuals sacrificed for the greater good of the Church. The pope judged what the good of the Church was. John of Salisbury put it clearly: such were the pope's difficulties and needs that he would sometimes use the licence of his power and procure by dispensation what was said to be expedient for the commonwealth, even though it was not expedient for religion.[2] He weighed up the dangerous times and acted according to circumstances, as it was his duty to do. Intellectuals of the Church developed a theory of sovereignty which secular princes took over for their own purposes. Similarly the concept of *raison d'état* was a gift from the Curia. The Becket conflict had peculiar side effects. It forced scholars to think about the relationship between principle and expediency, not only in practice, which was commonplace, but also in theory. Alexander was the theorist of expediency.

---

[1] *Mat.* iii, 352–4: Quod autem tacite arguendo me dicitis quod ad Magistri consilium tempus redimere debuissem, super prudentia vestra satis admirari non possum. Et si super illo Magistri verbo sanctorum interpretatio, sicut generalis et necessaria, ita vera est, iam non arbitror sed certissime scio me tempus hoc redemisse. Nec enim Magister ibi docet temporis redemptionem, ubi ecclesiasticae libertatis dispendium vertitur; . . . Ecce quod Magister . . . minime intelligit temporis redemptionem ubi servitute introducta ecclesiasticae libertatis deperit honor; verius quippe ibi quam temporis redemptio, temporis perditio, et ecclesiae ignominiosa abiectio est. . . . Videte itaque, fratres, si placet . . . si non redemerim tempus, qui temporalia dedi pro tempore; qui ecclesiae Cantuariensis divitias et honorem, pariter et domini mei regis gratiam et gloriam, pro mea et cleri mihi crediti libertate et pace dereliqui . . .

Magister in Herbert's biblical allusions always stands for St Paul. The words *tacite arguendo* refer to the slight cast on Becket in the pope's letter (sent some years after the interview at Sens!). The words *sanctorum interpretatio* refer to the *Great Gloss*, covertly alluded to in the pope's letter.

[2] ibid. vi, 20; see above, pp. 104–5.

VII
The Case against Becket

We should look for the case against Becket before his canonization clouded the issue. Henry's version of it is difficult to reconstruct because he never committed to writing any clear account of his case against his archbishop. He propounded verbal arguments. John of Salisbury reports an interview with Louis VII in 1165:

> The king of England put forward much for himself and much against you, so as to influence light, floating minds, now with promises, now with threats, now with various deals, as is his way.[1]

The report hardly suggests a reasoned defence of the claims of *regnum* against *sacerdotium* on a theoretical level. The same would apply to the only manifesto in the *Materials* where Henry defended himself to the Curia. It was drafted probably soon after mid April, 1165, since he refers to marriage negotiations with an embassy from Frederick I at Rouen.[2] The king relies on *ad hoc* excuses. The pope has shown gross ingratitude for Henry's services to his cause; Henry recognized Alexander freely and forced others to do likewise. In fact, Henry had taken a bribe in the form of papal permission for his son's marriage, and he had no need to force Alexander upon willing bishops. He answered the reproach that he communicated with schismatics by protesting that he had not known of the ban on Frederick, claiming to have had a verbal assurance from the pope that he did not regard Frederick as excommunicate. An assurance sent by word of mouth was obviously unverifiable. Therefore, Henry argued, he had committed no fault in arranging to marry his daughter to Frederick's son, just as his

[1] *Mat.* v, 161.
[2] ibid. vi, 78–81. See Eyton, 78. The marriage arranged between Henry's daughter Eleanor and Frederick's eldest son at this meeting with the imperial embassy never took place; see Poole, 328.

grandfather Henry I married his daughter to the emperor Henry 'of good memory'. Mention of Matilda's marriage to Henry V, most anticlerical of all twelfth-century rulers, shows defiance rather than tact; perhaps it was meant to. The manifesto then glances at political theory, only to turn aside. Henry 'acknowledged' that he held all his power and possessions from God. It was an implicit denial of the High-church doctrine that he held the material sword mediately from the pope. He withdrew from the ground of theory to take his stand on the customs of his ancestors. He would persevere in loving the pope if the latter would allow him what his holy predecessors had allowed to earlier kings of England. Henry had not impeded appeals and recourse to Rome except to the same extent, for the same reasons and in the same manner as had been done before, according to the customs and rights of the kingdom. The older and wiser men of the kingdom, both clerks and laymen, still remember and speak of these customs and rights. Turning to his quarrel with Becket, Henry accused him of sending himself into exile, just in order to make trouble. Then came a promise: Henry would repair with the advice of his clergy and barons whatever he could be shown to have done amiss acording to the customs, rights and honours of his kingdom. A threat followed: any man who should try to infringe them would be held as his public and private enemy, openly hostile to both king and kingdom. He ended by denying that he had ever oppressed either churches or parsons in his realm, as God and his conscience bore witness.

The manifesto certainly contains more 'threats, promises and suggested deals' than sustained argument. The core of Henry's case, as presented here, is his right to the customs of his forebears. He urged it consistently. Becket ought to have observed the ancient customs, as the five preceding archbishops had done, of whom some were holy men and had worked miracles, he told Louis VII at Montmirail.[3] His reliance on custom, *qua* custom, begged the question, raised at canon law, of whether his customs were 'good' as well as ancient. No custom, however ancient, would stand at canon law, unless it were good and approved by the Church. Did Henry present his customs as 'good'?

Herbert of Bosham tells us that Henry defended them as promoting 'the peace of his people'.[4] Henry, so Herbert tells us, had advice from counsellors skilled in both civil and canon law. They put

[3] *Mat.* vi, 508.   [4] ibid. iii, 266–7.

forward a commonsense argument on the punishment of criminous clerks: the threat of corporal punishment was needed; mere spiritual penalities would not deter miscreants from their evil deeds. Henry took a leaf out of the theologians' book: more is demanded from him to whom more is committed; hence clergy deserved to be penalized all the more severely when they broke the law, seeing that they enjoyed a more privileged and honourable status than laymen. He went on to quote Gratian on the handing over of recalcitrant clerks to lay tribunals. He then argued from civil law that sentence of exile was reserved to Caesar, the temporal lord of the land; it could not be imposed by churchmen. His final argument came from Scripture and troubled Becket, as we have seen:[5] the Old Law did not exempt priests and levites from its tariff of penalities. Henry could therefore stigmatize privilege of clergy as 'new':

> It would be a wonderful novelty at law and a new sort of holiness if crimes which disturb the peace of kingdoms, violate royal justice and profane all sanctity should be shielded by the privilege of their perpetrators.

It was left to Herbert to report this impressive case for the crown. He may even have strengthened it according to the scholastic method of alleging all possible reasons and authorities *contra*. Fitzstephen's account of Henry's exchanges with Herbert makes the king force him to grant that other kingdoms had 'bad customs' as well as England, though they carried less danger because they were not written down. Henry does not claim that his customs were 'good' ones.[6]

He further shelved the issue of principle by bringing personal charges against Becket. John of Salisbury exposed the trick in a letter to the bishop of Exeter, 1166:

> Those who persecute the archbishop of Canterbury do not persecute him as Thomas . . ., but because *he shows* God's *people their wicked doings* ... and calls upon princes to obey God's law. . . .
>
> Evil custom and divine equity now confront each other alone.

---

[5] Above, p. 131.   [6] Above, p. 63.

There is no longer any mention of the financial charge, which was trumped up at first and which was null in reality.[7]

A modern student of the conflict will supply Henry with many reasons for attacking privilege of clergy and may be surprised that he failed to mention them. A look at his chancery will suggest one answer. We have no detailed study of the style of royal letters, as distinct from that of royal scribes and of diplomatic.[8] We do know, however, that *dictamen*, the rhythmical Latin or *cursus* used in papal and imperial chanceries, penetrated the English in a slow, halting manner in the late thirteenth century and no earlier.[9] *Dictamen* was a branch of rhetoric or propaganda; a trained rhetor would justify his employer's policies with reasons and theories calculated to impress his readers or hearers. He could produce them without using the *cursus*, but they normally went together. Henry's letter to Frederick I of 1157 is a fine specimen of rhetoric, though its drafter did not use the *cursus*. Flattery of Frederick as emperor serves as a *capatatio benevolentiae* to soften him up before he hears that his demand for the return of his treasure has been refused.[10] Henry's chancery may have suffered a brain drain subsequently, when Becket took some of the clerks into his service as archbishop. Geoffrey Ridel stayed behind to succeed him as chancellor. Geoffrey had the title of Master (presumably in Arts), but rhetoric did not interest him. The royal letters preserved in the *Materials* are businesslike, blunt and even rude in tone. Henry employed shrewd rather than polished administrators and diplomats.[11]

---

[7] *Mat.* vi, 102–3.

[8] T. A. M. Bishop, *Scriptores Regis* (Oxford, 1961).

[9] N. Denholm-Young, *Collected Papers on Medieval Subjects* (Oxford, 1946) 26–55; E. H. Kantorowicz, *Selected Studies* (New York, 1965) 213–46.

[10] See above, p. 60. Another example of a rhetorical letter, which does not use the *cursus*, is that sent to Pope Honorius III in the name of Henry III, then a minor, excusing himself for delayed payment of sums due to the pope in *Royal and other Historical Letters*, ed. W. W. Shirley (Rolls Series, 1862) 6–8. The letter ascribed to Henry II, *Foedera* i, 35, has been rejected as a forgery partly on the grounds of its rhetorical style; see Delisle, op. cit. ii, 9 and Lunt, op. cit. 132–3.

[11] A charter of 1156–61 is witnessed by 'magistro Gaufrido Ridello'; see Delisle, op. cit. i, 297. On his services to Henry as royal justice, see H. G. Richardson and G. O. Sayles, *The Governance of Medieval England* (Edinburgh, 1963) *passim*. On the chancery after Becket's retirement see Poole, 210–11.

M

They contrast strikingly with Frederick's servants. The imperial chancellor Rainald of Dassel had studied rhetoric in the Arts course; he used his skills in a masterly way to support Frederick's policies and claims. A modern student of Rainald admired him for passing through the Paris schools unscathed by the High-church doctrine which prevailed there. He had every chance to: the latest research on his career has cast doubt on the statement that he studied at Paris, and makes it certain that he never studied theology in any school.[12] Henry must have known about the methods of the imperial chancery. He received Rainald as Frederick's envoy at Rouen in 1165. But he had more resources and fewer pretensions than the emperor. A king who could bribe and force his opponents did not need to make propaganda for his cause. The limitations of his chancery may have been self-imposed. Jolliffe was right to say that the Angevins produced no theory to justify their will or their 'anger and ill will'.[13]

Henry had a deeper reason for keeping off theory in his case against Becket. His strength enabled him to win the game without changing the rules. He wanted to cash in on papal power over the Church for his own purposes. What mattered was to get in first and to prevent subjects from doing the same thing against his interests. His attitude to the papacy remained formally correct. He employed proctors at the Curia and he received papal legates; he allowed Peter's Pence to be dispatched and papal letters to be sent to England.[14] Alexander's biographer Boso dwells on Henry's reverence and humility before the pope in person.[15] The exiles' gloomy view of his aims support this interpretation in spite of themselves. Becket forecast that the authority of the Roman Church would perish in England, if the pope gave way to Henry;[16] but Becket

---

[12] A. Stelzmann, 'Reinold von Dassel, seine Reichspolitik', *Jahrbuch des kölnischen Geschichtesverein* xxv (1950) 60–82; J. Spörl, 'Reinold von Dassel', *Historisches Jahrbuch* lx (1940) 250–7; L. Minio-Paluello, 'The *Ars Disserendi* of Adam of Balsham "Parvipontanus"', M.A.R.S. iii (1954) 167; N. Rubinstein, 'Political Rhetoric in the Imperial Chancery during the Twelfth and Thirteenth Centuries', *Medium Aevum* xiv (1945) 21–43.

[13] *Angevin Kingship* (London, 1955) 13–130.

[14] Richardson and Sayles, op. cit. 298–9; Lunt, op. cit. 48–53; W. Holtzmann, op. cit. 295–306 and ibid. N.F. xxiii–xxv, 367–79; F. 3, xiv–xv, 311–15; A. Morey, *Bartholomew of Exeter, Bishop and Canonist* (Cambridge, 1937) 92–4.

[15] op. cit. 407–8, 425.   [16] *Mat.* vii, 182.

assumes that he will remain in communion with Rome. The king boasted of having both pope and cardinals 'in the bag'. He was thought to be imitating the ruler of Sicily, whose leverage on the papacy had won him the grant of a papal legateship in his kingdom. Henry also held that he had acquired his own grandfather's privilege of being papal legate, patriarch, emperor and what he would as king of England.[17] These rumours, for all their exaggeration, prove that he was suspected of squeezing the pope for grants rather than breaking away. A breach with Rome appeared to be imminent on two occasions only. The first was when he made overtures to the schismatics, the second when he banned recourse to the Curia and ordered that Peter's Pence should be paid into the royal treasury, 1169.[18] On each occasion he had special reasons to put pressure on the pope and archbishop. Even his hollow reconciliation with Becket shows that he needed an archbishop at Canterbury for the running of his government. Pope and clergy had practical uses for Henry; he could browbeat them by practical means; there was no point in exalting *regnum* above *sacerdotium* in theory.

Finally, Henry recognized the key role of the Paris schools in the formation of clerical opinion. He 'offered to submit his quarrel to the arbitration of scholars of different provinces, who should examine it fairly'. He made the offer at a late stage in the conflict, about 1169, together with an alternative: the court of the king of France or the French Church should arbitrate.[19] It was a safe proposal and a clever move. Henry must have known that Becket would never submit his suit to any tribunal other than the pope's. The panel of 'scholars from different provinces' would have been hand-picked and bribable, in any case: scholars were notoriously poor. Students and teachers of the *Artes* far outnumbered theologians and canonists. The latter would have been for Becket, the Artists not necessarily so. Henry flattered the Paris scholars without risk to himself. Ralph of Diss says that the offer swung academic opinion round to his side.[20] He was sensitive to the charge of tyranny brought against him by

[17] ibid. vi, 160, 254, 416–17; see F. Chalandon, *Histoire de la domination Normande en Italie et en Sicilie* (Paris, 1907) i, 347, ii, 103.

[18] Knowles, *Becket* 124–5.

[19] *Mat.* vii, 164; H. Rashdall, *The Universities of Europe in the Middle Ages*, ed. F. M. Powicke and A. B. Emden (Oxford, 1936) i, 3.

[20] *Opera* (op. cit.) i, 337.

Becket and his friends, realizing that it sounded bad to scholars and churchmen, and tried to ward it off.[21]

We turn to Henry's bishops. Of three outstanding intellectuals, Bartholomew of Exeter and Roger of Worcester were the most sympathetic to Becket; Robert of Melun, bishop of Hereford, felt the strain of conflicting loyalties. Most bishops concurred with the pope's view. It was right to stand up for ecclesiastical liberties in principle, but there was a time for everything and especially for giving way to Henry.[22] Arnulf bishop of Lisieux expressed it perfectly in a letter to Becket, March 1165. The writer had studied Arts and law; we have no evidence that he was a theologian.[23] A gifted rhetor and publicist, he fancied himself as a peacemaker, but tended to fall between two stools for his pains. His letter reads like a *Times* leader of the old style. He first put the case for Becket, beginning with principle. The archbishop had *set up a wall for the house of Israel* (Ezech. xiii, 5) and had braved terrors in defence of the Church. But his flight had been injudicious. Henry might have preferred to yield to him out of generosity, rather than as a tribute to his sufferings. Becket must now consider (1) his cause (2) his adversary (3) what support he could mobilize for his cause. Arnulf lays down the principle as firmly as the Becket circle could have done. The justice of his cause is manifest, since he contends for the liberty of the Church, which our Redeemer bought for us on the Cross:

> As faith is one, so liberty is one. . . . The wondrous sacrament of the Church's unity consists of this: as there is one faith, one spirit and one baptism, so there is one testament of perpetual manumission, by which divine adoption makes us not only free, but heirs jointly with Christ.[24] The faith is dishonoured when

[21] For accusations of tyranny by Becket and John of Salisbury, see *Mat.* v, 139, vi, 160, 96. For Henry's reactions see ibid. v, 137, vi, 149; Ralph of Diss, op. cit. i, 335.

[22] The bishops complained to the pope in Oct. 1164 that Becket had exposed them to the king's wrath, *Mat.* v, 136–8: . . . non considerans quoniam blandiri oportet, non detrahere potestati. . . . Ac si nesciat quod, etsi in illo iudicio aliquantulum ecclesiae dignitati derogaretur, dissimulandum erat pro tempore, ut pax ecclesiae redderetur.

[23] *Letters of Arnulf of Lisieux*, xiii–xix. Arnulf studied law in Italy. His connections make it probable that he studied Arts at Paris.

[24] From Eph, iv, 4–5; Rom. viii, 15, 17.

liberty is withdrawn. The same reason binds faith and liberty together. Both feel the same loss or increase.[25]

Hence to attack ecclesiastical liberty constituted an attack on the very being of the Church. Now Becket must weigh up his adversary. Arnulf dwells on Henry's cunning, strength, riches and power. As to supporters: the bishops have turned against him to the pope's dismay. Put no further trust in them. What is left? Just the sympathy of the lesser clergy, who can offer nothing but their prayers. The secular nobles are always anticlerical and delight in any excuse to oppress the clergy. Becket's friends overseas will cool if he outstays his welcome. Arnulf advises him to compromise, temporize and dissemble. He brings up the old argument on non-resistance to rulers: leave it to God to soften their hearts. Mutual collaboration will strengthen both *regnum* and *sacerdotium*.

'Put your principles in your pocket' is unhelpful advice to one who takes them seriously. Arnulf continues: make peace with the king; do not stick at separate clauses in the Constitutions; it can do no harm to promise to observe royal privileges and ancient customs in things which do not offend against God's law. Arnulf blandly ignored the fact that in Becket's eyes the Constitutions did offend against God's law. After the murder Arnulf wrote to the pope criticizing Becket for not having taken his advice. If he had done so, he would not have tarnished his martyr's crown by spitefulness.[26] Arnulf's advice had been simply: 'evade the issue; wait and see.' He did not dispute the question of principle; he just persuaded Becket to compromise and dissemble in the crudest of terms.

Gilbert Foliot should have presented a reasoned case, if anyone could. He was Henry's spiritual guide and political adviser and leader of the Henrician bishops. The Becket circle regarded him as their chief enemy. I shall tackle this daunting and controversial figure by trying to find out what he studied and what principles he professed to hold before the conflict. It is rather like prising open a clam, in spite of the scholarship which has been lavished on him recently.[27]

[25] *Letters of Arnulf of Lisieux*, 72, 77-8.

[26] ibid. 111: Utinam ille zeli feruorem temperasset ad tempus, quia, in causa ecclesie, quam suscepisset, sollerti mansuetudine utilius proficere potuit, si pacificus esset ingressus eius, si suas uindicare distulisset offensas, neque repentinis infestationibus iocunda noue corone gaudia denigrasset.

[27] My evidence for Gilbert's career and writings will be found in *Gilbert Foliot*, unless specially mentioned.

I shall start by summarizing, since investigation of his studies and teaching has to take account of his late as well as his early works. Gilbert came of a large, well-connected family. He was born about 1105–10 and set to letters at an early age. He studied the *Artes* and *divina pagina*. All we know about his masters is that Robert Pullen was one of them: Gilbert addressed Pullen twice as his 'dearest master' in a letter written to him as papal chancellor. The dates of their careers make it likely that Foliot studied under Pullen at Exeter, before Pullen moved to Oxford in 1133; his teaching periods at Oxford and Paris would have been too late for Foliot to have been his pupil there.[28] Foliot's skill in handling civil and canon law texts suggests that he studied law as well. On the other hand, it is difficult to fit a stay at Bologna or another centre of legal studies into the dates of Foliot's career. He may have worked on legal texts privately, and he had experts to help him in his episcopal household. After qualifying as a master of theology he held a school; we do not know where, but it was probably somewhere in northern France. He left his chair to become a monk at Cluny 'well before 1139'. He may have held the office of prior there[29] and he certainly acted as prior of Cluny's cell at Abbeville. He was elected abbot of Gloucester in 1139 and bishop of Hereford in 1148. Five years later he was translated to London, having been passed over for Canterbury. He died as bishop of London in 1187.

To begin with his scholarship: two dedications of books to him prove that he had a reputation for great learning. The first came from one Odo, who was English or at least wrote in England. Odo dedicated his book to 'Gilbert Foliot, master of scholars and father of monks' while Gilbert was abbot of Gloucester.[30] Odo writes in so obscure a style that he is barely comprehensible and quite un-translatable, but he sketches a recognizable picture of a master teaching in the early twelfth-century schools. Foliot had studied rhetoric; he was 'armed with eloquence'. Dialectic enters in, since Odo suggests that Foliot used to preside over what sounds like a *disputatio*.

---

[28] G.F.L.C. 84–5.

[29] There is no evidence in any known Cluniac source that he was ever prior there; see *The Letters of Peter the Venerable*, ed. G. Constable (Cambridge, Mass., 1967) 346.

[30] ed. A. M. Landgraf, *Ecrits théologiques de l'école d'Abélard* (Spic. sac. Lov. xiv, 1934) 287–9.

He would put forward cunning arguments to trap his opponents; he would calm the turbulent and stimulate the less excitable.[31] The exercise described here might have taken place within the framework of the study of theology: Odo presents Foliot as a great theologian, comparing him to St Paul as a refuter of Judaism, heresy and schism. He expounded the 'moral senses' in his wisdom, 'ran through poles and parallels', and meditated both on theology and on the divine economy.[32] The 'moral senses', theology and the divine plan of salvation presumably refer to his teaching of Scripture. The 'poles and parallels' make an odd filling to the sandwich, since they evoke the teaching of astronomy in the Arts course; but one can make a guess at the obscure phrase: it was customary to give instruction on cosmology in lectures on the Genesis account of Creation, so that the whole would fit into Odo's picture of Foliot as a master of the holy page.

The aim of the dedication is to advertise Odo's book in France. Foliot's virtuous life, his fame as a teacher, which is still vividly remembered, and his orthodoxy will commend it to a French audience.[33] The book which follows the dedication in the manuscript is the *Ysagoge in theologiam*. There has been some uncertainty as to whether the dedication originally belonged to the *Ysagoge* or whether it prefaced some other book and was tacked on later. Dr Luscombe has given good reasons to show that Odo was the author of both the *Ysagoge* and the prologue. The *Ysagoge* was written by a disciple of Abelard, though he did not agree with all his master's opinions. It is rated as one of the most interesting products of early scholasticism. It would point to breadth of mind on Foliot's part if Odo expected him to sympathize with and to

[31] ibid. 288: Recolit gloria illam Folioth facundiam mavigene talaribus et petaso discurrentem, perplexis sermonibus decipulas innectentem, argutiis perurgentem, in contione tumultuantes disertissime perorando sopientem, animequiores asperantem.

For *Mavigene petaso*, a reference to Mercury's cap, also mentioned in a letter from Foliot to John of Canterbury, see G.F.L.C. 94.

[32] Recolit et sophiam sensa moralia pandentem, polos et paralella percurrentem, tam theologis quam economie meditationibus insistentem.

Oeconomia in patristic Latin referred to the divine plan of salvation; see A. Blaise, *Dictionnaire latin-français des auteurs chrétiens* (Turnhout, 1954) 574.

[33] ibid. 289: Huic ergo tante prestantie, huic tante existimationis viro hoc opus devoveo, ut quod Gallie transmittit Anglia, celeberrime utrobique prudentie censura nitatur.

sponsor a book connected with such a stormy petrel as Abelard.[34] In any case, the dedication proves that Foliot had passed through the Arts course with credit and that he taught theology and *divina pagina* somewhere in northern France, the only place where Odo's account of his academic activities would be credible at the time.

The second dedication precedes a treatise on the book of Judges by the monk Osbern of Gloucester. The writer had taught in the schools himself before entering religion; he had been at Gloucester while Foliot ruled as abbot and sends the book to him as bishop of Hereford.[35] What he writes confirms the evidence given by Odo. He addresses the bishop as his devout son, but also as one priest to another: as priests they both have a duty to expound Scripture for the benefit of their fellows.[36] Osbern praises those scholars who lay aside the figments of the poets and the useless fables of secular science in favour of the study and teaching of Scripture. Foliot stands out among them as the ornament and glory of his day. He wears, as it were, two laurel crowns, philosophy and divine learning, and 'breathes out pure eloquence' (an implied allusion to the style of Livy). He puts his gifts at the service of others. He knows the value of his studies for the ordering of life, for rule and discipline, for the health of the soul, for the good of one's character, for resistence to vice and for divine contemplation. These lessons, derived from his

[34] D. E. Luscombe, 'The authorship of the *Ysagoge in theologiam*', A.H.D.L.M.A. xxxv (1969) 7–16.

[35] On Osbern see R. W. Hunt, The "Lost" Preface to the *Liber derivationum* of Osbern of Gloucester', M.A.R.S. iv (1958) 267–82. The treatise on Judges with other works of Osbern is in ms London, Brit. Mus. Royal 6.D. ix, late twelfth-century, from Gloucester. The dedicatory letter is on foll. 73ra–75ra: Incipit tractatus magistri Osberni Gloecestriensis monachi super librum Iudicum. Venerabili patri et omni honore digno Gileberto Herefordensi episcopo suus Osbertus (*sic*) devote subiectionis annisum.... Valeat sanctitas tua, dilectissime pater, tuique Osberni memor esto benigne.

Osbern says here, as in the preface to his *Liber derivationum*, edited by Dr Hunt, that he spent some time in the schools in his youth. He may perhaps be identified with an Osbern of Gloucester who was prior of a cell of the abbey in Wales, to whom Gilbert as abbot wrote a letter of encouragement; see G.F.L.C. 47.

[36] He compares preaching to the bells on the vestments of the Old Testament priest (Exod. xxviii, 35), fol. 73rb:... innuit ut nos, qui in hac extrema etate devenimus, qui et sacerdotum nomine censemur,... semper ad nos instruendos et ad alios corrigendos doctrine tintinnabula circumferamus, verbis insonemus, monitis et exhortationibus adinvicem conclamemus.

study of Scripture, he teaches signally in word and deed.[37] Osbern submits his treatise to Foliot for correction and asks for his judgement and protection, if he deserves it. As usual, the author mentions detractors. He seems to have great faith in Foliot's patronage against the wounding criticism of friends, which is hard to bear, and the poisoned stings of his enemies, who never leave him in peace.[38] His treatise on Judges is a conventional monastic work, showing little, if any, interest in new techniques of exegesis, though it would repay study as a sample of Benedictine learning in England. It is surprising that Foliot should have received two such contrasting books as the *Ysagoge* and Osbern on Judges, whose authors wanted him to approve them and to win them approval.

Osbern confirms what Odo tells us: Foliot was renowned for his skill in rhetoric and he had taught the Scriptures, indeed was still teaching them: Osbern uses the present tense. We know that Foliot gave *collationes*, edifying talks, to his monks at Gloucester. These are now lost, but we still have his letter to Hamo, the Cistercian abbot of Bordesley, who had asked to have them written down and sent to him; Foliot sent them with his letter.[39] Osbern probably

[37] fol. 74ra: Ex quorum numero te, pater Gileberte, nostri temporis decus et gloria esse affirmo, qui et vernanti philosophie flore et splendido divine scientie ornatu tamquam gemino donatus lauro, lacteam ubique respirans eloquentiam. Et cum exutoque ex Tantali scilicet fonte et ex plenis sapientie cisternis uberrime imbuaris, sic utroque prudenter cum expedit uteris, ut illam tamen scientiam, quam ex divinitatis fonte avidis memorie faucis hausisti, ubique gentium preferas, illam amantissime ... amplexeris, illam intentissime ad minus intelligentes instruendos impartiaris. Nostro revera ex huiusmodi studio vite ordinem, regendi formam, subdendi disciplinam, animi profectum, morum procedere ornamentum, et quanto quispiam in ea assiduus fuerit, tanto ... se a mundi illecebris liberius abstrahere et Deo coniunctius posse copulare.

St Jerome's prologue to the Bible, *Frater Ambrosius*, has the phrases 'Ad Titum Livium lacteo eloquentiae fonte manantem' and 'de Tantali fonte potantem' (*Rep. Bible.* no. 284). The comparison of Gilbert's eloquence to Livy's would be obvious to Osbern's readers who knew St Jerome's reference to Livy in his prologue; it formed part of the medieval Vulgate.

[38] foll. 74rb–75ra: Hinc est igitur, sincerissime pater, Osberni tui qualemcumque sudorem gratanter suscipe, tueque correctionis lime ut queque inculta, ut soles, ferventer adiunge. ... Tue igitur equitatis libre, tui iudicii censure hoc opus committo, quatinus et contra amicorum vulnera, que, licet ferenda sint, infirmo tamen homini gravia et gravius equo quandoque infixa, et contra virosos scorpionum aculeos, qui me nec bonis intendentem, nec in angulis habitantem vivere permittunt, pie defensionis clipeo, si merui, tuearis.

[39] G.F.L.C. 44–5.

used the present tense so as to include Foliot's teaching and preaching as bishop. Hereford had a school, like many English cathedrals. It became a famous centre of scientific studies in the later twelfth century.[40] No reference to a 'master of the schools' there has been found for the period of Foliot's rule. A bishop of his day would normally delegate his traditional duty of presiding over the schools of his diocese. Foliot may perhaps have found time to give some instruction himself in default of a *scholasticus*.

To complete the evidence for his studies in the Arts course: a passage in one of his homilies, written when he was bishop of London and perhaps addressed to Abbot Aelred of Rievaulx, ties up with the 'poles and parallels' mentioned by Odo. The latter gave us to understand that Foliot taught cosmology in lectures on the Days of Creation. In one of his homilies, he raises a number of *quaestiones naturales*. The excuse for bringing them in is a commentary on the word *heaven*. He has taken as the subject of his homilies St Peter and St Paul, here called 'the two keys of heaven'. The word leads him to raise questions regarding the firmament, the aether, the fixed stars and the planets and their rotations. One question is whether the firmament consists of 'aether or fire', which some call 'the measure of bodies', because bodily nature grows ever thinner as it rises in the scale and what is more subtle is no longer body but spirit. No source for this postulate has been found.[41] Foliot also asks whether the sky is really blue or whether we see it so on account of our faulty vision, just as we think we see black when we shut our eyes.[42] The closest parallel to this question, so far as is known, comes in a commentary on the Days of Creation by Thierry of Chartres. Foliot does not quote it *verbatim*, and Thierry says that people think they see

[40] For recent data and bibliography see B. Lawn, *The Salernitan Questions* (Oxford, 1963) 35–6, 64–5.

[41] MS London, Brit. Mus. Royal 2.D. xxxii (see G.F.L.C. 333–4, and below, p. 174), fol. 163: Firmamentum vero celum nominatur. . . . Quod utrum solidum sit . . . an vero summa sit et subtilissima pars aeris, qui ether vel ignis dicitur, qui et iuxta quosdam meta corporum appellatur, quia eo usque natura corporalis semper attenuando progreditur et si quid eo subtilius est id iam non corpus sed spiritus est, necesse est . . .

[42] ibid. . . . et color ipse saphirinus, quem circa partem illam videmus nobis cernere, an ipsius materie color vere sit, an defectu visus ex aeris profunditate videamur nobis huiusmodi aliquid intueri, sicut et clausis oculis nigrum quiddam videmus nobis conspicere, et cetera huiusmodi, dum super terram gradimur et peregrinantes a Domino foris sumus, non certe comprehendimus.

green, not blue.[43] Our only date for Thierry's commentary is 'before 1155', when he died or resigned from being chancellor of Chartres to enter a monastery.[44] It would be rash to suppose that Foliot was his pupil or even that he had read the book. At least, however, the likeness to Thierry on the Six Days suggests that Foliot remembered questions on natural science which were discussed in his school days. His conclusion, befitting a homilist, is that we have no certain understanding of such things in our present life.[45] Later still, in his commentary on the Canticle, he dragged in a piece on the functions of the seven liberal and the mechanical Arts. He paid special attention to the subject matter of astronomy (which he extends to cover astrology). That must have been his favourite part of the *quadrivium*. Here, too, the tone is derogatory: divine learning has precedence over secular, which is mere vanity.[46] Yet he never quite shook off his old interests.

Rhetoric, as studied in the *trivium*, continued in practical use after he had left the schools. Foliot alludes to his former study of Cicero in a letter written to the archbishop of York, 1155-7. It was over and done with,[47] but the letters witness to Foliot's expertise. He could make learned allusions when he chose to, though he seldom indulged in the luxury and did not go in for window-dressing: to quote Livy was a rare accomplishment.[48] Herbert wrote that he surpassed the other bishops in fluency and elegance of speech, except for Bishop Hilary of Chichester.[49]

[43] ed. N. Haring, 'The Creation and Creator of the World according to Thierry of Chartres and Clarenbald of Arras', A.H.D.L.M.A. xxii (1956) 188: Nam hoc quod quidam rudes dicunt se videre caelum, quando aer purus est, cum aliquid viride se fingunt conspicere, illud falsissimum est. Nam ubi visus deficit, ibi error sensus dat imaginationem videndi quod non videt, sicuti aliquis clausis oculis videtur sibi tenebras videre.

I have to thank Dr Brian Lawn for this reference. Foliot could have studied under Thierry, who was a master by 1121, when he spoke for Abelard at the council of Soissons. This might perhaps explain why Odo hoped for Foliot's sympathy, since Odo was an admirer of Abelard. There is no real evidence, however. For recent notices on Thierry see D. E. Luscombe. *The School of Peter Abelard* (Cambridge, 1969) 57-8 and Southern, 68-70.

[44] A. Vernet, 'Une épitaphe inédite de Thierry de Chartres', *Recueil de travaux offert à M. Clovis Brunel* ii (Paris, 1955) 660-70.

[45] See n. 42 above.

[46] P.L. ccii, 1174-6, on Cant. i, 1: ... *thy breasts are better than wine.* Foliot interprets *breasts* as divine learning, which he contrasts with the *wine* of the secular sciences in the form of the Artes.

[47] G.F.L.C. 171.　　　　[48] G.F.L.C. 315.　　　　[49] *Mat.* iii, 336.

The Arts course left its mark on Foliot. His scriptual studies made a more obvious impression. He could write gracefully in biblical language, deploying both the literal and spiritual senses. The opening of Machabees came to mind when he wanted to find a comparison with the wars of Stephen's reign: they recalled the conflicts among Alexander's children.[50] He used new devices. Abbot Hamo specially asked him to include *schemata* in the *collationes* he was to send:[51] Hamo probably referred to divisions of subject matter in schematic form. Peter of Cornwall, prior of Holy Trinity Aldgate, described his pleasure at hearing a sermon preached by Foliot as bishop of London sometime after 1170: Foliot exhibited the new technique of *distinctiones*, lists of biblical nouns in their various meanings.[52] He continued to write. It seems likely that his homilies on St Peter and St Paul were sent to Abbot Aelred of Rievaulx; in that case they date from the midst of the Becket conflict, 1164–7.[53] Their recipient had asked him not to use the brevity of the schools, but to spread himself; in other words, he should write as a monk and not as a former schoolman.[54] Even towards the end of his life, when suffering from blindness, he produced a commentary on the Canticle. This is a traditional treatment of the theme of the Bride as the Church or the faithful soul. The commentator contributed nothing new, but he made a well-worn subject his own, instead of copying his sources verbally.[55]

The most important problem concerning Gilbert's school days is: what did he learn and teach on doctrine as distinct from the study of Scripture? There is one reference in his letters. 'When I was in the schools,' he wrote in 1140, 'I heard diverse men put forward diverse opinions on poverty of spirit.' The context shows that the debate he remembered had turned on the nature of poverty as a way

---

[50] G.F.L.C. 64.   [51] ibid. 44.

[52] R. W. Hunt was the first to notice this interesting reference, 'English Learning', 33–4.

[53] *Gilbert Foliot* 70. The reason for thinking that these homilies were sent to Aelred is that they occur in the same manuscript as Aelred's sermons.

[54] G.F.L.C. 334; Foliot writes: Nam et hoc in prece complexus es, ne tuam scolarium more propositionem sub breuitate constringerem, sed . . . quod proposueras auctoritatibus cingerem, et id uerbis et sententiis dilatando, non in expositionem solummodo, sed in tractatum extenderem.

[55] P.L. ccii, 1150–13⌐⌐; H. Riedlinger, *Die Makellosigkeit der Kirche in den lateinischen Hohenliedkommentaren des Mittelalters* (B.G.P.T.M. xxxviii, 1, 1958) 199–201.

of life. Gilbert is comforting the dean of Hereford for his expulsion from his cathedral during the civil war. Poverty is personified in the letter: she accompanied the dean into exile; she goes with him on his way; she promises him the kingdom of heaven as consolation.[56] It is a clear allusion to the text Mt. v, 3: *Beati pauperes spiritu.* Where could Gilbert have heard a scholastic debate on poverty of spirit in the early twelfth century? I began the search by looking through the *quaestiones,* sentences and biblical commentaries of the school of Laon. It was a blind alley. The authors and compilers connected with Laon discussed the beatitudes (Mt. v, 3–11) as gifts of the Holy Spirit, developing the theme of correspondence between the seven gifts and the beatitudes (reduced to seven for the purpose) and the seven petitions of the Lord's Prayer. They did not analyse the separate virtues.[57] Gilbert does not fit into the Laon tradition; he avoided the 'sevens' technique in his commentary on the Lord's Prayer, written 1177–87.[58] Then it dawned on me that Gilbert was pointing to his master Robert Pullen. In his treatise on the Christian life Pullen discusses the precept: *If thou wilt be perfect, go sell all that thou hast . . .* (Mt. xix, 21). He decides that the gospel precept is the safest guide to perfection, but that it does not apply to married men with families; a man can save his soul by making right use of his riches. Pullen also refers to the *poor in spirit* as friends of Christ, who suffer oppression from powerful men, although they have not rebelled.[59] This could have applied to Gilbert's friend, the exiled dean of Hereford. Pullen compared the merits of the active life, which supposed worldly possessions, and the contemplative, which went with poverty, in his *Sentences.* If the teaching of the treatise on the Christian life and the *Sentences* reflect Pullen's earlier teaching, as is probable, then his school at Exeter may have set the stage for debates on the true nature of poverty. It was a burning issue of the day. Members of the new

---

[56] G.F.L.C. 35: Iam dudum in scolis positi de paupertate spiritus diuersa a diuersis audiuimus.

Should *paupertate* perhaps be emended to *pauperie*?

[57] O. Lottin, 'La doctrine d'Anselme de Laon sur les dons du Saint-Esprit et son influence', R.T.A.M. xxiv (1957) 267–95. A commentary on St Matthew of the Laon schools raises the question 'whether he who has one virtue has all' on the beatitudes, but without discussing the nature of poverty of spirit; P.L. cxlii, 1286. On this commentary see Lottin, 153–69.

[58] MS Worcester Cathedral Q.48, foll. 60v–69; G.F.L.C. 334.

[59] 'An unpublished treatise', op. cit., 207, 214–16.

religious Orders and wandering preachers on the one hand, and black monks, representing an older tradition on the other, engaged in controversy on 'the true apostolic or gospel life'. Their quarrels occasioned many treatises; but we have no record of scholastic *quaestiones* on the subject from this early period. Perhaps they took place at Exeter under Pullen.

Gilbert's reminiscence tightens his link with his master. This brings another problem on its heels. Pullen taught the doctrine of the two swords in his *Sentences*. It seems unlikely that he would have changed his mind and therefore probable that he taught the same doctrine at Exeter. John of Salisbury developed Pullen's teaching on the two swords. It would be strange if Foliot had drawn an opposite conclusion from the same teaching and upheld *regnum* over *sacerdotium*. We need not speculate. Gilbert put forward a more precise case for resistance to secular tyranny than either Robert Pullen or Robert of Melun. If he started from Pullen's theory, he carried it further. It is significant that he does so immediately after his allusion to the debate on poverty in his letter to the dean of Hereford. This rather suggests that he had another scholastic *quaestio* in mind: it could have arisen on the text Rom. xiii, 1–2. Foliot considers this very text in the light of the civil wars of Stephen's reign. His correspondent had resisted the troops who besieged Hereford, expelled him, turned the cathedral into a fortress and knocked down a wall. Some persons, unnamed, object to the dean's action in resisting them: Foliot defends the dean:

> What does their objection come to? They oppose to you the Apostle's saying: *Let every soul be subject to the higher powers*, and *he that resisteth the power resisteth the ordinance of God*. Quite true; but the secular power has a law to bind it and to set limits within which it should be obeyed. The secular power must keep the law, observe God's commandments and not presume to act rashly against him. If it oversteps these limits by shamelessly affronting the highest King, then it cannot claim privilege from him whose right it has spurned. The objectors make a further point on the dictates of prudence and discretion. A man of discretion, so they say, should not kindle his zeal against small faults; let him keep his anger to correct graver sins. The little matter of a wall, which has been partly destroyed by the prince, should have been punished more mildly. Their points are well made, but

according to Wisdom: he that contemneth small things shall fall little by little. (Ecclus. xix, 1.)[60]

Foliot goes on to approve the dean for his attempt to nip the evil in the bud, so as to prevent even worse damage to the holy places in his charge.

The next letter is addressed to the bishop of Hereford. Foliot urges him to cast fear aside and to use all the spiritual weapons at his command against the attackers of churches and clergy.[61] There are similar appeals to the bishops of Worcester and Salisbury on later occasions: they should excommunicate despoilers of churches or lay interdicts on their lands, or allow Foliot to do so instead. He reproached the bishops for cowardice.[62] A letter to an unnamed bishop, on the contrary, praises him for his fearless courage and discipline.[63] The abbot of Gloucester had a name for resistance to secular tyranny. Odo in his dedicatory letter writes of Foliot's 'triumphant victories over the truculence of tyrants'.[64] The tyrants who represented secular power at this stage of Stephen's reign were generally local men: 'We suffer as many kings as the castles which burden us', Foliot wrote.[65] They stirred him to confute the doctrine of non-resistance. The Gregorian reformers themselves had never proclaimed the duty of prelates to wield the spiritual sword against disobedient princes in a more militant way. As bishop of Hereford he also defended privilege of clergy. A letter to a lay lord who has tried a priest and a dean of the diocese in his court reproves him for usurping a power against the Church, 'which up to now kings and emperors have sweated to win from her in vain.'[66]

Logically Gilbert should have been a keen papalist, and he was. He referred to the pope as 'Vicar of Christ' as early as 1155–7.[67] He praised the Roman Curia to litigants as 'the throne and temple of justice'. Rome would never go against the truth, if it were known to her.[68] He would not presume to judge a papal writing.[69] He appealed to the pope when abbot and bishop. His letters show him

[60] G.F.L.C. 35. I cannot find any source for this discussion in commentaries on Romans or in *quaestiones*.

[61] ibid. 36–7.   [62] ibid. 38–40, 66–8.   [63] ibid. 48–9.

[64] op. cit. 288: adversus aerie nequitie phalanges strenuus agonites dimicans et de triumphata tyrannorum truculentia trophea reportans...; omnia sustinens, quasi nulla sentiens, totus aliis vacabat.

[65] G.F.L.C. 64.   [66] ibid. 158.

[68] ibid. 87, 140.   [69] ibid. 152.   [67] ibid. 167.

constantly seeking papal support and intervention. Crowning irony, as bishop of London he objected to Archbishop Thomas, 1163–4, that a London cleric should not have had his case tried in the archbishop's court, since he had appealed to the pope.[70] Foliot showed the courage of his convictions when he raised a lone voice in protest against Becket's election to Canterbury. That was to champion the teaching of the schools against royal use of the Church for royal ends. It would displease Henry and might have prejudiced Foliot's chances of getting something better than the see of Hereford. He exaggerated the risk to himself and his family later on;[71] but he had really stuck his neck out in defence of the Church. Becket before his promotion represented the bugbear of masters of the holy page: he was a courtier, untrained in theology and therefore as unfitted for pastoral care as he was unlikely to defend ecclesiastical freedom. He came to his office unprepared, not from the cloister or the schools, but from the royal court, as Herbert put it, to excuse the shame of Clarendon. Foliot's election to Canterbury, on the other hand, would have rejoiced the hearts of theologians. Foliot was both a master and a monk. He used his knowledge of the *Artes* to strengthen his preaching. He had proved himself to be a friend of the Church's cause both as abbot of Gloucester and as bishop of Hereford. It was natural that he should feel slighted at being passed over, and natural, too, that he would not accept Becket's conversion as genuine. That a curial bishop might change his spots was not in the textbooks. A professional normally feels jealous of a gifted amateur. Foliot was a professional theologian and a model of virtue.

His short experience as a monk at Cluny may help to explain his antagonism to Becket and his taking Henry's side against Becket when the conflict began. Foliot made an unusual choice when he joined the Cluniacs. Masters of the early twelfth century, who 'took the jump', as the saying was, by entering religion, generally went the whole hog and became white monks or canons; the austerity of the new Orders appealed to them. Alternatively they preferred the Austin canons, who encouraged learning. Cluny's laxer interpretation of the Rule and her time-consuming liturgy put scholars off. The cut-throat competition from other Orders reduced Peter the Venerable as abbot of Cluny to touting for entrants; only so could he keep up his supply of talent. Foliot may have realized that Cluny offered prospects of quick promotion in the circumstances. His

---

[70] ibid. 193–4.   [71] ibid. 231.

superiors later regarded him as a feather in their cap. Black monk houses outside Cluny would elect Cluniacs as their abbots, as at Gloucester. And the Cluniac ethos suited him. Patience and moderation were among the most admired virtues at Cluny. The *Lives* of her abbots show them as gentle, but dignified; they always kept calm in emergencies. Peter the Venerable exemplified Cluniac virtues in their most winning form. The choir monks submitted to an authoritarian regime, which Foliot approved of as abbot. He liked modesty and decorum. *Nemo repente fit optimus*; he quoted this proverb to a friend who had entered Clairvaux; we attain virtue by stages, beginning with the virtue of humility.[72] Becket was not a humble type and he leaped into sanctity. His behaviour at the council of Northampton, when he provoked Henry by carrying his cross, struck the Cluniac in Gilbert as ill-bred and hysterical. Hence his famous remark that Becket had always been a fool and always would be. It was non-Cluniac to exaggerate. His Order's tradition in politics may have weighed with him too. The Cluniacs avoided committing themselves, if possible. They supported Gregorian reform from motives of interest and principle;[73] but their debt to lay patrons inclined them to good relations with the secular power. Still, Gilbert did not always follow the abbot of Cluny in politics; he avoided the mistake of backing Victor IV against Alexander III.[74]

His experience as abbot of Gloucester and bishop of Hereford may have led him to support Henry II. His practice had not always conformed to his principles. He had to operate in a border territory, exposed to attack from both sides in the civil war and with kinsmen in both camps. He had to combine loyalty to the Angevins with obedience to Archbishop Theobald, who was loyal to Stephen when Stephen would let him be. Gilbert sometimes ran with the hare and hunted with the hounds. He pressed bishops to take action against tyrants; but when the bishop of Hereford set an example to his colleagues to shake off their sloth by interdicting the earl of Gloucester in 1143, Gilbert pleaded for mildness. The earl was his kinsman and the interdict affected some of the churches of Gloucester abbey.[75] Like the chroniclers of Stephen's reign he looked back to

[72] ibid. 149.
[73] H. E. J. Cowdrey, *The Cluniacs and Gregorian Reform* (Oxford, 1970).
[74] G.F.L.C., 174–5.
[75] ibid. 56. The author of *Gesta Stephani* praises the bishop of Hereford for setting an example of boldness to the other bishops in 'resistance to the

the time of Henry I as a golden age of strong government.[76] The civil war taught him to keep in with both sides and to appreciate peace and order. It was one thing to resist local lords, quite another to sabotage Henry II's rule.

His role in the Becket conflict has been closely followed. He was suspected of being hostile to the archbishop because he would have liked to be primate himself. He disclaimed any wish or scheme to be promoted to Canterbury; but he certainly wished and schemed to raise London to independent status. How far disappointment and pique influenced him is impossible to judge. We know that he formed the backbone of opposition to Becket after Clarendon, that he advised Henry and that he prejudiced the chances of reconciliation by assisting at the coronation of the young King Henry by the archbishop of York, thus provoking Becket to renew his excommunications. Did he consciously go back on his principles as a high-churchman?

Not in his own eyes. All through the conflict he presented himself as a loyal papalist and defender of ecclesiastical liberties. Gilbert's first reaction to Becket's appeal to Rome was to lodge a counter appeal. He used the weapon of appeal persistently with Henry's permission. His language to the pope throughout was more respectful than that the exiles sometimes indulged in. The last of his homilies on St Peter and St Paul has a passage in which Gilbert goes out of his way to exalt the pope as St Peter's successor and ruler over the Church. Just as an earthly king has 'consuls, centurions, tribunes and many other officials to administer justice, who carry out his power and will in all things,' so St Peter set up successors in his see to rule over the Church committed in perpetuity to his care.[77] The see of Rome itself undoubtedly hallows its occupants

abandoned recklessness of the rich'; ed. and transl. K. R. Potter (London, 1955) 104–6. The *Gesta Stephani* may have been written by Bishop Robert of Bath; he was a partisan of Stephen and therefore antagonistic to the earl of Gloucester; but his first loyalty was to the Church; see R. H. C. Davis, 'The authorship of the *Gesta Stephani*', E.H.R. lxxvii (1962) 209—32.

[76] G.F.L.C. 61.

[77] MS Royal 2.D. xxxii, fol. 166v: Hunc igitur in ecclesia velut regem in regno attendamus. Habet consules rex, centuriones habet, tribunos habet, quamplures iustitie ministros habet, qui dum regalia dispensant officia, ipsi quidem operantur, sed operatur ille potissimum, cuius in ipsorum manibus iustitia est, cuius eorum manibus exercetur potestas et voluntas in omnibus adimpletur. In hunc ergo modum beatus Petrus cum ex suscepta cura totius ecclesie in sua sibi sede statuat in perpetuum successores. . .

or else receives men already holy.[78] It is an echo of Gregory VII's *Dictatus papae*. Gilbert goes on to proclaim the pope's power to bind and loose, as given to him by God and transmitted by him to lesser ecclesiastical dignitaries.[79] The dire effects of excommunication are stressed. The sinner who dies excommunicate has no hope of salvation.[80] Gilbert wrote these homilies as bishop of London; if the recipient was Aelred of Rievaulx, they must have been written before Aelred's death in January 1167. It sounds like Gilbert's manifesto of loyalty to Rome during the crisis. He omits to mention the relations between the spiritual and temporal powers, but so did the bishop of Assisi in his official address to the Lateran Council of 1179. Their comparisons of papal rule over the Church to royal rule are very similar.

Foliot's deeds were as good as his words. He obeyed the pope's order to accompany the bishop of Hereford to visit Henry and expostulate with him.[81] He persuaded Henry to allow the collection of Peter's Pence and saw to its despatch.[82] Communication with the Curia remained open, with only the normal amount of friction,[83] thanks largely to Foliot's efforts; so he claimed. He had grounds for his plea that the 'sacraments, faith and morals' were safeguarded in England: an incursion of heretics in 1165 was stopped with high speed.[84] His assurance to Alexander of Henry's devotion sounds inconsistent with his threat that Henry, if thwarted, might recognize the antipope, expel the Alexandrian bishops and replace them with yes-men.[85] Both threat and reassurance, however, provided Alexander with a welcome excuse to temporize. Foliot pleaded with reason that he had always done his best for Alexander

---

[78] ibid. . . . . quos (successores) sedes eadem indubitanter sanctos facit aut sanctos suscipit.

Clause xxiii of the *Dictatus* reads: Quod romanus pontifex, si canonice fuerit ordinatus, meritis beati Petri indubitanter efficitur sanctus. . . . On this clause and on the origin of the *Dictatus* see W. Ullmann, 'Romanus pontifex indubitanter efficitur sanctus: Dictatus papae 23 in restrospect and prospect', S.G. vi, 229–64.

[79] fol. 166v: . . . quicquid ab istorum aliquo ligatur aut solvitur, aperitur aut clauditur, merito ab isto ligari aut solvi, aperiri aut claudi dicitur, cuius nimirum potestas ipsi a Domino traditur et ab ipso in alios derivata hoc ipsum ligare aut solvere, aperire aut claudere non negatur.

[80] fol. 168–168v.   [81] G.F.L.C. 202–6.

[82] ibid. 203, 206–7, 225–6, 249–51.

[83] As on the Pentney case: see *Gilbert Foliot*, 236–7.

[84] G.F.L.C. 207–10.   [85] ibid. 204–5, 219–22.

in the teeth of difficulties.[86] His reverence for the Holy See appears in his dread of an excommunication authorized by the pope. When it could be staved off no longer in 1169, he got Henry's licence to visit the Curia in order to defend himself. He turned back at Milan only because news reached him that the pope had arranged for him to be absolved by the archbishop of Rouen. The censure of 1170 evoked a crawling plea for absolution.[87] The murder of Becket may account for his abject tone; the plea was consistent with his whole attitude.

Foliot never presented the Constitutions as other than evil. He merely pointed to the difficulties of resistance. Bad customs, deeply rooted in time, could not be plucked up until careful digging had loosened the soil around them. Henry would respond if he were treated gently instead of being irritated.[88] It was the plea of expediency: withdraw from the border, while saving your title-deeds. Foliot himself claimed benefit of clergy for some criminous clerks in 1168–9.[89] Granted the principle, he thought that infringement of ecclesiastical liberties 'for the time' did not call for martyrdom.[90] Becket upset him by taking the line which he, as abbot of Gloucester, had put to the dean of Hereford: *he that contemneth small things shall fall little by little*. Foliot made an even worse mistake when he changed sides on the rivalry between Canterbury and York. As bishop of London in 1163 he wrote to Alexander to put the case for the primacy of Canterbury.[91] Then his alliance with the archbishop of York against Becket led him to take a more detached view of the old quarrel for primacy than was normal in a bishop of the southern province. He agreed to Henry's wish that his son should be crowned by the archbishop of York, in Canterbury's absence. Becket, like Anselm before him, saw the rights of his see as no borderline area, to be evacuated under fire, but as the very heartland of freedom.

Since he could not approve the Constitutions in principle, Foliot had to argue against Becket on personal grounds. *Multiplicem*, the famous letter of reproach to Becket in answer to his charges against the bishops, was probably drafted by Foliot and certainly approved by him.[92] It is a tissue of half-truths and inconsistencies. Henry terrorized the bishops into accepting his unsuitable nominee to the

86 ibid. 256, 283. 87 ibid. 289. 88 ibid. 240–1.
89 ibid. 268–9. 90 ibid. 239, 254. 91 ibid. 191–2.
92 ibid. 229–43.

archbishopric of Canterbury. He tried to impose the Constitutions on them in spite of their opposition. Becket's conduct then so inflamed his wrath as to make it perilous to resist him any further. Yet intermittently, here as in letters to Alexander, Henry appears as a model of sweet reasonableness, who meant no harm to the Church. It should be recalled, in fairness to *Multiplicem*, that Herbert of Bosham described the king, in the same letter, as both fiercely determined and easily cowed.[93] The main target of *Multiplicem* is Becket's character and behaviour. Its account of them comes straight from the school picture of the bad prelate. The royal favourite jumped straight from the court and the hunting field to serve altars. He was already a notorious oppressor of ecclesiastical liberties: witness the tax of Toulouse. He bought both secular and ecclesiastical offices. He gave way to Henry on the Constitutions, although he had a united bench of bishops behind him, when he refused to agree. He let them down by submitting. Then he changed his mind. He broke his promise to submit, betraying the king to whom he owed so much. What ingratitude! His flight into self-imposed exile left his colleagues to face the music. The indictment shows flaws at this stage. If it was right to reject the Constitutions in the first place, then Becket was right to repent of his submission, however tardily. *Multiplicem* then blames his actions in exile: he told lies about Henry, reporting that the king burned with a tyrant's rage and that he had expelled Christ's minister from his kingdom, which was quite untrue. Yet elsewhere in the letter Henry's wrath would suggest tyranny.

The author argued like a good Englishman; he went for tactics in preference to theory. The reproaches hinge on Becket's handling of the business. He showed 'an extraordinary lack of tact', as we should say. 'Tactless' is one of the dirty words in our language. We like to think that 'tact and understanding' can avert any conflict. It is a safe hypothesis: they are worth trying. More comforting still, the author of *Multiplicem* cited examples from history: tact had been tried and had succeeded.[94] St Augustine of Canterbury had borne patiently with pagan practices among a newly converted people, eliminating their errors slowly by dint of preaching and exhortation. The cardinal legate John of Crema at a council in England (Westminster, 1125) had brought Henry I to allow him to correct old customs by gentle persuasion, when force would

---

[93] Above, p. 67. [94] G.F.L.C. 240–1.

have got him nowhere.[95] The clergy of France had recently obtained redress of old grievances from their pious king in gratitude for the birth of his long-awaited heir; they begged rather than threatened, 'as we have heard'.[96] Becket appears in *Multiplicem* as a bad prelate by origin, a natural oppressor of ecclesiastical liberties. Yet he becomes a tactless, malicious bungler when he stands up for them.

There are theories in *Multiplicem*, however. There had to be, since the author needed to prove his learning in competition with Becket's *eruditi*. Our difficulty is to know whose theories they are.[97] Becket obeyed the royal summons to Northampton and stood to judgements on charges brought against him as a tenant-in-chief of the crown. Then he refused to submit and appealed to the Curia. His motives are open to speculation, since he did not consult his colleagues. The author suggests an argument against submission to the council: canon law forbids a bishop to answer on a civil or criminal charge in a secular court. The arguments for submission, which Becket might have had in mind, are first that the king has a religious character, given to him by unction at his coronation; hence he has a right to act as judge even in spiritual causes. This argument rested on an old-fashioned concept of royalty; it is doubtful whether Henry, let alone Becket, would have taken it seriously. The second argument is presented as weightier. The secular and spiritual powers are twins, each one supreme in its own sphere. Thus a bishop, however independent in spiritual matters, owes allegiance to his king for the temporalities of his see. This view expressed current practice and theory well enough. The author of *Multiplicem* does not take responsibility for it even so; he writes 'ut affirmant'. His own views are never stated. He concludes this section by praising humility as a Christian virtue. Would that Becket had practised it! But he did not. To drag this piece of moralizing into theory was to sidestep the issue.

[95] The legate 'had lately done Henry a very good turn and was now reaping his reward'; see D. Nicholl, *Thurstan Archbishop of York (1114–1140)* (York, 1964) 92–5.

[96] Redress of grievances is not recorded among Louis VII's benefactions in gratitude for the birth of his long-awaited heir Philip, 21 August 1165; but some rumour of it may have reached England with the news of Philip's birth; see A. Cartellieri, *Philipp II. König von Frankreich* i (Leipzig, 1899) 5–8.

[97] G.F.L.C. 236–8.

Foliot's writings, including *Multiplicem*, contain no clear statement on the relations between the two powers. Was one above the other or were both supreme in their respective spheres? His silence contrasts with Becket's outspoken doctrine; but Foliot had a lead from the highest quarter in being non-committal. On the right of resistance he was consequent, on paper at least. As abbot of Gloucester he held that the secular prince had limits set to his power by the laws. He told Alexander, when writing on behalf of the English bishops in 1166, that Henry regarded himself as being bound by the laws,[98] wishful thinking perhaps, but consistent with his earlier statement to the dean of Hereford. The Constitutions, designed to keep the peace, struck him as more tolerable than the turning of churches into castles and other outrages committed in warfare. The Church needed the protection of the temporal sword.

The second homily on St Peter and St Paul sets out Foliot's view of the nature and function of secular government. Likening the two apostles to *the two olive trees* (Zach. iv, 11-12), Foliot expounds the fable of the trees of the wood who sought a king to reign over them (Iud. ix, 8-15). The trees of the wood signify the instability of earthly rule, which is always passing from one realm or people to another; that was an allusion to the text Ecclus. x, 8, *de regno in regnum*, often quoted in discussions on *translatio imperii*. The olive and the fig tree in the fable of the trees of the wood declined the invitation to rule over the other trees: they signify spiritual men. The thorn tree accepted and proceeded to rule oppressively. Just so, the worst men seek temporal rule; but spiritual men resist them and suffer persecution rather than imitate their evil ways. There was no thorn tree in paradise. Secular rule, signified by the thorn tree, grew and spread as a result of Adam's disobedience.[99] It is a classic

[98] G.F.L.C. 220 . . . seque legibus alligatum principem, presto est in omnibus exhibere.

[99] MS Royal 2.D. xxxii, foll. 145v-146r: Ligna silvarum sunt reges et principes nationum, quorum dominatio et regnum totum in motu est, quia mobile et transitorium facile de gente in gentem et de populo transfertur ad populum. Respuit itaque inter ligna commoveri, qui non vult inter homines temporaliter dominari. . . . Ceterum regnum mobile ramno competit; libenter a ramno suscipitur. Ramnus arbor est spinis consita, quam si contigeris lederis. . . . Arborem hanc Adam, peccati iam servus et a paradiso eiectus, invenit. Quos igitur arbor ista significat, nisi (illos) cuos peccatorum vallat asperitas. . . .? Hii sunt qui mundi dominationem affectant. . . . Obest enim adeo dominatio pessimorum ut sanctos, . . . si ipsis moribus et vita conformare refugiunt, ignis persecutionis egressus persepe corporaliter absumat. Melius tamen

expression of the traditional patristic view of secular rule as originating in man's sin at the fall. Foliot could portray Henry as devout and virtuous or even as a would-be crusader.[1] A king might be a good man; but Foliot saw all temporal rulers, good or bad, and more likely bad, as a punishment for sin, and their government as the prickly condition of our life on earth. John of Salisbury had a more hopeful view of royal government than had the royalist bishop.

Gilbert Foliot miscalculated. He hoped that Alexander could be coaxed off the fence on to Henry's side. The pope had a personal regard for Gilbert and had made him Henry's spiritual adviser.[2] It would never do for Alexander to antagonize Henry during the schism; Becket might be forced to resign or submit. The bishops under London's guidance told Becket that love and loyalty to the pope and the Holy Roman Church ought to sway him.[3] They under-rated Becket's obstinacy and over-rated Alexander's inertia.

Foliot could not have made a case for *regnum versus sacerdotium*. It would have belied both his principles and his diplomacy. Gilbert was useful to Henry and to Alexander in the early stages of the conflict precisely because he was a good papalist and threw the mantle of piety over compromise. The event showed that he compromised too much and too long for his reputation. One can easily see why. Henry frightened him; Becket offended his sense of decorum and his common sense; Alexander's eventual support for Becket puzzled him. But he was a product of the schools, whose learning made him a match for Herbert and John of Salisbury. He never disputed the theories which he had learnt, for all his hedging and for all his personal attacks on Becket and for all the influences brought to bear on him since his schooldays. He looked into his mental mirror and saw there the image of the good prelate. Perhaps the blows which killed Becket may have cracked it for a moment: we cannot know what went on in his mind.

A lone voice cries out in protest. It cries out rather than argues. Stephen of Rouen was a monk of Bec. He qualifies as an intellectual.

---

est affligi corpore quam ramno subici et ex spinis corporali subferre molestie quam peccatorum tenebris obscurari.

The reference to the contrast between the active and contemplative lives sounds traditional, though I have not found Foliot's source for his interpretation of the parable.

[1] G.F.L.C. 241. [2] ibid. 189. [3] ibid. 224.

since the abbey continued to run a school. It had declined after the palmy days of Lanfranc and Anselm, but it still provided a good education. Stephen came of an abbot-producing family with aristocratic connections. He went to the school at Bec, became a monk there, and probably taught grammar and rhetoric. His writings show a wide knowledge of Latin classical historians and rhetors.[4] He wrote his *Draco Normannicus* as a verse history of the house of Anjou; Henry II is his hero. Stephen finished his poem soon after the Peace of Poissy in 1169 and therefore well before Becket's murder.

We need a modern study of the *Draco* and Stephen's other poems. He has displeased both medieval Latinists and historians. Dr Raby, most learned and sensitive of the former, referred to the *Draco* in a footnote as 'a pretentious historical poem of mixed content'.[5] Historians use it as a source, but it tries them sorely. 'No more choice contribution to English history could have been made than an account of these years, had the poet been less diffuse, and less intent on turning tricky verses', his editor wrote.[6] The absence of chronological order annoys us: Stephen keeps jumping backwards according to the rule of eulogy that if you praise a man you must also praise his ancestors. Students of monastic spirituality pass by him, holding their noses. The *Draco* has a secular theme, which demanded secular treatment. No monastic writer could shed his memories of *lectio divina* and of the liturgy altogether when he wrote in a secular genre, but he could cut them down. Stephen chose verse as a fitting medium to tell of heroic deeds. Legend figures in his tale: we meet Arthur and Merlin; niceties of accurate detail go by the board. Nevertheless, he shows us the still-living archbishop in the light of two strong prejudices, which may well have been current before he became a martyr. Stephen celebrated the Angevins as doughty fighters against the French, as good as the Normans on that score. As a monk of Bec, he cared little for the liberties of the Church, but much for those of his abbey. The dukes

[4] M. Manitius, *Geschichte der lateinischen Literatur des Mittelalters* iii (Munich, 1931) 690–4; A. A. Porée, *Histoire de l'abbaye du Bec* (Bayeux, 1901) 524–42.

[5] *A History of Christian Latin Poetry* (2nd ed. Oxford, 1953) 309n.

[6] *Draco* ix–x; L. Halphen describes it as 'poème touffu et désordonné', 'Entrevues des rois Louis VII et Henri II durant l'exil de Thomas Becket en France', *Mélanges Charles Beaumont* (Paris, 1913) 152.

of Normandy, the kings of England and not least the Empress Matilda had played their parts in its history as founders, benefactors and patrons. The popes, on the contrary, demanded money. Stephen recalls Matthew Paris when he complains of the taxes levied by a hard-pressed pope on the wealth of Bec.[7] He had the same dislike of the Romans. 'A plague on both your houses!' would sum up his comments on the schism of 1159. He slightly preferred the imperialist pope, perhaps because Victor was related to the house of Champagne: Stephen wrote a poem in honour of Count Theobald of Champagne, who died in 1152. He may also have noted that Henry II was friendly with the emperor at the beginning of his reign. However, Stephen refers to Alexander as *apostolicus* from the moment when Henry recognized him.

Theobald of Bec sets the standard for a good prelate. As abbot he knew how to display his wealth and magnificence; sanctity is not mentioned. As archbishop he loved Matilda and her sons and always remained loyal to Henry in spite of danger to himself.[8] That was a half-truth, but Stephen followed the maxim:

Iudicioque carens dicere cuncta cupit.[9]

Only a fool wants to tell everything; he does not. Becket has a minor role as a traitor and trouble-maker, contrasting with Theobald. Even as chancellor he pocketed some of the money which he received in office. As archbishop he forbade the marriage between Henry's younger brother and the daughter of the earl of Warenne. The poor young prince died heartbroken, for which Stephen holds Becket responsible. Then he fled to the pope at Sens with a trumped-up story about having been driven into exile. The pope answered that he was an exile too and that Henry was too strong to be resisted: better dissemble.[10] The French king and nobles pleaded for Becket with Henry (damning allies). They asked the king to give up the rights and customs of his forebears, which he very properly refused to do; he would not have new customs. Let Becket, he said, content himself with what was good enough for his holy predecessors, Lanfranc and Anselm, who had pleased God by serving their king. His case was sound. Becket should be judged 'by his peers'; the precise meaning of *chorus procerum* is not clear. Henry then threat-

[7] *Draco* 740, 752.   [8] ibid. 741.
[9] ibid. 590.   [10] ibid. 741–2.

ened him with perpetual exile if he would not observe the laws of his ancestors.[11] Becket in exile enjoyed the pleasures of France, while stirring up warfare between the two rulers. He wanted to put Henry off his throne if he would not give in.[12] Spite at the loss of his see led Becket to sabotage the peace talks between Henry and Louis at Gisors. Stephen is inaccurate and inconsistent here. Becket is not known to have attended the meeting between Henry and Louis in the Vexin on 4 June 1167.[13] The *Draco* makes Henry spurn the yoke of his overlord, 'as an untamed lion':[14] so on Stephen's own showing Louis had no need of Becket to turn him against his vassal. It is added for good measure that Becket deserved to lose his see, having been guilty of triple simony.[15] Finally his plans fell through. Louis deserted him and left him to face Henry: 'I don't know what he wanted', is Stephen's parting shot.[16]

Faithful, unquestioning service to one's prince: Stephen might have set a different standard had he tried his hand at hagiography. He was churchman enough to smear Becket as a simoniac and to neutralize the pope. Alexander advised Becket against resistance to Henry, another convenient half-truth, which enabled the poet to make Becket act wantonly as a traitor. Stephen's judgement will prove the rule. To find a case against Becket grounded in principle of any sort we must leave both the king and the bishops aside and turn instead to a student of rhetoric in a Norman monastic school. It took a monk scholar, versifying in a secular genre with its own conventions and its own type of selectiveness, to blame the future St Thomas. Stephen's lack of inhibitions comes as a breath of fresh air. The martyrdom shuts the door again. Intellectuals who considered the case afterwards had to start from the shrine at Canterbury.

[11] ibid. 756-7.

[12] ibid. 676-7.

[13] Stephen of Rouen probably conflated a number of meetings where Louis VII tried to mediate between Henry II and Becket; see L. Halphen, op. cit. 151-62 and Foreville, 193-8.

[14] *Draco* 664, 675.

[15] ibid. 677.

[16] ibid. 757: Thomas conticuit, meditatur regia dicta, / Nescio quid voluit, retro redire timet.

VIII
The Martyr

'Truly he is dead, but his power lives on,' said a voice to the bishop of Exeter when he was grieving for Becket's death.[1] Power manifested itself in miracles, leading to an immediate cult of the martyr. His friends eagerly forwarded his canonization, which took place on 21 February 1173.[2] Canterbury became a centre of pilgrimage for the whole of Christendom. The cult 'attracted barbarian peoples';[3] it spread from Iceland to Sicily and from Spain to Eastern Europe. Children told the tale of St Thomas and sang of his glory as they played in the streets.[4] A tourist trade flourished and had its complement in literature and art. The English talent for collecting marvels and miracle stories had full scope.[5] Research on the martyr's life, passion and miracles developed into an industry to cater for the demand for information. Artists were commissioned to represent his martyrdom. Versions of the tale in vernacular rhyme carried it to the less learned. Edward Grim's Latin *Life* was soon translated into French. An enterprising clerk from the Isle-de-France, Garnier of Pont-Saint-Maxence, visited England to collect eye-witness accounts. He saw money in it. His first draft was pirated, but he gained rewards from the prior of Canterbury Cathedral and from Becket's sister, the abbess of Reading.[6]

[1] Benedict, *Mat.* ii, 28.

[2] On the bulls of canonization see A. P. Frutaz, '*Auctoritate beatorum Petri et Pauli*. Saggio sulle formale di canonizzatione', *Antonianum* xlii (1967) 435–501.

[3] Alan of Tewkesbury, *Mat.* ii, 299.

[4] Fitzstephen, ibid. iii, 153.

[5] See Southern, 171–4.

[6] On vernacular *Lives* see E. Walberg, *La tradition hagiographique de Saint Thomas Becket avant la fin du XIIe siècle* (Paris, 1929), M. D. Legge, *Anglo-Norman Literature and its Background* (Oxford, 1963) 248–51. On Becket's sister Mary see W. Urry, 'Some People and Places in Canterbury connected with the Story of Thomas Becket', *Canterbury Cathedral Chronicle* no lxv (1970) 86–7.

The cult held something for everyone. The story had entertainment value: it told of success on two levels; St Thomas succeeded in life as chancellor and archbishop and then he won the crown of martyrdom. The drama of murder in the cathedral struck the imagination; so did Henry II's penance and the failure of the most dangerous rebellion of his reign simultaneously. Churchmen rejoiced that their cause was vindicated. Laymen were normally anticlerical; but St Thomas showed special favour to knights and their families, healing them and restoring their lost falcons.[7] Professor J. C. Russell has pointed to the political element in the cult of opposition leaders in England. 'In the person of Becket resistance to the king had been canonized.' Pilgrimage and reports of miracles always offered 'an unpunishable way' of criticizing the Establishment.[8] The French had their own reasons for annexing St Thomas. When the four nations of Paris university grouped themselves together in the second decade of the thirteenth century, each nation had its patron saints, whose festivals were kept as holidays. The French nation honoured St Thomas of Canterbury; the English nation chose St Edmund the martyr and other saints.[9] St Thomas had spent his exile in France. Louis VII had supported him against Henry II. The martyr had commended his soul to St Denis, the patron saint of France, at the very moment of his death.[10] William of Canterbury presented St Thomas and St Denis as reaching a friendly understanding in heaven. St Denis, intent upon 'symbolic and anagogic demonstrations, and meditating on the celestial hierarchies', overlooked the prayers of a Frenchman who was vexed by a devil. The French saint, therefore, handed over the cure to his fellow martyr, St Thomas, in order that he should become famous.[11]

The cult could spread through many channels, such as Plantagenet marriage alliances and trade routes. The Cistercian Order played a key part. The Cistercians joined a far-flung network of houses to a closely knit organization. The Chapter General of abbots legislated for all houses, and so could frame a common policy. The Order supported Alexander III in the schism and adopted Becket's cause

[7] *Mat.* i, 208–9.

[8] 'The Canonization of Opposition to the King in Angevin England', *Anniversary Essays in Mediaeval History presented to C. H. Haskins*, ed. C. H. Taylor (Boston, 1922) 279–90.

[9] P. Kibre, *The Nations in the Mediaeval Universities* (Cambridge, Mass., 1948) 87–8.

[10] *Mat.* i, 133, ii, 320, vii, 466.   [11] ibid. i, 304.

as its own. He took refuge at Pontigny. The Chapter General registered in its proceedings Henry's move to prevent his staying on there in 1167.[12] Abbot Odo of Ourscamp sent Becket a sermon at his request with the wish that the Lord might speedily 'crush your Satan [Henry II] under your feet'.[13] The future martyr foretold his passion to the abbots of Pontigny and Vauluisant.[14] His festival was observed throughout the Order as soon as he was canonized.[15] The Cistercians colonized the border areas of Poland, Bohemia, Austria and Hungary; wherever they had a settlement he was on their calendar of saints.

Propaganda also radiated from the schools. Foreign scholars benefited from his miracles. Innocent III made the pilgrimage to Canterbury while he was a student at Paris.[16] Scholars would carry the cult home with them. A Master Vincent, who studied in France, probably at Paris, in the 1180s, fostered the cult of St Stanislas on the Becket model when he became bishop of Cracow, 1207. A copy of the *Miracles* of St Thomas reached Cracow in the early thirteenth century. It was probably brought from France by Master Ivo, Vincent's successor to the see of Cracow.[17] Canonization had the further consequence that sermons would be given to clergy and people on St Thomas's festival. Preachers had often had their training in the schools; they could spread the cult from the pulpit.

Events conspired to give unrivalled opportunities to his former friends and disciples. They swam with the tide of enthusiasm. Biographers and compilers of *Miracula* had a captive audience. It was up to them to offer their story in the way which would do most good for the Church. The English authors agreed on the main lines of their propaganda.

First it served their immediate concerns. The schism in the papacy did not end until 1177; hence it was still necessary to attack the imperialists. St Thomas's miracles 'divided the light from the darkness' by witnessing that Alexander was the true pope. Otherwise St Thomas, who approved his election, would not have been

---

[12] J.-M. Canivez, *Statuta Capitulorum Generalium Ordinis Cisterciensis* i (Louvain, 1933) 75.

[13] J. B. Pitra, *Analecta novissima Spicilegii Solesmensis altera continuatio* ii (Paris, 1888) xlii.

[14] *Mat.* ii, 12.   [15] Canivez, op. cit. 102, 144.   [16] See above, p. 139.

[17] Mr B. Harónski kindly gave me this information. He is preparing a dissertation on the Polish Church in the twelfth and thirteenth centuries, which includes a study of the cult of St Stanislas.

the saint that his signs proved him to be.[18] The imperialists, it was said, feared that the honour paid to him would damage their cause: a schismatic bishop tried vainly to prevent a man of his diocese from making the pilgrimage to Canterbury.[19] At home the outstanding Henrician bishops came over. Bishop Jocelyn of Salisbury persuaded Gilbert Foliot to vow a pilgrimage when he was mortally ill; and he was cured.[20] Henry II gets off lightly and receives the gentle treatment due to a penitent. He made amends by his penance and by forwarding the cult. The authors rejoice in his victory over his rebellious son. They are not anti-royalist. On the contrary, they take pains to clear St Thomas from the charge of treason which had been brought against him.[21] Later writers would use the Becket legend as a stick to beat the Angevins. Gerald of Wales did so.[22] The anonymous writer of a *Life*, which survives in one copy in a Brussels manuscript, contrasts strikingly with the contemporary English writers. The anonymous has a double bias:

> Henry king of the English, coiling snake of England, began to take hold of ecclesiastical freedom in the coiling knots of his fraud.[23]

Becket takes leave of 'his beloved France' when he returns to England to be murdered. *Privilegium fori* is defended against the secular power. The anonymous proclaims that St Peter's sword has prevailed over Nero's. The world cries out that King Henry is guilty of the blood of the just and an open enemy of God, king of kings. God bestows both spiritual and temporal swords and has fought Henry with both in the day of wrath. English writers had the more difficult task of combining loyalty to their king with defence of ecclesiastical freedom.

St Thomas suffered for the liberties of the Church and it was a worthy cause. On that all agreed. But this narrow approach did not satisfy the English writers. The martyrdom had universal significance; it belonged to the divine plan of salvation. Edward Grim writes:

---

[18] *Mat.* ii, 24–5. [19] ibid. i, 374–5.
[20] ibid. 251 and for another version iv, 175.
[21] ibid. 134; ii, 17–18; 440.
[22] Baldwin, *Masters*; see index under Gerald.
[23] Edited in *Catalogus codicum hagiographorum Bibl. Reg. Bruxellensis* i (1886) 269–80; see below, p. 212. This *Life* is derivative as to content, but the writer's comments are his own.

Love grows cold and wickedness abounds, as though the author of our salvation cared less for the things of this earth; and so, just as once he assumed human nature to visit and redeem his people, the working of his unseen majesty ever calls on them to do better. Lest our present time should seem to lack such a grace, a new soldier of Christ and a notable martyr has come forward among us in St Thomas, mirror of holiness, rule of righteousness, persuasion to patience, example of virtue and invincible spokesman of truth.[24]

The new martyr surpassed his predecessors in that each of them acted mainly in his own cause, when they were forced to sacrifice to demons and to worship idols. St Thomas, on the contrary, bought the salvation of others at the price of his precious blood, judging that there is no greater charity than to give up one's life for one's friends.[25] Benedict of Peterborough contrasts him with earlier martyrs even more sharply: they acted each in his own cause, entering the fray for the sake of their own salvation, whereas St Thomas championed the cause of the Church universal; he fought against princes and tyrants and against men who were hirelings rather than pastors in God's Church (bad bishops); he allowed the knights to triumph over his body in her defence. Adherents of other religions killed earlier martyrs; the slayers of St Thomas were Christians and his own sons.[26] Thus his cult transcended all merely local ones, though his special witness to the rights of Canterbury was not forgotten.[27] He benefited the whole Christian people.

The last days at Canterbury made a bridge between his life and passion. St Thomas preached a sermon on Christmas Day, telling his hearers that he had returned from exile for no other reason than to lift the yoke of servitude from their necks or to suffer the pain of death both among them and for them. He chose his martyrdom freely.[28] It has been remarked that the iconography of his passion tended to be inaccurate in its historical detail. Artists would present him as saying Mass or praying at the altar, to bring out the horror and sacrilege of the scene. He kneels meekly to receive his wounds, just as earlier martyrs knelt before their torturers. The scuffle and angry exchanges with the knights are ignored.[29] But iconography

[24] *Mat.* ii, 354.   [25] ibid. 323; John of Salisbury, ibid. 301.
[26] ibid. 14.   [27] ibid. 25.   [28] ibid. 17–18.
[29] T. Borenius, *St Thomas Becket in Art* (London, 1932).

renders the biographers' interpretation, in that they fitted St Thomas into their pattern of martyrdom.

Their stress on martyrdom released a flood of longing, which had been swelling up and needed an outlet. It had a long history. In the early Church martyrdom was regarded as the proper climax of a truly Christian life. The idea had its roots in Jewish tradition; it lived on in the middle ages in the books of Machabees. Medieval Bible illustrations told readers of the heroic mother and her seven sons, all tortured to death because they refused to break their Law (II, vii).[30] The ideal of martyrdom gave way to that of asceticism when the Roman empire became Christian and persecution faded into a memory.[31] Then missions to convert the heathen brought martyrdom to the fore again. Asceticism began to look second-best. St Peter Damian in his *Life* of St Romuald tells how Romuald aspired to mission work and martyrdom. He had to give it up, as contrary to God's will for him; but according to Peter Damian his troubles and his self-imposed austerities amounted to martyrdom:

O golden age of Romuald, which did not lack voluntary martyrdom, even though it was spared the torments of persecution![32]

Damian protests too much. The crusades provided a chance to seek martyrdom of a different kind: 'How blessed are the martyrs who die in battle!' exclaimed St Bernard in his letter in praise of the new military Order of the Knights Templar (1128–36). Bernard quoted Machabees to justify the foundation of a military religious Order.[33] The failure of the second crusade took the gloss off the crusading ideal. Asceticism was favoured again as an alternative. A bishop of Auxerre, who resigned his see in order to become a monk at Clairvaux in 1167, 'entered upon the martyrdom of his time.'[34] Clairvaux offered a substitute for death in battle against the infidel or on the mission field. St Thomas combined secret asceticism with public persecution and murder. At last people had a real martyr

[30] See Professor P. Brieger's forthcoming catalogue of medieval Bible illustrations.

[31] W. H. C. Frend, *Martyrdom and Persecution in the Early Church. A Study of a Conflict from the Maccabees to Donatus* (Oxford, 1965).

[32] ed. G. Tabacco (Fonti per la storia d'Italia xciv, Rome 1957) 79–82, 105.

[33] *De laude novae militiae, Opera*, ed. J. Leclercq and H. M. Rochais, iii (Rome, 1963) 215, 221.

[34] *Gesta pontificum Autissiodorensium*, ed. cit. 420.

to intercede for them. There had been nothing so authentic since the apostles and martyrs of the early Church.

The Becket group went further: they likened their hero to Jesus:

> It would be hard, we believe, to find a passion of any other martyr whose likeness answers so closely to the Lord's.[35]

John of Salisbury compared Becket's passion with the Gospel in detail, Becket having a slight lead over Christ. St Thomas suffered within his church instead of outside on unconsecrated ground, and so on.[36] Herbert took up the theme in his more personal and possessive way. A modern Christian may find the comparison at worst blasphemous or at best impertinent. Medieval scholars recreated the past in the light of the present and modelled the present on the past. Christ was honoured in the cult of St. Thomas. Devotion to the Gospel would grow keener just because it had been re-enacted by a man who lived and died so recently. *By his stripes we are healed* had both fresh and continuous meaning.

The *eruditi Sancti Thomae* were resourceful advocates. John and Herbert in particular had helped to make the story by briefing their master on the teaching of the schools and encouraging him to defy Henry. Now they joined with others to shape it, so as to serve a much wider purpose. Becket's example could be fed back into the classroom. We shall see how it fared.

Early evidence comes from Oxford. Master Robert of Crichlade, prior of St Frideswide's 1141–*c.* 1174, was a man of learning and a book hunter.[37] The martyr cured him of a long-standing ailment and he wrote a *Life*, now lost, which served as a source for the Icelandic *Thomas Saga*. The canons of St Frideswide's did not hold a school for the students who were beginning to congregate in Oxford, but the Order of Canons Regular had a tradition of study; the prior must have had contacts with the masters of Oxford and their pupils. Master Robert composed homilies on Ezechiel towards the end of his life, designed to appeal to a learned audience, which would have included clerks of Oxford.[38] The homilies continue

---

[35] Benedict, *Mat.* ii, 18–19.

[36] ibid. 318, vii, 464–5.   [37] B.R.U.O. i, 513–14.

[38] The two surviving copies are in MSS O.3.x of Hereford Cathedral Library and Pembroke College, Cambridge 30, from the abbey of Bury St Edmund. I quote from the latter, since the former is incomplete, having only 38 homilies; the Bury MS has 42, with Robert's explicit; see M. R. James, *Descriptive Catalogue of MSS in Pembroke College Cambridge* (Cambridge, 1905) 33.

the exposition of Ezechiel from where St Gregory left off, in imitation of the Gregorian model. The author excuses himself for his presumption in undertaking such a task, while trusting to divine enlightenment. His homilies could have been preached, since he addresses 'dearly beloved brethren'; he also intended them to be read: he appeals to his readers and ends with a request for their prayers. A public versed in the holy page is presupposed by his attack on Richard of St Victor's exegesis of Ezechiel's vision. Richard had ventured to criticize St Gregory. Robert, keeping to old ways, argued strongly against the criticism.[39] He must have expected his readers or hearers to have had some notion of Victorine exegesis; otherwise they would have found his argument difficult to follow. Specific references to St Jerome on the Prophets and to Bede's *De Tabernaculo* point in the same direction; so do his discussions of pagan gods and their festivals.[40] The homilist wrote as a scholar for scholars.

The prologue is addressed to Reginald prior of Gresley, who had asked him to write the homilies. Gresley Priory in Derbyshire was a small house of Austin Canons founded by William de Gresley before about 1166 (the probable date of his death). A Prior Reginald of Gresley witnessed one of his charters. We do not know how long Reginald held the office of prior.[41] The homilies can be dated more closely by two passages on Becket's life and martyrdom. Fr. A. Squire has suggested 'one summer soon after 1170'.[42] Robert wrote at a time when 'the whole world venerated' the martyr, celebrated for his miracles, but probably before the official canonization,

[39] *Study of the Bible*, 109. There is an even stronger attack on Richard on fol. 62vb, hom. xv: Cogor sepius quasi invective loqui contra presumptores fatuos, qui etiam posuerunt os suum in sanctissimum papam Gregorium, doctorem peritissimum, dicentes quod litterali possit intelligentia comprehendi quod ipse beatissimus papa dixerat non posse secundum litteram stare. Quod si non potuerint, a fatua presumptione sua supersedeant.

On St Gregory's influence on medieval exegesis in the twelfth century and earlier, see R. Wasselynck, 'L'influence de l'exégèse de S. Grégoire le Grand sur les commentaires bibliques médiévaux', RTAM xxxii (1965) 157–204; 'La présence des Moralia de saint Grégoire le Grand dans les ouvrages de morale du XIIe siècle', ibid. xxxv (1968) 197–240, xxxvi (1969) 31–45.

[40] foll. 66rb–va, 97va–98ra.

[41] F. Madan, *The Gresleys of Drakelowe* (Oxford, 1899) 172–6. William de Gresley's son succeeded to his knights' fees in 1166.

[42] *Aelred of Rievaulx* (London, 1969) 136, 169. Fr. Squire was the first to notice these references to St Thomas.

which is not mentioned. The author calls himself 'Prior of St Frideswide's'; we know that he died or retired about 1174.

The first passage on Becket defends him as an example of perfect patience. The tone is interesting, because it shows that Becket was still being criticized for rushing indiscreetly to his death. His patience had to be insisted on:

> What shall I say of Thomas, glorious bishop and martyr, who merited the crown of martyrdom in our time? He neither feared the king's threats nor yielded to the promise of worldly honours, but despised them all in the fullness of his Christian charity, and offered himself up as a sacrifice to Christ for the liberty of the Church. Receiving his assailants' sword strokes without fear, he neither bowed his head nor parried the blow by hand or any other means, but stayed still and unflinching. So he fell to his glorious death.
>
> Who is so mad as to dare say that his patience was not perfect? Now the whole world venerates him whom the wicked knights did not fear to slay.[43]

In the second passage Becket is added to a list of martyrs, who were all pillars of the Church; it runs from St Stephen to St Laurence. St Thomas is hailed as a new martyr and saviour of the Church's tottering walls:

> . . . we have seen and known [him]; many of us had his friendship. Now in our days and before our eyes, the palm of martyrdom has added him to the fabric of the Church. Not only that. He is set as a big strong pillar to hold up the fabric, which was just nigh to ruin.

Robert goes on to tell the story of Becket's career and to draw lessons from it. He probably took the details from his own *Life* of the saint, since he does not quote verbally from the other *Lives*.

---

[43] Hom. vi, fol. 33rb: Quid dicam de gloriosissimo martyre et pontifice Thoma, qui in nostris temporibus martirii coronam promeruit, qui regis minas non timuit nec temporalium honorum blandimentis cessit? Caritate enim Christi repletus omnia despexit et seipsum Christo pro libertate ecclesie hostiam optulit. Ictus gladiorum iminentium sine terrore suscepit, nec capite declinavit nec manum nec aliud aliquid ictui opposuit, sed imperterritus et immobilis permansit; sicque gloriosa morte occubuit. Quis ita demens est qui audeat dicere quod ista patientia non fuerit perfecta? Nunc autem totus mundus eum veneratur, quem satellites pessimi occidere non verebantur.

Becket acquired the archdeaconry of all England (Canterbury), the famous provostship of Beverley and many prebends even before he became chancellor. As chancellor he was the king's *alter ego*. His mere word counted as a writ or charter when the king was abroad. As archbishop he changed his way of life. His conduct had been worthy before; now he surpassed himself:

> He rejected the king's friendship in order to be the friend of Christ. . . . Finally he despised this earthly life, although he was in the age of manhood, when to live is sweeter, that he might be worthy to come to Christ, who is our life.

The martyr's example shames us. We pile up wealth, or want to, if we lack the means; we revere kings and powerful men of the world, as though they were God; we bask in their smiles and rely on their often illusory promises:

> When we think upon our fathers, the patriarchs and prophets, the apostles and martyrs and this one (St Thomas) in particular, whom God has celebrated by ineffable miracles before our eyes, and God's other chosen men and their works, we ought to blush for ours, if we be not unfeeling.[44]

[44] fol. 91ra–vb: Veniamus ad beatissimum pontificem et martyrem Thomam, quem vidimus, quem cognovimus, cuius familiares plerique sumus, qui in his diebus quasi in oculis nostris non solum martyrii palmam huic fabrice additus est, sed appositus quasi columpna maxima et fortissima ad sublevandum fabricam iam iam fere ruentem. In eo utique, si bene metimur nos per vitam ipsius et facta, inveniemus quidem unde liquide erubescamus. Antequam fieret cancellarius regis multas habuit possessiones, archidiaconatum scilicet matris ecclesie totius Anglie, preposituram nominatissimam Berverlaci, prebendas plurimas. Factus cancellarius, tantam invenit gratiam coram rege ut non modo secundus ab eo, sed alter ipse videretur. Quando(que), rege existente in transmarinis partibus, non cartas nec regis brevia secum ferebat, sed que fieri verbo iubebat fiebant, et que autem prohibebat nemo facere audebat. Tandem apicem archiepiscopatus adeptus, statim mutatus est in virum alterum, et licet in vita preterita se honestissime egisset, seipsum honestate et sanctitate superavit. . . . Ut Christo familiaris esse posset, regis familiaritatem repulit. . . . Et ne longius protraham sermonem, vitam despexit temporalem, licet esset in ea etate, scilicet iuvenili, in qua vivere homini est dulcius, ut illuc mereretur pervenire ubi Christus, qui est vita nostra. Quando consideramus patres nostros, patriarchas et prophetas, apostolos et martyres, et hunc precipue, qui in oculis nostris clarificatus est a Deo ineffabilibus miraculis, et ceteros electos Dei et opera eorum, si insensibiles non sumus, in omnibus operibus nostris erubescere debemus.

Robert may have been exaggerating Thomas's power as chancellor; the

The prior of St Frideswide put a forceful stamp on the pattern of hagiography. He dwelt on the opposition between service to Henry and service to God and he saw the martyrdom as a new and glorious page in the Church's history.

We shall now follow the tale to the schools of France. It soon reached Orleans, a noted centre for the study of the Latin poets. William of Canterbury, who collected his *Miracula* 1172–4, begins by relating the dream of a certain clerk, who was studying secular science at Orleans. The clerk dreamed that he was sitting in a master's chair, lecturing on Lucan's *Pharsalia* to many attentive pupils. He had reached the place in his text where Cato dies after suffering persecution, when it seemed to him that his own master came up to him and ordered him to reread his text, since he had omitted to explain a verse. He looked back in surprise and found that it had escaped his notice. No wonder: it was a piece of doggerel, miraculously added to *Pharsalia*:

> Sic vobis, Scitici, mors est ignota Catonis;
> In bellis didicit bella timere timor.

Reflecting afterwards, he understood that it foretold St Thomas's martyrdom. The 'Scyths' signified the English; Caesar, who persecuted Cato, signified Henry II.[45] William of Canterbury's tale might be dismissed as pure fiction, circumstantial as it is, if we did not know that Master Arnulf of Orleans commended Becket in his lectures on *Pharsalia* at this very time. Master Arnulf was a famous commentator on classical texts; Dante used his glosses on Ovid.[46] The context of his reference to Becket is precisely the death of Cato:

> He was a true father of his country and far worthier than others, who have since been granted this title, to have altars raised in his memory. One day, when we are finally freed from slavery, if that ever happens, Cato will be deified.[47]

chancellor normally accompanied the king wherever he went; but Henry sent him back to England alone on hearing the news of Archbishop Theobald's death and there may have been other rare occasions when the chancellor had to give orders on his own account.

[45] *Mat.* i, 139–40.

[46] C. A. Robson, 'Dante's Use in the *Divina Commedia* of the Medieval Allegories on Ovid', *Centenary Essays on Dante by members of the Oxford Dante Society* (Oxford, 1965) 9–21.

[47] Robert Graves's translation, *Pharsalia* (London, 1956) 187–8.

Lucan puts the question: 'whether it is enough to be virtuous without troubling to be successful?' Arnulf answers:

A good man, who begins some worthy task and cannot carry it to completion, is no worse than one who does. The lord archbishop of Canterbury, for instance, began to uphold strict justice against the Englishman. Death prevented him from completing that worthy task; but its worth would have been no greater had he accomplished it in full.

This part of the lecture course must have been given before Becket's canonization, 21 February 1173, since Arnulf refers to him as 'archbishop', not as 'saint'. The date fits well into our scanty knowledge of his teaching career.[48-9] It seems certain that he was the master who appeared to the Orleans clerk in the dream. His comparison of Becket to Cato had an echo at Canterbury. The miracle had its origin in a lecture, which was antedated so as to become a prophecy. At Orleans, then, the martyr was celebrated as a new Cato, resisting tyranny according to the classical virtue of *honestas*.

We now move over to the schools of theology at Paris. Theologians would have to provide a Christian framework for the story; but first they had to decide whether Becket's cause sufficed to make him a martyr. The question had been raised and debated already as a hypothesis in the household of Robert of Melun, when he was bishop of Hereford.[50] It continued after the murder. The Cistercian Caesarius of Heisterbach noted it in his *Dialogus miraculorum*, 1219–23. He tells us that there had been discussion in plenty. The dispute arose because the archbishop had worked no miracles in his lifetime. Opinions varied. Some argued that he was executed as a traitor to the realm, others that he suffered righteously in defence of the Church. A debate was held at Paris on the question whether he was a martyr. A 'Master Roger', Caesarius says, swore that Becket deserved to die, even though the mode of executing him was

---

[48-9] *Arnulfi Aurelianensis Glosule super Lucanum* ed. B. M. Marti (American Academy of Rome, Papers and Monographs xviii, 1958) 466 on ix, 571. Hitherto the *Glosule* have been dated from Becket's murder in 1170 to 1211–1214, when they were quoted in *Faits des romains*. We can now date them back to a date soon after the murder.

[50] Above, p. 57.

wrong. Master Roger rated the saint's constancy as mere contumacy. Master Peter the Chanter on the contrary swore that he was a God-worthy martyr, having died in the cause of the Church's freedom. Caesarius concluded that Christ had solved the question, when he glorified Becket with so many and so great signs. He went on to compare the English archbishop to St Anno of Cologne, who had many detractors after his death; they regarded him as a despoiler of churches and an oppressor of his townsmen; but God vindicated his sanctity by the signs wrought at his translation.[51] The comparison, given Anno's character, is not very flattering to Becket. Caesarius had reason to warn his readers that Becket must not be preferred to the apostles and other great martyrs on the score of merit, although they have fewer miracles ascribed to them. The *Dialogus* is an interesting witness to the climate of opinion at Paris before Becket's canonization. The difficulty about accepting it as accurate in detail is that we have no other evidence to show that Peter, who became Chanter of Notre Dame in 1183 and died in 1197, was teaching as a qualified master so soon after the murder of December, 1170.[52] Master Roger, on the other hand, has been plausibly identified with Master Roger the Norman, a former student of civil law at Bologna, canon of Rouen from 1166 and later dean of the cathedral. He taught Arts at Paris in the 1170s. As a servant of the strong Henrician, Archbishop Rotrou of Rouen, Master Roger may well have argued that Becket was a traitor.[53] The propagation of his miracles settled the question of martyrdom once for all.

Caesarius was certainly right in presenting the future Chanter as a defender of Becket, whether his story of the Paris *quaestio* is authentic or not. The Chanter propagated the Becket legend in his teaching. In a lecture on Hebrews he quoted the *Great Gloss* on xi, 4: *By faith Abel offered to God a sacrifice exceeding that of Cain, by which he obtained a testimony that he was just. . . . And by it he being dead yet speaketh.* The Glossator explained that Abel *yet speaketh* 'because his example teaches others to be just. Death

---

[51] ed. J. Strange (Cologne, 1851) ii, 139–40. Archbishop Anno of Cologne, who died in 1075, was canonized in 1183.

[52] J. W. Baldwin, 'A debate at Paris over Thomas Becket between Master Roger and Master Peter the Chanter', *Studia Gratiana* xi (1967) 121–6.

[53] ibid. and S. Kuttner and E. Rathbone, 'Anglo-Norman Canonists of the Twelfth Century', *Traditio* vii (1949–51) 289.

destroyed him, but not the memory of his glory.[54] The Chanter added:

St Thomas of Canterbury speaks likewise by the example, decision and word which he left us.[55]

The second Cato has become a second Abel.[56] Henry II appears in the role of Cain, shedding the blood of the righteous man. The Chanter, when discussing in his *Summa* a question concerning the ultimate responsibility for a crime, tells the story of how Henry complained that none would avenge the wrongs which Becket had done him, as he said, and how the murderers took him at his word: was not the king himself the culprit in this case?[57] Becket's stand for the privilege of clergy decided the Chanter to favour it:

There is a custom in some churches that if a clerk be degraded on account of a grave crime he should be handed over at once to the secular court and the executioners. In my opinion this should never happen, for the reason that St Thomas the Englishman refused it to the king of England and died later on for that and other causes.[58]

The same theme, that Becket incurred the king's hatred by refusing the *traditio curiae*, recurs elsewhere in the Chanter's works.[59]

The saint's conduct as archbishop as well as his martyrdom served as an example. The Chanter spread a story that Becket, on returning from exile, forbade his chancellor, Master Arnulf, to take any fee or perquisite for affixing the seal to a document issued by the archiepiscopal chancery;[60] that would have meant an unheard-of departure from twelfth-century standards of administration. As the editor of his *Summa* pointed out, the Chanter 'did much to increase the intransigent archbishop's popularity in France'.[61] This master

---

[54] P.L. cxcii, 490.

[55] Baldwin, op. cit. 127–8. He does not mention the quotation from the *Great Gloss*, which makes the Chanter's allusion clearer.

[56] As in one of the *Passions*: Consummavit ergo noster Abel in martyrii gloria...; *Mat.* iv, 194–5.   [57] Baldwin, *Masters*, i, 256–7.

[58] *Pierre le Chantre, Summa de sacramentis et de animae consiliis*, ed. J. A. Dugauquier (Analecta mediaevalia Namurcensia xxi, 1967) 388.

[59] Baldwin, *Masters*, ii, 102.

[60] ibid. i, 181. Becket was also said to have resigned his see into the pope's hands on the grounds of unworthiness; ibid. 172.

[61] Dugauquier, op. cit. (Analecta mediaevalia Namurcensia vii, 1957) 277.

formed the centre of a group of Paris theologians who interested themselves in practical moral questions, dealing with the relations between secular and spiritual authorities *inter alia*. The Chanter's influence as a master and colleague ranged widely. Professor Baldwin has proved that his pupil Robert Courson, later cardinal, echoed and appropriated the master's opinion of Becket and his cause, when he compiled his Summa (1208–12/3).[62]

Stephen Langton may have studied under the Chanter and certainly quoted him. Langton's teaching period ran from about 1180 to 1206, when he left the Paris schools to become a cardinal.[63] Like Peter the Chanter, he invoked the Becket legend in his lectures on Scripture. Nehemias, building up the walls of Jerusalem in defiance of his enemies, signified the good prelate who stood for the liberties of the Church. Such a man would answer those who urged him to desist with the words of St Thomas to the bishop of London (Gilbert Foliot):

I hold the rudder and you call upon me to sleep.

Nehemias refused to shut the doors of the temple against those who sought his life: *Should such a man as I flee?* So St Thomas refused to bar the doors against his murderers.[64] The good prelate, like Jonathan in the book of Machabees,

does not cease through fear of death to rebuke princes who attack the Church; he fears not to throw himself into the breach to defend her freedom; on her behalf he demands of the prince that he may enjoy his rightful privilege.

As the Machabees won freedom from the Romans, so ecclesiastics should have theirs *registered on tables of brass*, so that they may enjoy their privilege in quiet.[65] Langton's pupils would supply the example of Becket both here and in other contexts, as when the master commented on the disobedience of Saul. The prophet Samuel had commanded him not to spare Amalec; *Saul took Agag the king of Amalec alive: but all the common people he slew with the sword*:

[62] Baldwin, *Masters*, i, 19, 25 and *passim*.
[63] ibid. 25–31.
[64] On II Esdr. vi, 3, 11, quoted in *Study of the Bible*, 252.
[65] On I Machab. xiv, 26, quoted ibid. 252–3.

Many (prelates) do just the same. They slay the common people, that is, they correct and rebuke lesser men; but they dare not correct the greater.[66]

These lectures on Kings, Esdras and Machabees probably belong to the late 1180s and early 1190s.[67]

King John had good reason to oppose Langton's appointment to Canterbury, quite apart from the fact that he was a protégé of Innocent III. John objected on the pretext that Langton was personally unknown to him and that he had been living in enemy territory at Paris. It could have been no secret that Langton taught his pupils to follow the example of Becket. Master Stephen had the reputation for being a famous teacher of the holy page. He had held his school at Paris for some twenty-five years. John would fume at the thought of a new Becket at Canterbury.

Lecturers on canon-law texts made the same sort of references. A set of glosses on the *Decretum* record the opinions of a number of masters who taught in England in the 1190s. 'Events and protagonists of the Becket controversy crop up frequently.' Two examples have been printed from the glosses. When Gratian refers to the rudder of a ship, the glossator quotes the same tag from Becket's answer to Foliot as Langton did. The text *I am sacrificed freely* recalls the words of St Thomas at his passion.[68] It would be interesting to know whether contemporary glosses on canon-law texts from Bologna include allusions to Becket. We shall have to wait until more of the vast manuscript material has been studied and published. Alanus Anglicus taught canon law at Bologna in the years around 1200. He was both an Englishman and an extreme papalist, the most extreme of his canonist colleagues.[69] One would expect him to honour the Becket tradition, although there is no evidence so far.

[66] On I. Reg. xv, 8. MS Oxford, Bodl. Canon. pat. lat. 186, fol. 196ra: Hec ad litteram multi faciunt. Vulgus interficiunt, id est minores corripiunt et reprehendunt; maiores autem non audent corripere.

[67] Langton refers to the capture of Jerusalem several times in his commentary on I Reg.. which dates it soon after 1187. As he commented on the historical books of the Old Testament in sequence, he would have come on to Esdras and Machabees soon afterwards; see *Study of the Bible*, 198.

[68] Kuttner and Rathbone, op. cit. 319.

[69] J. A. Watt, *The Theory of Papal Monarchy in the Thirteenth Century. The Contribution of the Canonists* (London, 1965) 49–54; R. L. Benson, op. cit. 413 for index of references to Alanus.

Two further illustrations will show how Becket took his place in the expanding Bible of the schools. The Austin Friars of Bordeaux had a copy of the *Historia scholastica* with marginal glosses, now at the Departmental Library of Bordeaux. The manuscript and its glosses were written in the second half of the thirteenth century, but the glosses may have been copied from earlier ones, originating at Paris or in some other *studium* of the Order. When Jesus foretells his passion to the disciples (Mt. xx, 17–19), a glossator has added:

So the glorious martyr Thomas of Canterbury foretold his passion to the admirable Catholic King Louis, when he crossed to England after making peace with Henry, king of England.[70]

The *Bible moralisée* throws a bridge between the Paris schools and a royal or princely patron of scholars. It consists of a selected, simplified text of the whole Bible; each extract from the Bible pairs with an allegory or morality; both are illustrated by pictures set in medallions beside the columns containing the script. There are over 5,000 medallions in the volumes which have come down to us. We know little about the authorship, sources, date and transmission of this huge enterprise, but its purpose is clear.[71] Some Paris theologian or a group of them, probably of the Dominican Order, prepared the *Bible moralisée* for some wealthy layman, to whom expense was no object. Around 1230 would be a possible date. The author must have chosen the texts and their glosses; some of the latter derive from known sources; others may have sprung from his own invention. He adopts a 'told to the children' technique for the benefit of his

---

[70] On Hist. schol. in Evang. cxiii, P.L. cxcviii, 1595, MS Bordeaux 14, fol. 129: Sic gloriosus martir Thomas Cantuarinen (*sic*) predixit passionem suam laudabili et catholico regi Ludovico, dum facta pace cum rege Anglie Henrico transiret in Angliam.
From William of Canterbury's *Life*, Mat. i, 76.

[71] I refer to the version reproduced by A. de Laborde, *La Bible moralisée illustrée* (5 vol., Paris, 1911–27). Dr R. Hausherr is preparing a systematic study of the problems arising from the *Bible moralisée*; see his 'Templum Salomonis und Ecclesia Christi. Zu einem Bildvergleich der Bible moralisée', *Zeitschrift für Künstgeschichte* (1968) 101–21. He shows that the Laborde version as reproduced in full represents a copy, not the original. My reasons for suggesting a date around 1230–40, and a Dominican authorship, are based on the content of the Laborde version, without prejudice to forthcoming data.

patron or patrons, as when he calls the Philistines 'Saracens'. The pictures, which the artists would have painted under the author's direction, make the Bible story and its teaching vividly comprehensible to less learned readers. The illustrations to the Bible text show 'what happened'; the pictured moralities bring its teaching up to date by showing contemporary scenes: sinners indulge in their various vices with hearty enjoyment; monks pray and ring the bell for choir; friars preach, hear confessions and set penances; scholars study in order to teach and preach in their turn. The author introduces St Thomas into his world of types, good and bad, in several places.

Esau, who troubled his mother while still in her womb (Gen. xxv, 22) signifies princes and knights such as those who have killed holy men, bishops and others; they killed St Thomas, who was slain 'in his mother's womb', that is in the bosom of the Church. The picture shows him kneeling to receive their blows.[72] The author draws an even sharper lesson from the slaughter of the priests of Israel, ordered by Saul because they had given bread and a sword to David (I Reg. xxii, 13, 18–19). Saul is depicted as presiding over and encouraging his knights to massacre the priests, falling under their blows. This signifies that bad princes kill prelates of the Church because they want to protect her freedom and to keep good customs. The morality is illustrated by an exact parallel to the Old Testament scene: knights murder a kneeling prelate, whose pastoral cross is held up in the background, while a king stands beside them, giving his order. No names are mentioned in the text, but a contemporary hand has written underneath it: 'as the king of England...'. The note has been scrubbed out, so that only the first words are legible; but the illegible words obviously meant St Thomas.[73] The allusion to his keeping 'good customs' referred to his objection to the 'bad customs' of the Constitutions of Clarendon. Henry II resembles Saul in being directly responsible for the murder of a priest. The owner of the manuscript, which was in England at the time of the Reformation, had to erase the note to comply with royal orders. Other versions of the *Bible moralisée* pair St Thomas with St Denis; both were martyred for love of Jesus. Their prototypes are the men of Israel, who wept before the Lord, asking

[72] Laborde, i, pl. 17.
[73] ibid. pl. 141. The words do not show in the manuscript under ultraviolet ray.

him whether they should continue their fight against sinful Benjamin, and were told to persevere (Iud. xx, 26–28).[74]

The *Bible moralisée* has a leading idea. Its teaching adds up to more than the sum of individual scenes. It has a hero in God himself, the author of the Bible and of all history. It has a heroine in Holy Mother Church. She appears from the very beginning, personified as a lady, robed and crowned, signifying *terra firma* at the Creation. Then she takes part in the story or watches as a spectator right through to the Apocalypse. St Thomas, as a witness and faithful servant, belongs to God's plan for salvation through the means of his Church. Youngest of all the saints recorded, Becket ranks as high as the apostles and early martyrs.

His success makes a challenging contrast to the failure of another murdered prelate, whose cult never got off the ground until the early seventeenth century. St Albert of Louvain was murdered in 1192. His feast day was authorized only in 1612, a year after the translation of his relics to Brussels. Albert's friends and his biographer realized that his story had much in common with Becket's; they tried to make capital out of the likeness; yet their efforts failed. It is worth asking why.

Albert resembled Thomas in that he led a worldly life until his election to a bishopric, though unlike Thomas he came of a noble family and had his path smoothed for him.[75] As a younger brother of the duke of Brabant, he was expected to make his way in the Church. Benefices accrued to him from the age of twelve onwards. Nevertheless the prospect of a clerical career so displeased him that he tried to thwart his family's plans by renouncing his clergy in order to be knighted and to go on crusade. Only under pressure did he return to his former state. Then he was elected to the bishopric of Liège at the age of twenty-four. It was a disputed election. The *maior et sanior pars* of the chapter chose him in preference to a minority candidate, of a rival noble family. The emperor Henry VI seized on the occasion of a disputed election to exercise a right claimed, but never enforced, by his father Frederick I: if the electors to a bishopric of the empire disagreed, it was claimed that the emperor had a right to intervene. Henry VI put in a third candidate of his own choosing. Albert took up the challenge in defence of

---

[74] ibid. iv, pl. 678, 679, 758.

[75] E. de Moreau, *Albert de Louvain* (Brussels, 1946); R. H. Schmandt, *Speculum* xlii (1967) 639–60.

ecclesiastical freedom. He braved Henry's wrath by appealing to Rome and proceeding to the Curia to plead his cause in person. The emperor kept watch over the main roads, but the elect foiled him, arriving at Rome in a dirty disguise after a devious journey. Here he succeeded in convincing pope and cardinals that his election to Liège was valid at canon law. Celestine III was a firmer character than has sometimes been supposed.[76] He overcame his reluctance to offend the emperor and risk a conflict. Albert received papal confirmation of his election and became a cardinal. The pope ordered the archbishop of Cologne to consecrate him; should Cologne refuse from fear of the emperor, as indeed proved to be the case, the archbishop of Rheims was to do so instead. Celestine threatened to excommunicate the imperialist candidate unless he withdrew, and carried out the threat later. Archbishop William of Rheims, still ever-ready to protect those exiled in a good cause, consecrated Albert bishop of Liège and gave him hospitality, since the emperor kept him out of his see. Albert settled at Rheims with a few faithful companions, living in such dire poverty that he could hardly go out of his house, except to church. His brother, Duke Henry of Brabant, gave him neither political nor financial support. Creditors dunned him. Meanwhile a party of German knights had joined his household on pretence of being refugees from the imperial court. They set upon Albert and murdered him a few months after his consecration, when they were riding together in the country outside Rheims. The tale has a 'ruthless rhyme' flavour: the bishop's creditors took his murder in bad part because his assassins had ridden off with his horse, which had been pledged as surety for his debt. All his servants were thrown into prison in consequence. The Germans made straight for the emperor to announce their news. He received them in such a way as to leave contemporaries in no doubt that he had suggested the murder in the first place. But Albert's stand in defence of the Church was vindicated, although there was no spectacular penance, as at Canterbury after Becket's murder. Henry VI banished the culprits eventually; he allowed his candidate to vacate the see at the pope's command; he made some reparation by endowing altars and masses.

Parallels to the Becket conflict leap to the eye. Albert had as good or even a better cause: he defended freedom of elections and his right to appeal to Rome. He suffered exile, which was forced upon

[76] P. Zerbi, *Papato, Impero e 'respublica Christiana' dal 1187 al 1198* (Milan, 1955) 97–102.

him, not self-inflicted. He was murdered, probably with the emperor's consent, for refusing to waive his claim to his see. His *Life* was written only two years or so after the murder by Werric abbot of Lobbes, who had been his devoted companion in exile and who knew him well.[77] The abbot exploits the resemblance to the Becket story. Albert, like Thomas, 'put on a new man' and became more devout at his consecration; he predicted his murder on the day it happened.[78] But Werric writes with the freshness of familiarity and brings out the contrasts as well as the likenesses. Albert in exile displayed just those virtues which John of Salisbury had preached to Becket in vain. The exiled bishop genuinely wished for peace; he would not allow his wrongs to be used as a *casus belli*. He neither cursed his enemies nor allowed jokes to be made against them at his table. He lamented his plight ruefully and yet half-laughingly; you never knew whether he was joking or serious:

> I'm well-born. I used to be a rich, jolly, highly placed clerk. Now I'm a poor exiled bishop. No bishop has ever lived in such poverty as I. It doesn't hurt me. At least I shall die humble and not proud. Seven feet of earth will suffice me.[79]

Werric makes an explicit comparison with Becket in Albert's favour, after telling of the murder. The emperor behaved worse then Henry king of England, who had St Thomas put to death. King Henry at least did not receive the murderers at his court, as the emperor did. The whole world cries out at Albert's murder, marvelling at its manner and cause. Albert tried to make peace with the raging emperor, who banished him from the realm. He spent his exile in meekness and quiet. His murderers were more cruel than those of St Thomas: they betrayed him as their host; they gave him no chance to reply; they inflicted twenty-three wounds on his body instead of three, after which they cut it to pieces. Werric then produces testimonials from friends of Becket. Archbishop Conrad of Mainz among others 'detested the deed'.[80] Conrad had been a close friend of Becket and fellow exile. The trump card has waited until near the end. Werric gives the verdict of Dean Ralph of Rheims:

> When they were mourning for Albert at Rheims, his death was compared to Thomas's. Dean Ralph of Rheims, a man greatly

[77] It survives in an incomplete form; ed. M.G.H., SS. xxv, 139–68.
[78] ibid. 151, 161.   [79] ibid.   [80] ibid. 168.

revered in the Church, put a word in: 'Behold a greater than Thomas here!' He was English by birth and had been one of St Thomas's companions in the Frankish kingdom during his exile for many years. He was learned and well known for his worthy character. He used to praise 'his' Albert, whom he knew well, for his innocence and for his good cause, with truly pious affection. He devoutly stated and believed that Albert was a martyr of God, who died in innocence, betrayed by the guilty, for the sake of the liberty of God's Church, which the emperor Henry wanted to subdue.[81]

The emperor's designs on the Church are enlarged upon to prove that Albert's resistance was well grounded.

A glance at Ralph's career will bring out the value of his testimony. He was the Master Ralph of Sarre in Kent to whom John of Salisbury addressed his famous letter on the Council of Pavia, denouncing the Germans and their claims.[82] Ralph of Sarre had belonged to Archbishop Theobald's household, but was a member of the chapter of Rheims, perhaps as a canon, by 1165. John of Salisbury recommended him for the office of dean, writing that none was worthier or more generous to the poor. He became dean in or soon after 1170 and died about 1196. He showed zeal in reforming his chapter and seems to have been on friendly terms with Peter of la Celle, now abbot of St Remigius of Rheims.[83] Peter had subscribed to Becket's cause and had befriended John of Salisbury. Ralph kept in close touch with Canterbury. Archbishop Richard of Dover, a former chaplain of Becket, referred to Ralph as 'our very dear son' in a confirmation of the possessions and liberties of the monks of St Martin of Dover, 1177–88; he was then holding the prebend of Dale.[84] The monks of Christchurch relied on him to back their cause abroad in their quarrel with the archbishop. His friendship with Pope Gregory VIII, 1187, raised their hopes; they begged him for advice and praised him as a man of good counsel.[85] Ralph left his

---

[81] ibid.

[82] *Letters* i, no. cxxiv, p. 204–15, written June/July 1160; see p. 204 for the evidence on Ralph's career.

[83] P.L. ccii, 562.

[84] B. E. A. Jones, *The Acta of Archbishops Richard and Baldwin 1174–1190* (London University Ph.D. thesis, 1964) 562.

[85] *Ep. Cant.* xliii–xliv, 13, 88, 113, 220, 229, 281–2.

P

library to Christchurch. He had a fine collection of glossed books of the Bible and John the Scot's commentary on the *Celestial Hierarchy*, with other Pseudo-Dionysian texts.[86] His interest in Pseudo-Dionysius links him to John of Salisbury as a scholar. Herbert of Bosham gives him a place among the *eruditi sancti Thomae*: Ralph suffered exile along with his aged parents, although he did not belong to the archbishop's household or family. He deserved to end his life as a bishop, as did other *eruditi*, but at least he was promoted to be dean of Rheims.[87] Werric could have found no better expert on martyrdom to bring into the witness-box. A man of impressive learning, as his library shows, a companion of St Thomas in exile, sympathetic to the cause of ecclesiastical liberty, especially against the imperialists, as we gather from John of Salisbury's letter, and adviser to the monks of Christchurch in what they and their friends (including Herbert) regarded as a fight against tyranny, Dean Ralph should have succeeded in putting Albert on a level with Thomas.

Only one copy of Werric's *Life* survives in a manuscript of the thirteenth century, which belonged to the White Canons of Heylissen in the diocese of Liège; it is now at Brussels. Albert's *Life* by Werric follows immediately after the anonymous *Life* of St Thomas, which I mentioned earlier as hitting hard against the secular power in the person of Henry II.[88] There are no other hagiographical pieces in the manuscript.[89] The pairing of the two martyrs, both victims of the secular power, was intended to stress their likeness and to put Albert in the best possible company. But Werric had only two miracles to record.[90] Chroniclers mention the story of Albert; but it does not figure in scholastic works or in *exempla* as far as I know.

Two reasons for the disparity between Albert and Thomas suggest themselves. Albert lacked propagandists. He had no institution behind him to forward his cult. He had been a stranger at Rheims;

---

[86] ibid. 559; *Ancient Libraries*, 86–7; *Medieval Libraries*, 29–35; H. Dondaine, 'Les *expositiones super ierarchiam caelestem* de Jean Scot Erigène', A.H.D.L.M.A. xviii (1951) 245–7.

[87] *Mat.* iii, 526.   [88] Above, p. 193.

[89] J. Van den Gheyn, *Catalogue des MSS de la Bibliothèque royale de Belgique* i (Brussels, 1901) 101. Heylissen was founded in 1129. The mark of ownership is in a seventeenth-century hand. The *Lives* in this MS (no. 221, 723–7) are written in a different hand from the other items in the volume (foll. 114vb–137ra). They look like mid-thirteenth century to me.

[90] *Vita*, 156–66. They are commonplace: a woman was healed at the tomb and some townsmen saw lights shining over the place of the murder.

the canons of Liège neglected him; he had no ties with the Cistercians: he had no *eruditi*. Albert himself was not without learning, though not a *magister*. He had probably studied at Liège and he compared favourably with the minority candidate for the bishopric, who was 'dull and unlettered'. A Master Gerard, canon of Liège and 'a keen investigator', was one of Albert's chaplains. Albert used to chide him goodnaturedly for being 'too clever and eager'.[91] But Master Gerard was no Herbert. Albert's friends, Dean Ralph of Sarre and Archbishop Conrad, were too old to agitate in his cause by 1192.

The second reason for neglect goes deeper. The climate of academic opinon changed in the late twelfth and early thirteenth century. Albert's 'passion' was an epilogue, the last phase of the Investiture Contest in Germany.[92] One cannot bathe twice in the same river; the masters did not try. Two martyrs in the same cause made one too many. We have heard a lot of sabre-rattling at Paris *apropos* of Becket's defence of *sacerdotium*. It sounds against a background of disappointment. Peter the Chanter and his circle, while admiring Becket, noted that his doctrine failed to take account of facts. The most ardent churchmen at Paris admitted what the lukewarm had always acted upon: they were fighting a losing battle against compromise. Popes and bishops connived in practice at what they forbade in theory. There was evasion and hairsplitting. Men could not be forced to obey the clergy.[93] Masters and students had won the right of privilege of clergy as members of the schools. That was what really mattered to them. Application of the principle of clerical immunity elsewhere lost its urgency, though it still formed a subject for *quaestiones*.[94]

Paris theologians lost interest in the problem of the relationship between the two swords or preferred to shelve it. We have our exception to prove the rule. An anonymous commentator on Gilbert of la Porrée's *Media glosatura* on St Paul, teaching in the last third of the twelfth century, decided strongly for the High-church theory held by Becket and his circle on the superiority of the spiritual sword. He stood alone. No later commentator on the crucial text Rom. xiii, 7 bothered to discuss the relations between *regnum* and *sacerdotium*.[95]

---

[91] ibid. 154, 160-1.   [92] E. de Moreau op. cit. 13.
[93] This conclusion emerges from Baldwin, *Masters*.
[94] Baldwin, 'A debate at Paris', op. cit. 129-31.
[95] Affeldt, op. cit. 174-249, 295.

Stephen Langton, as far as we know, would never commit himself on the question of the two swords. He raised it only to drop it inconclusively. His lectures on the Twelve Prophets (about 1200) contain arguments for the overall superiority of the spiritual power. As the sun lights up the moon, so the spiritual power gives its light to the secular. A similar argument is drawn from the two swords, Langton says. He assumes that his pupils will know the argument on the two swords of the Gospel and does not specify any further, except to comment: 'But that is questionable.' He twists the metaphor round. The moon, signifying he secular power, receives the light of doctrine and the splendour of faith from the sun, signifying the spiritual power. But each power suffers eclipse from the intervention of the other. Now we have reached such a pass that *the sun is turned into darkness* of sin, *and the moon into blood* of spoil (Joel ii, 31).[96] The same problem came up in one of his *questiones*:[97]

> It seems that both swords belong to the Church by virtue of her authority and power.

Langton cites the gospel text on the two swords and adds a text from Gratian's *Decretum* to support the proposition. But this is disputed:

> The Romans say 'yes' because Constantine gave Sylvester the sword of the west, keeping that of the east for himself. Therefore (they argue), the pope transferred the power inhering in the emperor to King Charles (Charlemagne), committing the empire to him. The pope could not have done so (they argue) unless he already had the authority of the sword. The emperor's party contest it.

Resolving the question, Langton inclines to the view that the Church has held the power of both swords from the time of Abel. He adds a rider which takes away the force of his decision in favour of the papalists against the imperialists: 'I do not say the pope, but the Church'. Hence he doubted whether the pope held both swords, though he would ascribe them to the Church. The debate ends: 'But we shall pass this over, since it is an old quarrel.' The burning ques-

---

[96] *Study of the Bible*, 261–2.

[97] J. Leclercq, 'Questions des XIIIe et XIVe siècles sur la Juridiction de l'Eglise', *Studia Gratiana* xii (1967) 321–3. For discussion and bibliography see Baldwin, *Masters* i, 164–7, ii, 19–21, 110–11. Langton's *quaestiones* cannot be dated precisely.

tion of yesterday is dismissed as stale and tiresome! Langton goes on to consider more detailed questions on the relations between various groups and officials. These had more immediate interest for him than the general question of relations between the two powers.[98]

Langton venerated St Thomas, whose resistance to tyranny set a good example; but he entered on his own career as archbishop with a more sophisticated, down-to-earth outlook. The stark simplicity of the two-swords theory broke up into numbers of separate problems. Scholastic *quaestiones* came to include so many reservations and distinctions that it is difficult to know what personal views a master put forward. Attention shifted from ecclesiastical liberties to ecclesiastical discipline. The Becket conflict marked high tide in the defence of *sacerdotium*. Albert of Louvain came too late to be noticed. New problems and new ways of thinking engaged the thirteenth-century schoolmen. The tide turned even sooner in England than it did at Paris.

[98] Leclercq, op. cit.: Sed hoc pretermisso, quia vetus est querela, queritur de hoc singulatim.

IX

Second Thoughts in England

Herbert of Bosham took a gloomy view of Becket's successors at Canterbury:

> Concerning the two who succeeded my lord in the metropolitan see, whom I saw for myself while I was writing the martyr's story, I raise no question now nor make any complaint at all, since I owe them reverence as spouses of my mother, the holy church of Canterbury, and ought not to raise any question or complaint against them. They know what benefits them; let them see to it.

He urged Archbishop Baldwin to imitate St Thomas's zeal, without much hope that the lesson would be heeded.[1] His gloom was justified. The clergy gained a circumscribed *privilegium fori*. Otherwise Henry II went his own way, as successfully, if more deviously, than before his settlement with Alexander at Avranches. His men got their bishoprics. The more loyal of Becket's *eruditi* found posts abroad. The disloyal did well for themselves. Even Herbert compromised with his principles eventually by taking service with the chancellor bishop, William Longchamp. Becket's first successor, Archbishop Richard of Dover, was notoriously pliable. Both Richard and Baldwin worked well with Henry, contenting themselves with fatherly admonition on occasion. Both applied themselves to routine administration, as they needed to, after Becket's long exile and the vacancy which followed the murder.

Passions ran high again at Canterbury under Baldwin's rule; but this time it was no straight conflict between *regnum* and *sacerdotium*. The archbishop quarrelled with the monks of his cathedral. He planned to establish a college for secular canons to provide for the secular clerks of his household; a monastic chapter could not finance them. The college was to be endowed partly from Christchurch property. The monks resisted the raid on their revenues and were

[1] P.L. cxc, 1403–4; 1073–4.

afraid of losing their electoral rights. They appealed to Rome. Ex-communications and street-fighting followed. Henry favoured the archbishop, but did not feel strongly enough to force a decision: the dispute affected the Church rather than royal government. Both parties appealed to the memory of St Thomas. Baldwin claimed that the saint had anticipated his plan, and promised to dedicate the new church to St Stephen and St Thomas. The monks appealed to the martyr's stand for the liberties of Canterbury. That probably explains why Herbert backed them in fighting for their rights against both king and archbishop.[2] They made much of a local incident when the rival faction at Canterbury caught a nephew of St Thomas, threw him into prison and later sacked his house:

> The martyr's blood is still fresh. If his nephew is not spared, then who will be?

The martyr's nephew, the monks claimed, had suffered with his companions in the outrage for their religious zeal: they had refused to communicate with excommunicates. The Church's name was abased in the ill treatment meted out to them.[3] Yet it was the arch-bishop's men, not the king's, who persecuted the martyr's relative. Times had changed.

What did Baldwin think of his canonized predecessor? His edu-cation and career suggest that he would have sympathized with the martyr's cause.[4] Master Baldwin studied and perhaps taught at Exeter; he also acted at tutor to a nephew of Pope Innocent II at Ferentino before 1150; probably he had gone abroad to study law in Italy. As archdeacon of Totnes and close friend of Bartholo-mew, bishop of Exeter, he corresponded with John of Salisbury during the exile. John wrote to him as one scholar to another and re-garded him as a strong supporter of Becket.[5] Baldwin entered the

---

[2] Above, p. 72.

[3] *Ep. Cant.* 200–1, 209–10; the letters quoted are dated April 1188. See Urry, op. cit. 87–8.

[4] G.F.L.C. 531 and *passim.* B. E. A. Jones, *The Acta of Archbishops Richard and Baldwin 1174–1190* (London University Ph.D. thesis, 1964) gives a useful account of Baldwin's career and of his archiepiscopate. On his spiritual works, see *Dictionnaire de spiritualité* ed. M. Viller i (1937) 1285–1286. Not all have been published. Apart from the pieces printed in P.L. cciv, see *Baudouin de Ford, le sacrement de l'autel*, ed. J. Mor with a foreword by J. Leclercq (Paris, 1963).

[5] *Mat.* vi, 71, 87, 317–19.

Cistercian abbey of Ford about 1169. The Becket conflict may have influenced his decision to become a monk, but he certainly had a vocation. His many writings as monk and abbot of Ford show a combination of theological doctrine and monastic spirituality which was becoming rare in the second half of the twelfth century. That they answered a contemporary need appears from the number of manuscript copies and from their use by compilers of 'select extracts'. The Dominican Robert Holcot was quoting Baldwin's homily to priests as late as the 1330s.[6] While abbot of Ford, he was elected to the bishopric of Worcester in 1180 and then to Canterbury in 1184. Opinions varied on his policies as archbishop; most people would have agreed with Gerald of Wales that he was 'distinguished for his learning and religion'.[7] His learning included not only theology, homiletics and canon law (he was a great decretal collector), but interest in geography and history. He appreciated Gerald's *Topography of Ireland* and he wished his nephew, Joseph of Exeter, the poet of the Trojan War, to write a history of the Crusade. Finally, the old archbishop made a tour of Wales in order to preach the cross there. Gerald, who escorted him, praises his success in recruiting would-be crusaders and his endurance in travelling through the wild countryside. He accompanied Richard I on Crusade and died during the seige of Acre, 19 November 1190. He was remembered as a man with a dry sense of humour.[8]

We can compare Baldwin's first and second thoughts on Becket. He treats of martyrdom in his *Sacrament of the Altar*, written while he was abbot of Ford and therefore within ten years of Becket's death. Baldwin defines martyrdom so as to cover defence of a just cause and not only witness to the faith against infidels. He does not mention St Thomas by name, but the allusion to him is recognizable:

Wine is changed into blood when righteousness rejoices and it is decided to resist unrighteousness at the cost of bloodshed. That is righteousness perfected. Of imperfect righteousness the apostle says, writing to the Hebrews: *For you have not yet resisted unto blood, striving against sin* (xii, 4). If a righteous man girds

---

[6] B. Smalley, 'Robert Holcot O.P.', *Archivum Fratrum Praedicatorum* xxvi (1956) 48.

[7] *Itinerarium Kambriae* Opera VI, ed J. F. Dimock (Rolls Series).

[8] ibid. 125; S. Runciman, *A History of the Crusades* iii (Cambridge, 1954) 7–8.

himself with the sword against trial or persecution, if he judges it
better to die than to depart from righteousness . . ., if he is found
faithful in men's sight when he is brought to judgement for
confession of faith or for defence of righteousness, then he shall
be ranked with Christ in the judgement to come. . . . A man of
this sort is worthy to be called a martyr and appears as a faithful
witness, testifying in the land.[9]

The passage reads as a vindication of Thomas as a true martyr,
with an implied reproach to his royal persecutor. It is interesting to
find that a copy of *The Sacrament of the Altar* in a manuscript
formerly at Clairvaux is followed by an account of St Thomas's
martyrdom, the bull of canonization and a list of eminent visitors
to his shrine.[10]

Baldwin's second thoughts on Becket occur in a treatise on *The
Evil Ways of Clergy and People.* Its authoritative tone sets it in the
period when Baldwin was archbishop. He associates himself with
the clergy while denouncing their sins; he would not have done so
when he was still an abbot, addressing religious. The treatise probably represents sermon material.[11] It belongs to the hell-fire genre.
The burden of Baldwin's complaint against the clergy is that they
have proved themselves to be unworthy of their privilege and
deserve that laymen should persecute them. The clergy, therefore,
must take the blame for St Thomas's martyrdom. They were
responsible for it indirectly but certainly:

> Laymen find nothing in our conduct to imitate; they find what
> they would rather persecute. They persecute us with calumnies;
> they persecute us with injuries; finally they persecute us with the
> sword. Recently the fury of their persecution has wounded us in
> our head, when they persecuted the Lord's St Thomas our arch-
> bishop unto death for his glorious defence of the freedom of the
> Church. . . . If it is true, as report has spread and as the con-
> science of many has feared, then our disordered life was the cause

[9] *Le sacrement de l'autel,* 218–20.

[10] ibid. 55. The pieces on the martyrdom come from Ralph of Diss.

[11] P.L. cciv, 415. The treatise probably represents a reworking of earlier
material, since Baldwin refers to the murder as having taken place recently
and calls St Thomas 'our archbishop'. The printed edition gives Baldwin
the title of archbishop, but this may not have manuscript authority. We
know that he continued to write after leaving Ford; see *Gilbert Foliot,* 72.

of this great evil and furnished the springs of hatred. *Man* did
not *so account of us as the ministers of Christ and the dispensers
of the mysteries of God.* (I Cor. iv, 1). . . . We seemed, perhaps,
to be unworthy of those ancient privileges which the indulgence
of popes and of noble kings of old accorded to the clergy for their
liberty and peace . . .

Does not the blessed martyr, who offered up his life for our
sake, bring a charge against us? . . . Did he not die for our fault?
Did he not die by reason of our fault? Our fault did not cause
his death, but it gave the pretext. . . . Rightly must it be charged
to our fault that the secular power claims ecclesiastical cases for
itself, that it is not governed by the authority of the Church, that
it neither uses nor relies upon the counsel of the Church, that
Peter's sword has been blunted, that Peter's keys are dishonoured,
that the sacraments of the Church are scorned, that perjurers take
God's holy name in vain, that due reverence is not paid to Holy
Church, that her parsons are not respected as they should be, and
that the worthy name of holy religion is debased. All this . . .
must be laid at our door.[12]

The moral is that all would go well again if the clergy would mend
their ways.

St Thomas is presented as a victim of clerical indiscipline. Lay
anti-clericalism and the murder itself resulted from the sins of the
clergy. Baldwin seems to take a grim pleasure in turning the
martyr's significance upside down. His sermon amounted to a
manifesto of his own aims as archbishop. The clergy needed discipline rather than privilege. Only by setting his house in order could
he hope to conciliate the lay power. The zeal which Herbert recommended should be turned against the clergy, not the laity.

It is surprising that Baldwin's friend Bishop Bartholomew of
Exeter left no written sermon on the martyr. He preached in the
cathedral at Canterbury at the invitation of the prior and convent
when it was reopened after the closure following on its desecration,
21 December 1171. Nothing but his introductory text has been
recorded.[13] Bartholomew put together in writing the sermons which
he preached as bishop of Exeter to various congregations on Sundays

[12] P.L. cciv, 416–18.
[13] A. Morey, *Bartholomew of Exeter, Bishop and Canonist* (Cambridge,
1937) 35.

and holy days.[14] His devotion to St Peter appears in the number of sermons allotted to St Peter's festivals. One includes a strong statement on Petrine supremacy:

The Good Shepherd, who laid down his life for his sheep, exalted St Peter, whose feast we are keeping, and set him up as chief shepherd after himself, as prince of the apostles and as ruler over all rulers, that is over kings, emperors and bishops.[15]

This taste of Bartholomew's doctrine whets the appetite for more; but there is no sermon in honour of St Thomas. Bartholomew may perhaps have had his sermons written down at some time in his long episcopate (1161–84) before the canonization of 1173. If so, he did not care to add a supplement on the new festival. Perhaps he thought that silence was golden.

We have evidence that one of the *eruditi* changed his mind in his old age. Gervase of Chichester has left ample material for a comparison between his first and second thoughts on the martyrdom. Herbert listed Gervase among the *eruditi* immediately after Matthew, then dean of Chichester (1180/1–1196/7),[16] and described relations with Becket in much the same terms:

After Matthew, Gervase, also of Chichester by origin and name. He was young at the time and praiseworthy for his character and learning. He too (like Matthew) did not leave his country, since he was not called upon (to go into exile).[17]

Gervase had the title of master. He must have studied theology at some stage in his career; he refers to himself as a theologian, using the *Artes* as subsidiary to theology, in his homilies on Malachias.[18]

[14] ibid. 109–12. The sermons are preserved in MS Oxford, Bodl. 449 (2396), from the chapter library of Exeter.

[15] fol. 59rb–va: Pastor iste bonus, qui pro nobis ovibus suis mortem sustinuit, beatum Petrum apostolum, cuius hodie sollemnitatem colimus, adeo sublimavit ut eum post se summum pastorum suarum ovium, principem apostolorum, rectorem quoque omnium rectorum, videlicet regum, imperatorum atque pontificum constituerit.

[16] On Master Matthew see *The Acta of the Bishops of Chichester*, ed. H. Mayr-Harting (Canterbury and York Soc. cxxx, 1964) 11, 211, 213.

[17] *Mat.* iii, 526–7.

[18] MS Brit. mus., Royal 3.B.x, fol. 93rb: . . . immo etiam et omnis artium liberalium vel cuiuslibet literature scientia, dummodo fidei catholice sanctioni non obviet, Dei et ecclesie cultoribus est applicanda.

Bishop Hilary of Chichester may have trained and patronized him in his early days. By 1158 he had entered the royal chancery under Becket and presumably went with him to Canterbury with other chancery clerks in 1162. He joined Bishop Hilary's household when Becket went into exile, and was a canon of Chichester by 1165–9. Gervase was witnessing Chichester documents in the 1170s and 1180s.[19] It is notable that Herbert did not blame him for deserting the marytr's cause and serving a royalist bishop. The local patriotism of a Bosham man may have influenced Herbert; he did not pass adverse judgement on Bishop Hilary either.[20] Further, Gervase's learning made him an ornament to the list of *eruditi*. He claimed to have been attached to St Thomas in his lifetime and made good any defection by his enthusiastic cult of the martyr.

Two sermons preached by Gervase soon after the murder have been preserved for us by a lucky chance in a sixteenth-century transcript made by a sub-dean of Chichester called Nicholas Hickett. His transcript is now in MS 14 of Westminster Abbey.[21] The two sermons are rubricated as 'preached in the chapter of Chichester on the feast of St Thomas the martyr in the first year of the ordination of the said Gervase', and 'preached by Gervase, priest of Chichester, in the chapter in the second year when the Church was in perturbation'. The 'perturbation of the Church' mentioned in the second rubric must refer to the murder and its consequences. The second year of perturbation would have fallen between 29 December 1171 and 1172, and therefore before the canonization of 1173. Gervase anticipates it, since he says that Thomas is the author and patron of the day's celebration. He preached the first sermon, according to the rubric, on St Thomas's feast day in the first year of his ordination. He must have been ordained sometime in 1172, being a priest in the year 1171–2. It looks as though the second sermon in Hickett's transcript was preached first; the first in the transcript, preached after the second, would have been given on the first festi-

---

fol. 93vb: Omnem enim decimam inferimus, dum in cordis nostri horreo perfectam theologie scientiam obsequiis dominicis subservituram recondimus.

On this MS see below, p. 248.

[19] *Acta*, op. cit. 11, 118, 136, 138, 145; *Select Documents of the English Lands of the Abbey of Bec*, ed. M. Chibnall (Camden Soc. 3rd series, lxxiii, 1951) 4.

[20] Dr Mayr-Harting pointed this out to me.

[21] See below, p. 247 for Appendix ii on Nicholas Hickett and the MSS of Gervase.

val to be held in honour of the newly canonized saint, December 1173, 'in nova novi martyris solempnitate.'

The earlier sermon addresses priests on their duties on the text: *I am the good shepherd* (Io. x, 11). Thomas was both a *good shepherd*, who laid down his life for his sheep, and an *atoning sacrifice* (Num. v, 8), who expiated the sin of the English Church. He preferred a glorious passion to apostasy from the divine law. He defeated the forces of evil by choosing to die. Gervase describes his victory as follows:

> He felled the beast of war with the ferocity of his divine daring and exposed himself to danger of his own free will, so as to slay the enemies of the Law, being slain, and to smite the smiters of the Church, being smitten down. He unmanned the brutal force of lay fury by giving himself up to be trampled on by brutal men. Like another Phineas in his zeal for the Law, he pierced evil livers with the dagger of his tongue, that it might be set down to him for righteousness forever (Num. xxv, 7-13), and wrought atoning vengeance for his brothers' guilt.[22]

The comparison to Phineas shows what Gervase had in mind. Phineas drew his dagger upon fornicators in Israel and was remembered forever as a good priest; he signified a prelate who corrected his sinful subjects.[23] The emphasis is laid on what St Thomas won for the Church by defending God's law.

The sermon on his feast day elaborates the theme. Gervase describes the martyr's austerities as proved by the vermin found in his hairshirt.[24] He draws the familiar parallel with the passion of Christ. Then he points to a contrast: Christ redeemed us from eternal bond-

---

[22] MS Westminster Abbey 14, fol. 124v: Quemadmodum gloriosus ille solempnitatis hodierne patronus et auctor eximius, Thomas scilicet, moderna ecclesie anglicane hostia placabilis, fortiter egisse cognoscitur, qui iuxta quandem constantiam gloriosa pre-eligit occumbere passione quam divine legis apostatare transgressione. . . . Qui etiam . . . bestiam belligerem audacis divine ferocitate prosternens, sese voluntario subiecit periculo, ut legis inimicos occisus occideret et ecclesie oppressores oppressus opprimeret. Quatenus bestialem laicalis violentie furorem enervaret, dum se bestialibus hominibus prosternandum substerneret. Qui rursus velut alter legis emulator Phineas, ut sempiternam sibi reputaretur ad iustitiam, carnaliter agentes lingue sue pugione transfodit et placabilem fraterni sceleris vindictam exercuit.

[23] See Raban Maur's commentary on Numbers, P.L. cviii, 770. Gervase would assume this interpretation of the Numbers text.

[24] foll. 120v-121.

age, St Thomas from temporal. We give thanks to them both.[25] God uses the reprobate to benefit the elect, as events now prove. The martyr's death has exalted the Church. Christ appeared weak in his passion, great in his burial and greatest of all in his resurrection. Similarly St Thomas was inglorious in death, but famous in his burial place, and his triumphant death has spread his glory over all the earth. Thus the prophecy of Isaias, *his sepulchre shall be glorious* (xi, 10) can now be said to apply to St Thomas as well as to Christ.[26] The climax of the argument is that the martyrdom has saved *sacerdotium* in England:

> Unless our new Abel, the righteous man, had been slain by his brother's, nay, by a filial sword, which was even more cruel, as new first fruits offered up to God and to the good fight, so that one might die for the many, the whole of our order in England might perhaps have perished. But the offering of his holy blood and brains, scattered on the pavement for our sake, has reunited God's scattered children.[27]

Gervase ends his sermon by calling upon his hearers to show themselves worthy of the sacrifice which St Thomas made on behalf of their order. He agreed with Robert of Crichlade, preaching in the same years, that St Thomas had saved the clergy by his resistance to secular oppression and by his martyrdom. It was a shared illusion.

The homilies on Malachias for the instruction of priests were written in Gervase's old age. They survive in one medieval copy, which belonged to Gloucester abbey and is now MS Royal 3.B.x

[25] fol. 120: ut oves iam libere eternaliter per Christum ac temporaliter per Thomam a servilis claustro detentionis eiecte, utrique nostre liberationis auctori, illi quidem omnimodas, huic vero multimodas, gratiarum referamus actiones.

[26] fol. 122: Sed sicut iste in passione modicus, in sepulchro magnus, in resurrectione apparuit maximus, ita et discipulus in morte quidem ignominiosus, in sepulchri autem cespite famosus, post mortis vero triumphum ubique terrarum extitit gloriosus, adeo ut de sepulchro Domini illud Esaie propheticum sepulchro Thome veraciter iam dicatur adaptatum: *et erit sepulchrum eius gloriosum*.

[27] fol. 123: Nisi enim novus ipse noster Abel iustus fraterno, immo crudelius gladio filiali, quasi nove Deo et agone primitie immolatus, ut unus multo moreretur pro populo, anglicana forsitan ordinis nostri gens tota deperiret. Sed sacrata sanguinis ac cerebri carnisque conscissa hostia, pro nobis pavimento dispersa, dispersos Dei filios in unum congregavit.

of the British Museum.[28] In his prefatory verses Gervase says that he continued to study in his old age and that he expounded the prophet Malachias by request in order to instruct and to reform the conduct of bishops and priests. After that, he turned his mind to the story and merits of St Thomas. His love for the martyr, to whom he was attached in his lifetime, puts him under obligation to hold up St Thomas as an example to prelates. St Thomas's virtues, exile, courageous death and many signs and cures all set an example:

> Take heed then, shepherd, when you read my writings, that you rule your fold as I teach you.[29]

A set of homilies on St Thomas originally followed the homilies on Malachias in the Gloucester manuscript; but some twelve leaves have been cut out, so that only the tailpiece of the last homily remains. It was probably done at the Reformation. The surviving fragment shows that it belonged to a different set from the sermons transcribed by Hickett in the Westminster Abbey manuscript. The two columns of text which are left suffice to show that Gervase's attitude to the martyr has changed. The effects of his martyrdom have broadened out. Instead of presenting him as the saviour of ecclesiastical liberties, Gervase makes him redeem religion in general and set a moral example:

> A clerk outwardly, a monk inwardly and wearing a hermit's hairshirt, which was more, he mediated at the cost of his life for the general redemption of English religion in order to bring monks and clerks, together with all ranks of religion, to enjoy the portion of his lot.[30]

The homilies on Malachias register second thoughts in plenty. Gervase addressed 'all the priests of Christ in the Church of the English', as their fellow priest.[31] He will instruct them, as requested, by moralizing Malachias. Moralists often quoted the denunciations

---

[28] Warner and Gilson, *Catalogue of Western Manuscripts in the Old Royal and King's Collections in the British Museum* i (1967) 72–3. The hands are English, of the late twelfth or early thirteenth century.

[29] fol. 1.

[30] MS Royal 3.B.x, fol. 113vb:... Ut qui clericus exterius, monachus interius, intime plus hiis heremita ciliciatus, pro generali religionis anglicane redemptione anime sue pretium interposuit, (ut) monachos et clericos cum omni religionis gradu in sortis sue portionem introducat.

[31] fol. 2ra.

of this prophet, adapting them to the contemporary priesthood. Gervase was the first to provide a full commentary. He modelled himself on St Gregory's homilies on Ezechiel. His work has much in common with Robert of Crichlade's, except that Gervase wrote with a more specific purpose and did not burden his pages with so many learned allusions.[32] Like Crichlade he intended his homilies for both preaching and reading: he addresses his public as 'dearly beloved brethren', 'holy fathers' and 'scribe or reader'.[33] He aimed at reminding them of what they knew rather than teaching novelties.[34] He broke through the bonds of convention, nevertheless. His criticisms of his contemporaries are precise and well informed in a genre which lent itself to banality.

The English clergy are more prone to unchastity than those in other Catholic countries. Splendid church buildings and furniture are preferred to the worship of the heart. Patrons think only of their kinsmen when they give benefices, whence it happens that unlearned priests teach heresies, profane novelties, apocrypha and dubious doctrines. Bishops and religious engage in litigation, disturbing the Church as though by civil war. Even the Roman Church, mother of all churches, cannot cope with so many lawsuits.[35] Turning to the laity, Gervase complains that fraud is widespread. Husbands want to repudiate their wives as soon as they get rich, so as to better themselves by making more advantageous alliances. Yet a clever, wise and good woman can help her husband better than one chosen for her wealth alone.[36]

The homilist draws a moral for the clergy from this dark picture. They have brought their troubles on themselves. God subjected laymen 'under our feet' for as long as and no longer than our holiness surpassed theirs. Nowadays clerks cause more scandal than laymen. If we have to investigate matter for just reproof in any parish, we can go straight to the house of the priest. The result is that clerks are scorned by laymen and even reduced to begging. Many clerks wander about 'sine titulis'; others put off their clergy so as to earn their living by taking secular office.[37] Gervase is making the same

---

[32] Gervase makes some unspecific references to St Gregory, brings out the odd tag of verse and makes a list of pagan deities to illustrate the meaning of 'false gods' in his text (fol. 41va).

[33] foll. 25va, 40rb, 112vb.   [34] fol. 6ra.

[35] foll. 4va, 16rb, 26rb–va, 34va, 45va.

[36] foll. 50va–53rb.   [37] fol. 46va–vb.

point as Baldwin: the clergy have forfeited their right to privilege by abusing it.

He advises them on the attitude they should take *vis-à-vis* the secular power. After warning them not to incur God's wrath in their anxiety to evade the displeasure of princes who offend God by persecuting priests and humbling the Church, he goes on to the delicate question of what sanctions they should use against princes. 'Go slow' is his answer. Respect even bad rulers. Oppose the shield of patience, should madness or human frailty kindle their anger against prelates. Admonish them gently. Moderate talk may quench the flame which their power kindles. In the last resort, if the prince is obdurate, then he must be smitten with the spiritual sword. It is better to help the prince in the exercise of his authority; but if he robs churches he should be forced to return what he has taken by spiritual censures. A definitive sentence should not be pronounced lightly, however. Indiscretion may inflame the offender. It may even be well for the prelate to flee for a time, thus giving the ruler time to see reason. Distance may prove more effective than talk at close quarters.[38] Gervase never uses the emotive terms 'excommunication' or 'the liberties of the Church'. He hoped that censure and an open breach might be avoided and thought them unlikely to do much good. He never raises the question of the relationship between the two swords.

Grudging permissiveness replaces caution when Gervase discusses the rights and wrongs of clerical service to secular princes. Bishops and priests, he says, ought not to go to court as a habit, but only when necessary; nor should they spend the money of their churches in the house of a lay magnate.[39] But he makes a proviso:

> We do not forbid clerks to do honest service to princes; we only detest the fact that they do it by reason of obsequiousness and greed and that they enjoy it so much. . . . It will not detract from churchmen's worth and merit if they decide to attach themselves to princely courts and follow laymen's camps, provided that their motive is love and desire to correct the princes or to forward the business of churches, and providing that they do not harbour ambition secretly.[40]

[38] foll. 17vb–18ra, 47ra–48ra, 89vb, 109va.   [39] foll. 71va, 88rb.

[40] fol. 88rb–va: Nec tamen principibus exhibendum honestum clericis inhibemus obsequium, sed inordinatam obsequii causam et cupidum obse-

Q

A powerful man must be loved as a neighbour; the prince must be honoured as a lord and protector, not because he confers benefices. It is more praiseworthy to convert a rich man than a pauper by frequent correction; the rich man's opportunities expose him to greater temptation.[41]

The homilist realized that secular service had come to stay. He defended it by disingenuous excuses: the prelate in civil service will act as a spiritual mentor at court; but defend it he did. To read the homilies on Malachias is to hear the Becket thunderstorm rolling away into the distance. Gervase was still praising Becket in his old age; but he dropped the martyr as an example except in very general terms. Bow to the altar and go about your business, conciliating princes and serving them as courtiers. The canon of Chichester resembled the Paris masters in adjusting his theories to practice.

Herbert himself had second thoughts when he was writing the *Life*. It was sad that the friendship between Henry and Thomas should have broken like glass. Harm came of their quarrel to both *regnum* and *sacerdotium*. Insecurity made Henry unduly anxious to have his son crowned king. The coronation led to the young Henry's wicked rebellion against his father. The clergy suffered and sees were left vacant. Most telling of all, Herbert admitted that Henry II was moved by zeal for his people's peace, just as Becket was moved by zeal for his clergy's freedom. Herbert never doubted that Becket was in the right, but he could observe the consequences of the clash of their rival zeals.[42]

The *Lives* and letters of Becket's *eruditi* offer a paradox which helps to explain why the climate of opinion changed. They could have made out a better case for Henry than he did for himself or than his bishops did for him. Writers of the *Lives* use the term 'public power' to denote royal government. Becket called the sheriffs 'ministers of the public power';[43] Fitzstephen called Ex-

---

quentium detestamur affectum. . . . Sic et viri ecclesiastici principum curiis adherentes, si dilectionis ac correctionis eorum intuitu aut ob promovenda ecclesiarum negotia laicorum castra sequi decreverint, non utique condigno privabuntur merito, si mentis ambitione priventur in occulto.

See H. Mayr-Harting, 'Hilary Bishop of Chichester and Henry II', E.H.R. lxxviii (1963) 219–20.

[41] fol. 88va–vb.   [42] *Mat.* iii, 263, 314–15, 272.

[43] ibid. i, 12, 47. Becket referred to the Count of Troyes also as exercising 'public power'; ibid. vi, 374–7.

chequer officials 'receivers of the public money'.[44] The term 'public power' appears in contexts where 'royal will or anger' might have seemed more appropriate: 'The public power upsets everything!' exclaimed Becket's cross-bearer at Clarendon.[45] Becket, according to one account, confessed to the pope that he owed his election to 'the terror of the public power', meaning that Henry had engineered his promotion to Canterbury.[46] The Church was oppressed 'on the pretext of public power'.[47] John of Salisbury wrote that the ports had been closed 'by public edict' and that courtiers held church property 'by the authority of public power' during the exile. He hoped that 'the ensign of the faith and of the public power might shine from the royal heads' when the quarrel was over.[48] It is true that Becket's supporters opposed the liberties of the Church to the public power. As Grim put it, the royal counsel and will decreed that clerks guilty of public crimes should be subject to the common law of the realm (which presumably would have been to the public advantage); but the archbishop objected to the plan as destructive of ecclesiastical liberties.[49] Yet 'public power' carried overtones of respectability; it had its origin in antiquity and had never been quite forgotten. It could lead on to the notion of 'the common good' and the needs of 'the community of the realm'.

Henry's servants used the term 'public power' less often. Richard Fitzneal in his *Dialogue of the Exchequer* prefers 'royal power' or 'the king's advantage'. He mentions 'public power' in several contexts, as when he writes that the royal prerogative belongs to the office of public power.[50] But he excuses the unpopular service of King's approver as follows: 'whatever contributes to the peace of the realm is undoubtedly to the king's advantage.'[51] The author of the treatise *On the Laws of England* sets the tone in the first line of his prologue; he begins with the words *Regiam potestatem*.[52]

---

[44] ibid. iii, 51.
[45] ibid. ii, 324.
[46] ibid. 343.
[47] ibid. i, 5.
[48] *Letters* i, 221–4; *Mat.* vii, 407–8; vi, 185.
[49] ibid. ii, 385–6.
[50] ed. and transl. by C. Johnson (London, 1950) 84, 94, 100.
[51] ibid. 88. Fitzneal combines the two ideas, ibid. 43: ut igitur regie simul et publice prouideretur utilitate.
[52] *Tractatus de legibus et consuetudinibus regni Anglie qui Glanvilla vocatur*, ed. and transl. by G. D. G. Hall (London, 1965) 1. The author has the prologue to the *Institutes* in mind. On the authorship of *De legibus*, see ibid. xxx–xxxiii.

Fitzneal and the author of this treatise had a good grasp of the realities and working of Angevin government; they were less forward-looking than Becket's friends in conceiving it as representing public power. The mere use of the term suggests a hidden ambivalence in the case made for Becket. His apologists realized that there were two sides to the question, if one looked at it from the point of view of 'the common good'. They suppressed the case for Henry in the heat of passion. After the conflict they acquiesced in manifestations of public authority which they had objected to earlier. Second thoughts had always been there.

The dean of St Paul's is jogging my elbow. Master Ralph of Diss has a right to the last word, since he crops up at each stage of the conflict, and then he narrated it in his *Histories*. Ralph took his name from Diss in Norfolk (latinized as Diceto).[53] He had several periods of study at Paris. Fitzstephen described him as 'a man of great worth, outstanding for his learning in the holy page'.[54] Gilbert Foliot commended him for his learned doctrine and his worth of character.[55] Ralph must have taught the holy page as well as studying at Paris: he left his commentaries on Ecclesiasticus and Wisdom to the cathedral library of St Paul's. Unfortunately they are lost, like so many other books of this library.[56] Ralph was archdeacon of Middlesex from 1152 until 1180, when he became dean of St Paul's. He died in 1202. The cathedral school grew and flourished during his tenure of office. He gave a striking example of the efficiency of a scholar turned administrator, combining moderate reform with realism. Thus he made provision for the practice of non-residence by the canons, which could no longer be prevented, while ensuring that some would reside to perform their duties in the cathedral. As well as legislating, he acted as judge delegate and made a survey of lands and churches belonging to his chapter. He was remembered as 'the good dean'.

[53] C. Duggan, *Twelfth-Century Decretal Collections and their Importance in English History* (London, 1963) 10–11. For notices on Ralph's life and writings see W. Stubbs' introductions in his *Radulphi de Diceto Opera Historica* (Rolls Series, 1876); M. Gibbs, *Early Charters of the Cathedral Church of St Paul, London* (Royal Historical Society, Camden 3rd series, lviii, 1939); C. N. L. Brooke, 'The Earliest Times to 1485', *A History of St Paul's Cathedral and the Men Associated with It*, ed. W. R. Matthews and W. M. Atkins (London, 1957) 1–99; *Gilbert Foliot* and G.F.L.C. *passim*.

[54] *Mat.* iii, 143. [55] G.F.L.C. 316.

[56] *Medieval Libraries*, 120–1.

Ralph's conduct in the Becket conflict was what one would expect of a master of the holy page who was also an archdeacon, a friend of Gilbert Foliot, and devoted to royal interests, as Gilbert assured Henry II.[57] Fitzstephen says that he 'wept much' on the fatal day at Northampton, but he did not take Becket's side and remained on good terms with both Henry and Gilbert.[58] However, he answered 'yes' to Richard of Ilchester's question on whether to submit to Becket's excommunications. His reason was that ecclesiastical discipline ought to be observed. To flout it would set a bad example to the people, always inclined to rebel against their superiors.[59] Ralph wanted order to be kept in both spiritual and temporal matters. He upheld the supremacy of the Church, headed by the pope, in principle. This comes out in his short treatise *On the two swords*. He quotes the usual texts on submission to Caesar in temporal matters and sets forth the usual account of the temporal power as having originated in man's sin at the fall. But the prelates of the Church are girt with the spiritual sword to draw upon the guilty, just as St Peter slew Ananias and Saphira. St Peter and his successors have power to bind and loose the soul, which is worthier than the body. They receive the power from God. Hence we must take our starting point from God's house, the Roman Church, which St Peter ruled manfully and which he adorned with his martyrdom.[60] Ralph has made a conventional statement; he does not draw consequences likely to offend anyone. Nor did he do so in practice.

He began to compile his major historical work, the *Imagines historiarum*, after 1183; it was in progress in 1188 and nearing completion by 1190. Ralph continued adding to it until his death in 1202. Presentation of the Becket conflict posed grave difficulties. Becket had long been a canonized saint. Ralph did not wish to criticize him. At the same time he thought that Henry II had been an admirable ruler. The dean identified royal government with 'public power' and the public good. His description of Henry's measures to prevent corruption and to punish crime for the public good is famous: Stubbs included it in *Select Charters*.[61] Ralph also wrote that there was no 'public power' in Ireland to enforce justice before Henry's intervention.[62] He went much further than Gervase

[57] G.F.L.C. 316.
[58] *Mat.* iii, 59; vi, 66; M. Gibbs, op. cit. xxxiv.
[59] *Opera* i, 319.   [60] ibid ii, 180.
[61] ibid. i, 434.   [62] ibid. 350.

of Chichester in defending the holding of secular office by churchmen. The king chose bishops as royal justices because they were less
likely to take bribes. Canon law forbade the practice, it was true,
but bishops could defend themselves for flouting the canons: they
could plead 'the king's importunity and his pious intention and their
own performance, which was fit to please God and to be praised
by men.'[63] Ralph told William Longchamp, royal chancellor and
bishop of Ely, that his tenure of the chancellorship and consequent
delegation of his episcopal duties to subordinates need not redound
to his discredit.[64] This is more than unwilling acceptance; Ralph set
a positive value on royal service by bishops. He judged that it
worked well in the empire too: Rainald of Dassel was both chancellor and archbishop. Henry had this sensible arrangement in mind
when he wanted Becket to retain his chancellorship after his promotion to Canterbury.[65] How was Ralph to reconcile his conflicting
loyalties and judgements when he told the story of St Thomas?

First of all, he gives us a pointer to his method as a historian.
It occurs in a scrapbook of excerpts which he compiled as a preface to his *Abbreviations of Chronicles*. Ralph ascribes this particular cutting to a chronicle of Hugh of St Victor; he was probably
right.[66] Hugh explains how we should store up the treasure of
wisdom in our hearts. Divine wisdom (history included) resembles
earthly treasure in being of diverse kinds – gold, silver and jewels.
They should be arranged separately. To keep one's files in order is
to gain enlightenment and to aid the memory: *dispositio ordinis
illustratio est cognitionis*. If we mix things up we may overlook or
forget them. What better advice could be offered to the research
student? Hugh illustrated his meaning by a topical example, which
would have appealed to Ralph as a businessman. It relates to the
Paris *Bourse* and shows that the Victorine could observe street
scenes. Money-changers use a marvellous sort of wallet, containing
many separate compartments, though you would never think so
to look at the outside. By keeping diverse kinds of coinage in
separate compartments, they can effect their exchanges so swiftly

---

[63] ibid. 435.   [64] ibid. ii, 179.   [65] ibid. i, 307–8.

[66] ibid. 31. On Hugh's authorship see R. Baron, 'La Chronique de Hugues
de Saint-Victor', *Studia Gratiana* xii (1967) 167–80. The text quoted by Ralph
has been edited by W. M. Green, 'Hugo of St Victor, *De Tribus Maximis
Circumstantiis Gestorum*', *Speculum* xviii (1943) 488–9. Ralph's quotation
corresponds almost verbally to the original. I have summarized Hugh without
attempting a full or close translation.

and accurately that the people standing round them gape and even laugh to see the same wallet producing so many different kinds of coinage. It looks like a miracle to bystanders. We should do the same with the diverse kinds of wisdom.

Ralph adopted the method of pigeon-holing one's *fiches* and applied it to historical presentation. He divided his narrative into secular and ecclesiastical history. Each has its sign in the margin, a crown or a crozier, to distinguish it from the other. A special sign denotes conflict, where a clash between *regnum* and *sacerdotium* is recorded. Thus Becket's resignation of the chancellor's seal when he became archbishop is recorded among the causes of conflict.[67] The beauty of the method was that the historian had no need to comment or to express his opinion on the rights and wrongs of the case; the facts went under separate headings. Much thought must have gone into the invention of this thought-saving device. Ralph used rather the same technique in an account of the conflict which he sent to the monks of St Colomba at Sens. They had received Becket and given him hospitality after his forced departure from Pontigny. It was a fitting gesture to offer them a 'little book' on the conflict and its sequel of martyrdom and canonization. Ralph pieced the story together from his *Imagines*.[68] He lists the causes of the dispute between king and archbishop; he quotes letters, including his own advice to Richard of Ilchester to respect Becket's anathemas; he records the murder and Henry's subsequent reconciliation with the pope at Avranches. Last come the bull of canonization and a list of distinguished pilgrims to the shrine. Ralph 'lets the facts speak for themselves.' His only personal comment is a discreet advertisement:

> Whenever you meet the name of Thomas, glorious martyr, as numbered among the archbishops of Canterbury, never pass over in silence his praiseworthy life, his excellent deeds, his exile, his passion, his constancy in death, and the many miracles which he wrought after passing from this mortal life to his heavenly home.[69]

Richard Fitzneal may have anticipated the system of pigeon-holing. He refers in his *Dialogue of the Exchequer* to a history of England under Henry II arranged in three columns:

> I called it the *Tricolumnis* because I arranged it all in three

[67] *Opera* i, 269.   [68] ibid. ii, 279–85.   [69] ibid. 280.

columns. The first column dealt with the affairs of the English Church and some papal bulls. The second dealt with the King's noble deeds, which are beyond human belief. In the third are various matters of public and private interest, and also judgements of the King's Court.[70]

He wrote it as a young man before his *Dialogue of the Exchequer*, the first draft of which was probably finished in 1179.[71] Fitzneal was a royal servant and admirer of Henry; he admits in his *Dialogue* that he is afraid of appearing to be too favourable to clerks.[72] Yet he was a clerk himself and would hardly have wanted to argue the case for Henry against Becket. His three-column arrangement provided him with a good alibi. Still, the *Tricolumnis* is lost; we do not know whether Ralph of Diss had read it or even knew of it. The dean holds the patent of invention for the time being. He had precedents in that pagan and Christian history had been written in parallels; it was new to put the events of near contemporary history into watertight compartments.

Prophetic method! Historiography has often tended to become a vast system of filing, though historians make spasmodic efforts to shake out the contents of their files and rearrange them in a pattern of their choice. The pigeon-holing system dispenses the historian or chronicler from analysis or synthesis. At the same time it has had the advantage, as Ralph understood, of permitting the record of facts which might have been suppressed as irrelevant or inconvenient. The Becket conflict affected historiography as well as political theory.

---

[70] *Dialogue of the Exchequer*, op. cit. 27.
[71] ibid. xvii–xxii.   [72] ibid. 123.

Conclusions

It seems honest to begin by stating what I expected to find before tackling 'The Becket Conflict and the Schools'. Yes: I had a presumption in favour of Marsilio and Hobbes, who described the schoolmen as agents of the papacy. The Protestant view that interpretation of Scripture according to the four senses supported 'papal usurpations' struck me as likely to prove correct. Looking back, I can see that my presumptions were too weak; I under-rated the case. The masters of the holy page depended on the Church financially. They needed ecclesiastical revenues and benefices for their livelihood; they needed protection and privileges for their safety. The centralization of ecclesiastical government led them to turn towards Rome. The popes on their side relied on theologians to give them ideological and political backing. Masters indoctrinated their pupils. Masters and pupils alike were potential prelates; their actions might decide the future of the Church. The development of teaching techniques, of political allegory in particular, enabled masters to find what they needed to find on the holy page. If the interests of *regnum* and *sacerdotium* should clash, then masters would propagate the cause of *sacerdotium*. Robert Pullen, Robert of Melun and Geoffrey Babion are early examples. Of course Marsilio's historical background was faulty. The popes did not 'usurp' civil power in the west: it was thrust upon them. Nor did the masters have any alternative to their alliance with the Curia. The civil power in its twelfth-century form lacked the means to finance or control the education of clerks. 'Leisure and liberty for the treating of truth' could be procured from one quarter only. There were strings attached, as there always are. I have concentrated on theologians. Teachers of *Artes*, medicos and lawyers may have been more independent and more lay-minded. Members of these faculties may have had less occasion than theologians to involve themselves in politics except occasionally. They did paid services for their employers,

Did theologians commit themselves to the cause of the Church and the papacy from motives of self-interest or from principle? That question eludes the historian. He can discern interest well enough. His judgement on the element of principle will be subjective. I can only report my impression of twelfth-century lectures on Scripture. It seems that the masters felt free to do what they wanted: they did not feel constricted by their obligations. What they wanted was to evangelize. They hoped to lead their pupils to choose a good way of life and to send them as missionaries to Christians and heathens. They had a mission to rebuke anticlerical princes and to defend the liberties of the Church; but this belonged to a wider programme. Opportunities were opening up. New things were taking shape all round them. The schools and scholasticism were new. The Gospel was old; but its preaching must now be intensified and must reach a wider audience. The tympanum of the Madeleine at Vézelay expresses these aspirations marvellously.[1] Christ in majesty sends his disciples to convert all peoples of the earth. St Peter and St Paul and the other apostles prepare to obey. The peoples, including dogheads and pygmies, to signify the ends of the earth, await the Gospel, while a *river of the water of life* proceeds *from the throne* to purify the world (Apoc. xxii, 1). The *Artes* serve the queen of the sciences in the presentation of the scene. Pagan lore has contributed to the depiction of the heathen, and Christian learning to the amalgam of texts shown in the central group of figures. Christ commands his disciples to preach to all peoples, as in the Gospel; they receive the Holy Spirit after the Ascension, as in Acts: there is a reference to the calling of the gentiles. The conflation of scenes goes back to patristic commentaries. The Fathers explained that the evangelization of the gentiles became possible only after the Ascension and Pentecost; they emphasized the importance of preaching.[2] The Madeleine tympanum has been dated about 1125–38, about the time that Robert Pullen and Geoffrey Babion were giving their lectures, or soon before. The Madeleine

---

[1] F. Salet, *La Madeleine de Vézelay* (Melun, 1948) 116–35.

[2] F. Bovon, *De Vocatione Gentium. Histoire de l'interprétation d'Act. 10. 1–11, 18. dans les six premiers siècles* (Beiträge zur Geschichte der biblischen Exegese viii, Tübingen, 1967) 251–9. The *Gloss* sums up the tradition on the story of Cornelius, Act. x, 7: Tres misit Cornelius ad Petrum, quia credens Gentilitas apostolicae fidei Europam, Asiam Africamque subegit, partim studiis militaribus, hoc est instantia praedicandi, partim domesticis negotiis occupando.

iconography is unique; but its vision of the Church was reflected in the schoolroom, where masters of the holy page saw themselves as successors to the apostles of Vézelay.

The reality differed; and that, too, found its epitome in the abbey's history. St Bernard preached the second crusade at Vézelay in 1146: infidels were to be killed instead of converted. Becket excommunicated his enemies there in 1166: it would not have displeased him if civil war had broken out as a sequel. The abbot of Vézelay had some heretics burnt in the following year. As for preaching to Christians, the flood which poured from the schools watered a small section of the clergy and dried to a trickle before it reached the laity. But illusions, especially academic illusions, supply a driving force in history. Something came of the masters' teaching, though less than they hoped for or than the artists of Vézelay showed in their 'universal moment' of the Church militant.

The Becket conflict demonstrates the masters' success on a narrow front. The archbishop was suggestible. He had friends to 'put ideas into his head and purpose into his heart'. The shadow of the good prelate fell between Thomas the chancellor, the royal servant, and Thomas the archbishop, servant of God's Church and of Christ's vicar, the pope. He betrayed the Church on leaving Theobald's household; it troubled his conscience, as is proved by his wish to be friends with Peter of la Celle and his request for Master Gebuin's sermons, 'St Bernard for junior forms'. As archbishop he surrounded himself with 'high-minded men' (read *exaltés*) and 'noble scholars'; so his critics complained. The evidence leads me to suppose that theologians influenced him more than canonists and that his theological advisers were less restrained than his lawyers in their claims for privilege of clergy. Becket translated theory into action. The good prelate refused to compromise. He pursued his defence of his Church and his people to the climax of martyrdom. His choice dismayed even Herbert and John of Salisbury; but they, too, accepted the consequences of what they had taught him. Herbert sacrificed his ambitions, though grudgingly. John did the same. In John's case it meant that he had to revise his admiration for Cicero, as well as living in poverty and exile.

Then the problem of hostile reactions confronted me. Some theologians took Henry's side; others did a balancing act. The difficulties of following the lead of a good prelate, when he moved from the pages of the textbook into life, proved insuperable. Henry's bishops and Alexander III had their hands tied; but office prevented them from keeping their mouths shut. How did they square the teaching of the schools with opposition or compromise? Henry James's description of 'muddlement' in his preface to *What Maisie Knew* was a comfort here:

> The great thing indeed is that the muddled state too is one of the very sharpest of the realities, that it also has colour and form and character, has often in fact a broad and rich comicality, many of the signs and values of the appreciable.

It emerged from the muddle of anti-Becket propaganda that Henry II had no coherent theory of royal power to oppose to Becket's defence of the Church, or preferred not to state it, if he had one. Gilbert Foliot did not help him. Foliot's reticence surprised me until I had dredged up evidence for his schooling and the statements of principle scattered about in his writings. He had fastened on the concept of the good prelate as firmly as any other master. Foliot made no case against Becket on grounds of principle; his attacks focused on the archbishop's personal character and tactics: Becket's moves were ill-judged and ill-timed; moderation would have won more for the Church. The bishop of London ate humble-pie in the end; but it resulted from his actions; he did not have to withdraw his principles. Stephen of Rouen, a monk of the ducal abbey of Bec, and a Master Roger, canon of the very Henrician see of Rouen, criticized Becket as a traitor to his king. Theologians would have none of it.

Alexander III suffered dreadfully from the muddled state of politics. The schismatics and the Henricians, who might join forces, threatened him on one hand; Becket, supported by the French schools and the French Church, clamoured and lectured him on the other. But muddle never entered the pope's clear mind. His dilemma stimulated him to think up a theory which would save him from his wild men. Alexander neither stated nor denied extreme theories on the superiority of *sacerdotium* over *regnum*. He justified his slowness to commit himself to Becket's side by his theory of *raison d'Eglise*. The principle of ecclesiastical liberty is sacred. To act on it may be inexpedient and may harm the true interests of Christendom. The pope was supreme ruler of the Church; Alexander pronounced explicitly on that point. It was for him to judge at a given moment what policy would forward the good of all. The theory did not endear him to the Becket circle, who execrated his caution. It bore hard on Foliot when the party line changed unpredictably. But his theory saved the pope's face all of the time and Foliot's face some of the time.

After his murder scholars exploited the Becket story for all it was worth. Theologians had influenced him in his life; now his passion added a new page to the expanding Bible of the schools. The process looks like a hall of magnifying glasses. St Thomas's deeds and martyrdom served two purposes, the narrow one of ecclesiastical freedom and clerical immunities, the wider one of evangelization: his passion brought men closer to Christ's. Again one thinks of the tympanum at Vézelay. The cult of St Thomas spread to distant lands and barbarian peoples. The masters had some success on their wider front, thanks to St Thomas's martyrdom.

My journey had gone smoothly so far. Masters of theology were committed in politics up to the hilt. Some acted on their principles when they left the schools; others admitted their belief in principle when they invented reasons for waiving it *pro tem*. They all accepted the academic picture of the good prelate and used it to measure reality. Then suddenly a rift in the landscape appeared. The cult of St Thomas had screened it off. I had not reckoned with the fluidity of opinion in the schools: the masters both reflected and guided fluctuations in politics. The Becket conflict marked high tide in the claims of *sacerdotium* against *regnum*. It was exciting and noble while it lasted. By the end of the century it had begun to pall. The masters had had enough of the quarrel as a stark and simple issue. They had grown out of it. They failed to exploit the murder of Albert of Louvain, although he died in the Church's cause, and although the emperor Henry VI fitted the role of anti-clerical villain better than Henry II. The younger men concerned themselves with detailed study of Christian problems. They were less inclined to generalize. Links between Rome and the faculties of theology remained strong; but theologians came round to *raison d'Eglise*. It made them more useful to the papacy.

The Paris masters did not need to justify their boredom; it was a negative attitude. English theologians had to acknowledge their positive approval of Angevin rule. 'The public power' in Henry's hands had struck at the liberties and authority of the Church in the person of Becket. His martyrdom had little effect on the working of royal government. But Henry's regime benefited men of property, including churchmen. 'The public power' advanced 'the public good', including the clergy's. It was wise to collaborate. Becket broke with Henry by resigning his seal according to a strict interpretation of canon law. Both Gervase of Chichester and Ralph of Diss conceded that bishops could hold secular office, notwithstanding the canons: bishops made better officials than laymen and so contributed to the public good. The observation, if pursued, would have led to a revision of the ideal of the good prelate. School tradition put the ideal beyond the reach of criticism. Wideawake thinkers had to accept double standards and live with them. It had ceased to be a question of good theory versus bad practice: now there were two kinds of good. Ralph of Diss told the story of the conflict in parallel columns. King and archbishop could be honoured side by side. Herbert had written in the heat of the quarrel:

> The king's peace which we seek and our justice which we cherish, his rule and our priesthood, cannot meet.[3]

Ralph devised a method of ensuring that they need not meet, at least in the pages of his *History*. He came to terms with the irreconcilable.

One more admission before I stop. The masters whom I have studied were all secular clerks or priests, apart from Robert Crichlade, an Austin canon, and Gilbert Foliot, who entered Cluny after teaching as a secular. These masters assigned themselves a special role. Their active life as teachers and preachers was equal, if not superior, to the religious life of contemplation in their judgement. Pullen defended the mixed life of the prelate as best; masters of the holy page were training their pupils for prelacy. Robert of Melun was noted for his pride in his calling. Peter the Chanter and his circle would make similar claims. It was borne in on me that their teaching reflected their status: they made more allowance for secular values than monastic moralists. Pullen told rich men how to get to heaven. Herbert was a self-confessed worldling, who compensated for his inaptness to receive 'theophanies' by extraordinary feats of scholarship. He threw a bridge between St Thomas and his worldly milieu. John of Salisbury anticipated the Latin *Politics* when he presented the art and practice of government as potentially virtuous and creative. Gervase of Chichester and Ralph of Diss shared

[3] *Mat.* vii, 265–9.

his view implicitly. Gilbert Foliot, on the other hand, true to his monastic vocation, saw earthly rule in the patristic tradition as a remedy for man's sin after his expulsion from paradise; it was just a nasty chore. Hence the secular masters seemed to be on the way to playing down *contemptus mundi* and developing a more tolerant ethos. It was not quite consistent with their commitment to *sacerdotium* against *regnum*; but it fitted into their aim to evangelize the laity. The clergy would supervise secular rulers and their officials. I need not apologize for the untidiness of history.

My journey ends on the edge of the thirteenth century. The foundation of Mendicant *studia* brought a new type of intellectual to the schools. The friars tended to smother the seculars as biblicists and homilists. The seculars concentrated more on theology proper, covering their withdrawal from the teaching of Scripture by loud protests against Mendicant privileges and the Mendicant claim to monopoly of the perfect way of life. Further exploration would lead into a new climate and a landscape full of hidden ditches.

APPENDIX I
Robert Pullen's Sermons

Nineteen sermons, written consecutively and each one ascribed to 'Doctor Robert Pullen', are found in MSS 458 of Lambeth Palace Library and O.2.viii of Hereford Cathedral Library. The Lambeth MS is late twelfth-century, of unknown provenance, and the Hereford MS late twelfth- or early thirteenth-century and belonged to the cathedral. Some of the sermons occur in other collections, either singly or in groups. Fr. Courtney has listed and numbered them.[1] Their content gave him the impression that these so-called sermons derived from Pullen's lectures on Scripture at Oxford or Paris or both, just as the *Sentences* may have derived from the classroom and been reorganized. I think he is right. It is worth while to go into the evidence for the origin of the sermons in more detail. We have no other samples of Pullen's lectures on Scripture. Commentaries on part of the Psalter and on the Apocalypse ascribed to him are now lost;[2] a commentary on the first fifty psalms ascribed to him in a sixteenth-century hand in MS Royal 3.C.v of the British Museum is certainly not his.[3] If the sermons can be shown to have originated in lectures, they will tell us something of Pullen's teaching. I have used the Lamebth MS and checked it from a microfilm of the Hereford MS.

Fr. Courtney pointed out that the sermons were addressed to clerks, who could be expected to understand an allusion to Aristotle's *Categories* and who were supposed to be students. We have further evidence in the form of the pieces: the material has

[1] Courtney, op. cit. (above, p. 39) 32–6.

[2] ibid. 52–3; *Rep. Bibl.* no. 7479.

[3] Warner and Gilson, i, 75. This commentary on the Psalter, complete in other MSS, has some relationship to the Psalter-commentary of Master Ivo of Chartres, a pupil of Gilbert of la Porrée; see *Rep. Bibl.* no. 5337, 5340, 7477, 7478. I compared the only one of Pullen's sermons which starts from a text of the Psalter (no. 12, on Ps. xcvii, 1) with the copy of the commentary in MS Magdalen College, Oxford, 207 on this text. There is no resemblance at all.

not been worked into sermon form. No attempt has been made to gear the separate items to the liturgical year or to suggest themes for sermons. Each item has an opening address, *fratres carissimi*, and concludes with a prayer. But lectures also began and ended with prayers. It is always difficult to draw a line between *lectio* and *praedicatio* in lectures of the homiletic type. Lectures served as material for sermons. We can draw a parallel with the sermons of Master Geoffrey Babion, Pullen's contemporary. It has been suggested that they represent a revision of the lectures which he gave as *scholasticus* at Tours.[4] Pullen's sermons are closer to the parent lecture course than Babion's; they are even less like real sermons. Pullen sometimes gives his opinion on a disputed point. Is it wrong, he asks, for unworthy prelates and priests to pray that their people's sins should be forgiven? He dare not affirm it; but he holds it for true that such prayers are neither good nor useful, and he gives his reason for thinking so.[5] The question and answer would have been more appropriate in a lecture than a sermon.

The range of texts opening the sermons also suggests lecture courses. Set in their order in the Bible, the opening texts would show Pullen lecturing on Genesis to Leviticus inclusive, on Kings I and III, on the Psalter, on Ecclesiastes and the Canticle, on St Matthew, St Luke and the Apocalypse. There is some continuity. The first and second sermon of the collection expound the same text of the Apocalypse and the second refers back to the first:

> Heri, fratres carissimi, de bono conscientie vobiscum sermonem habuimus.[6]

The choice of biblical books fits into what we know of early twelfth-century lectures. Pullen leaves out the Old Testament prophets altogether. According to Abelard, the prophecy of Ezechiel was *inusitata* in Anselm's school at Laon.[7] The rarity of contemporary commentaries on any of the prophets bears him out. Pullen's omission of the Pauline epistles could be explained by the fact that

---

[4] J. P. Bonnes, op. cit. (above, p. 117).

[5] MS Lambeth 458, foll. 156v–157: Affirmare non audeo malum esse quod huiusmodi homines pro peccatis aliorum orationes faciunt. Illud autem dico: pro vero estimo quod orationes (quas) faciunt (nec) bene sint nec utiles. Quis enim est ille servus qui suum dominum pro conservo suo intercedere presumat, cum ipsum dominum contra semetipsum iratum sentiat?

[6] fol. 112.

[7] *Historia calamitatum*, ed. J. Monfrin (Paris, 1959) 69.

R

he was giving moral instruction rather than teaching theological doctrine. His *Sentences* may perhaps derive from lectures on St Paul in the first place. His opening texts sometimes come from the same part of a book, as Num. xxi, 21 (18), 23-30 (17), Cant. iii, 6 (15), 7 (14), 11 (11). Pullen sometimes comments on one long passage per sermon, as on the whole of Gen. xiii (5). Sermon no. 7 deals with the history of Israel from Exodus to the entry into Canaan. That again fits into what we know of contemporary lecture techniques: masters did not always go through their text consecutively, but picked out the passages in it which interested them. If Pullen followed this selective method in his lectures, it would have been easy for him to cut out bits and to present them separately as material for sermons. His comments are discursive, in the Gregorian style. He generally begins with the literal or historical sense of his text and goes on to the allegorical or moral sense; but he is not systematic. In this respect, too, he resembles his contemporaries. Even so, he must have made many digressions and probably broke off his lectures unfinished; he could not have expounded a whole book at the same length as he does certain texts chosen from it. Oxford commentators on Scripture from Robert Bacon O.P., lecturing in the 1230s, to William Woodford O.F.M., lecturing in the late fourteenth century, preferred a discursive, homiletic style to the comparative brevity of Paris masters. It may be far-fetched, but it is worth suggesting that if Pullen gave this type of homiletic lecture at Oxford, he started a fashion which proved congenial and had a long future there.

The content of his teaching with its advice to clergy and prelates looks forward to that of Master Ivo of Chartres, lecturing on the Psalter in the 1150s.[8] It has much in common with that of 'the biblical moral school' of Peter Comestor, Peter the Chanter and Stephen Langton. It would be useful to discover what immediate sources Pullen used, but they have eluded me. He did not use the *Gloss* compiled by Anselm of Laon and his circle, which became the standard textbook on Scripture in the second half of the twelfth century. Nor did he use Paterius' excerpts from St Gregory, a favourite book of the glossators. Pullen drew on a common stock of tradition: there are reminiscences of Jerome, Augustine, Gregory, Bede and Raban Maur; but he seldom quotes verbally and he does

[8] B. Smalley, 'Master Ivo of Chartres', E.H.R. 1 (1935) 680-6; *Rep. Bibl.* no. 5337.

not follow any of them consistently. He probably referred to compilations from the Fathers, perhaps in the form of glosses, of a type which circulated before the *Gloss* replaced them in classrooms.[9] This, too, belongs to the pattern of teaching which one would expect to find in the 1130s and early 1140s.

A second collection of sermons, twenty-seven in all, is ascribed to 'Master Robert Pulo', a variant of Robert's surname. Fr. Courtney has listed them. I have read them in a MS which should be added to his list; it now belongs to the Roman Catholic cathedral at Southwark. The hand is late-twelfth-century French and the provenance unknown.[10] The ascription to Robert Pulo, both here and in the other MS, is in a hand nearly contemporary with the text. None of these sermons occurs in the first collection, except the last, which is no. 11 of the first collection. It is difficult to accept the second collection, apart from the last item, as genuine work of Pullen, in spite of the ascription. These sermons were written by a religious for religious. The preacher refers to himself as a religious and addresses men who have made their vows and have left the world.[11] He puts his comparisons of the active and contemplative lives into a monastic framework: a monk should seek the security of solitude in the heat of his youth; he should return to minister to Christ's family in his experienced old age.[12] Moreover they are real sermons;

---

[9] R. Wasselynck, 'L'influence de l'exégèse de S. Grégoire le Grand sur les commentaires bibliques médiévaux', R.T.A.M. xxxii (1965) 157–204; B. Smalley, 'Les commentaires bibliques de l'époque romane: gloses ordinaires et gloses périmées', *Cahiers de civilisation médiévale* iv (1961) 15–19. I have compared sermon no. 12 on Ps. xcvii, 1 with a number of early twelfth-century commentaries on the Psalter without finding any resemblance.

[10] See N. R. Ker, *Medieval Manuscripts in British Libraries* i (Oxford, 1969) 331. The provenance of this MS is not known. I am very grateful to the Archbishop's Chancellor, the Rev. J. McGettrick, for letting me study it. For the list of MSS and incipits see Courtney, 41–4.

[11] MS Southwark, fol. 3: Confugisti in claustro ad Iesum...; fol. 34v: Nulli enim convenientius quam homines monastice professionis intelliguntur regni celorum negotiatores. . . . Conveniunt ergo in publico foro monasterii Iesus et monachus . . .; fol. 40: Moraliter angeli significant sacerdotes nostros et doctores. . . Isti angeli nobis de Sodoma seculi exeuntibus cotidie clamant: salvate animas vestras in claustris monasterii et nolite respicere post terga ad illecebras seculi.

There are other examples.

[12] fol. 30–30v: Itaque strenuus supplantator (Iacob) et mane et meridie laborat in agro, quia in exordio etatis et fervore iuventutis separare se debet a mundi periculoso turbine et exercere se in solitaria securitate. Ad vesperam

their titles allocate them to special feasts: 'the common of the saints', apostles, martyrs, confessors, doctors and virgins.[13] They are uniform, in that all begin with a text from the Gospels. The last sermon, no. 11 of the first collection, has been tacked on at the end. A blank space has been left over the incipit, since it has no title. It starts from the text Cant. iii, 11. There is no mention of religious in it, but there is a mention of prelates.[14] It looks as though this last sermon, which is certainly Pullen's, was added to the second collection; that would explain why the whole of the second collection came to be ascribed to him.

Fr. Courtney argues for Pullen's authorship of both collections. He points to resemblances of subject matter and style; but these are not distinctive enough to prove that Pullen wrote both. The second argument is that Pullen belonged to the Order of Canons Regular, and therefore could have referred to himself as a religious. This is not convincing. The evidence for making him a Canon Regular is too flimsy. It conflicts with the known facts of his career and with his outlook in his *Sentences*, *Treatise* and authentic sermons. In all these Pullen writes consciously as a secular master. It is better to reject the second collection of sermons (1–26) as spurious. On the other hand, it seems safe to count the first collection as derived from his lectures and therefore as evidence for his teaching.

vero de agro revertitur, quia in senectute iam perfecte decoctus ab illa interna quiete ad familiam Christi dispensandam affectu caritatis egreditur.

[13] fol. 2: Beatus iste apostolus, cuius sollemnia colimus. . .

[14] MS Lambeth 458, fol. 144: In qua est (Christus) corrector morum, per vicarios suos nos instruendo. . . . Et quia sunt multi qui bonis suis sepe superbiunt, subiunxit Salomon, quasi dicat: De bonis vestris ne superbiant. .

APPENDIX II

Nicholas Hickett

This Chichester man brings the Becket story into the sixteenth century. Nicholas Hickett belonged to the clergy of Chichester cathedral in February 1539, our earliest reference to him. He took part in chapter business as a vicar choral and then was presented to the subdeanery or vicarage of St Peter the Great, 20 July 1554. He also held a cathedral chantry in 1548 and earlier. He vacated his subdeanery on being instituted to the vicarage of Pulborough in Chichester diocese, 10 November 1558.[1] Hickett died as vicar of Pulborough between 15 May 1585, when he wrote his will, and 10 July of the same year, when his will was proved. The vicar 'bequeathes his soul to the Trinity, directs burial in Pulborough church chancel, and mentions working tools, great and small, brass still-pot and pipes for making aquavite'. There is no mention of books in his will.[2]

MS 14 of Westminster Abbey[3] contains transcripts of Gervase of Chichester's homilies on Malachias (lacking the first few leaves, which were lost before binding) and of two sermons preached by Gervase at Chichester. The rubrics are as follows:

[1] J. E. Ray, 'Sussex Chantry Records', *Sussex Record Society* xxxvi (1931) 47, 143–4; R. Garraway Rice, 'Transcripts of Sussex Wills', ibid. xli (1935) 309, 347; W. D. Peckham, 'The Acts of the Dean and Chapter of the Cathedral Church of Chichester 1472–1544 (The White Book)', ibid. lii (1951/2) 57, 63, 69–70, 126–7; 'The Acts of the Dean and Chapter of Chichester 1545–1642', ibid. lviii (1959) 14, 23–6, 532; 'A Diocesan Visitation of 1553', *Sussex Archaeological Collections* lxxvii (1936) 97; 'The Vicars Choral of Chichester Cathedral', ibid. lxxviii (1937) 50.

[2] Mr W. D. Peckham very kindly answered my request for a dossier on Nicholas Hickett by sending me the list of printed notices given above and added an unprinted note on his will. He hopes to publish further information on Hickett.

[3] J. A. Robinson and M. R. James, *The MSS of Westminster Abbey* (Cambridge, 1909) 73. The date of the inscription of ownership has been misread; it is 1563 not 1562. Hickett is not identified as subdean of Chichester.

Explicit editio Gervasii presbiteri Cicestrensis super Malachiam prophetam de ordinis sacerdotalis instructione.

Sermo eiusdem Gervasii habitus in capitulo Cicestrensi in festo S. Thome martyris, anno ordinationis eiusdem Gervasii primo (fol. 119v)

Sermo Gervasii presbiteri Cicestrensis habitus in capitulo Cicestrensi anno 2° cum in perturbatione fuisset ecclesia (fol. 123v)

The second sermon breaks off unfinished in the middle of a page. The two last leaves of the volume are blank. An inscription inside the front cover reads:

Liber Nico' Hickett subde' 29 Julii, anno 1563

There is an erased inscription just below these words. It does not show up more clearly under an ultra-violet lamp. What little of it can be read suggests a note of purchase, pawn or loan: there are some numerals and 'Promiss. . .'. The transcripts of Gervase's works are in a sixteenth-century hand, large, clear and rather copperplate in type. A specimen of Hickett's hand in the *Acta* of Chichester chapter shows that the same person wrote the Westminster transcripts; there is perfect identity.[4] The 'Promiss . . .' of the erased inscription is also in his hand. The inscription of ownership is not. It is written in a different ink and the letters are formed quite differently. Another puzzle is that he is called 'subdean' in 1563. There was no subdean of Westminster of that name,[5] and Hickett vacated the subdeanery at Chichester when he was instituted to the vicarage of Pulborough in 1558. One can only suppose that the person who acquired the volume, perhaps a pawnbroker, wrote Hickett's name and the date, and got his title wrong; it could also mean that he was known to have made the transcripts while he was subdean of Chichester. It is not known how the manuscript came to Westminster Abbey.

The two sermons on St Thomas are not found elsewhere. We have the homilies on Malachias in MS Royal 3.B.x of the British Museum, which belonged to Gloucester Abbey. Hickett may have

[4] Mr Peckham gives a photographic plate of Hickett's autograph from the Chapter *Acta*, op. cit. *Sussex Record Society* lviii, pl. 1 and p. xi.
[5] The Assistant Librarian at Westminster Abbey kindly gave me this information and helped me to examine the manuscript.

used this manuscript for his transcript. It came to the British Museum via Lord Lumley's library. Lord Lumley's collection incorporated that of his father-in-law, the earl of Arundel, who acquired books from monastic libraries at the dissolution.[6] Hickett may have had access to the former Gloucester Abbey manuscript through Lord Arundel's connections with Chichester. This is not certain.[7] There was at least one other copy of Gervase on Malachias in circulation in the fifteenth century. The 1418 catalogue of Peterhouse, Cambridge, lists 'Gervasius super Malachiam cum quibusdam sermonibus'. This item is now lost.[8] The sermons following the homilies on Malachias in the Peterhouse copy may perhaps have been the two transcribed by Hickett. On the other hand, the Peterhouse copy may have had the same sermons as MS Royal 3.B.x, which has a different set from Hickett's. Perhaps Hickett found the two sermons in Chichester cathedral library.

The most intriguing question of all is why he took the trouble to copy out a very long twelfth-century text (Gervase on Malachias is in twelve books) and two sermons, one of which is for St Thomas's feast day; the other mentions St Thomas explicitly. Local patriotism would explain Hickett's interest in Gervase as a former canon of Chichester. Sympathy for the old religion would account for his inclusion of the two sermons on St Thomas. Hickett probably transcribed them during Mary's reign, 1553-8. He must have conformed to the Elizabethan settlement as vicar of Pulborough, but many conformed to it without enthusiasm. The cult of St Thomas revived at Canterbury under Mary's restoration of the Catholic faith. The Canterbury cathedral accounts record payments for writing the St Thomas legends, for 'pricking of St Thomas' story' (preparing the leaves of a book or liturgical music) and painting his altar. The townsmen of Canterbury restored the 'march-

[6] *The Lumley Library. The Catalogue of 1609*, ed. S. Jayne and F. R. Johnson (London, 1956) 376.

[7] I have collated specimen passages and found that Hickett's text of Gervase's homilies on Malachias is practically identical with that of MS Royal 3.B.x. There are a few differences, in that the rubrics of the homilies have been expanded: Hickett gives Gervase's name and the full title of the homily at the beginning of each of the twelve books. His transcript has some marginal references to biblical texts quoted by Gervase. An invocation 'Spiritus sanctus assit michi gratia' on the recto of fol. 1 is not in the Royal manuscript.

[8] M. R. James, *A Descriptive Catalogue of the MSS in the Library of Peterhouse* (Cambridge, 1899) 9.

ing watch' of St Thomas.[9] If news of these celebrations reached Chichester it may have encouraged Hickett to make his transcripts. Gervase's early sermons on the martyr would have been lost otherwise.

[9] Cathedral Library, Dean and Chapter Miscel. Accounts, 40 (unfoliated), 1555–1558; Cathedral Library, City Act Book 2, fol. 93v; City Accounts, F/A 15, foll. 75v–77v. Mr Peter Clark of Magdalen College kindly gave me these references.

ADDENDUM

Hickett was actually cited as a Marian priest in the metropolitical visitation of 1569, when he was parson of Pulborough. He had connexions with the deprived Marian archdeacon of Chichester, Dr Alban Langdale (d. 1587–9). Langdale was probably the private chaplain of Lord Montague, the most important Roman Catholic in Sussex at the time; see R. B. Manning, *Religion and Society in Elizabethan Sussex* (Leicester, 1969) 42–4, 54, 160.

INDEX I

Persons living before c.1500

INDEX II
Persons living after c.1500

Editors and translators of texts are not included unless the texts are anonymous

INDEX III

Manuscripts